D1436211

TANKS IN BATTLE

THE CHIEFTAIN

By courtesy of The Ministry of Defence

THE IMPERIAL SERVICES LIBRARY
Volume VIII

TANKS
IN
BATTLE

By
COLONEL H. C. B. ROGERS
O.B.E.

LONDON
Seeley Service & Co.
Limited

Seeley Service & Co. Ltd. 1965

ISBN 0 85422 009 7

PRINTED IN GREAT BRITAIN
by Robert Cunningham and Sons Ltd.
Alva, Scotland

TO MY WIFE,

who saw,
mirrored in a tank,
the armoured chivalry of England

CONTENTS

LIST OF PLATES

8

9

MAPS

Introduction

THROUGHOUT military history armies have been composed of three main types of fighting troops: cavalry, infantry and artillery. That is not to say that these three arms have always been present in all military forces; for, indeed, those of the more primitive countries or peoples have often consisted solely of either infantry or cavalry.

These three arms exist, and have existed, to perform particular functions in war, though equipment and weapons have been dependent on local resources and technical ability. Infantry have always fought on foot; but the weapons of the artillery have progressed from stone flinging catapults, through gun-fired projectiles to the rocket missiles of to-day; and cavalry is an all embracing term applied to troops who have gone into action in chariots, on horses, elephants and camels, and in armoured cars and tanks. The boundaries between these arms have sometimes been blurred. There have been mounted infantry, for instance, as the bulk of our opponents in the Boer War, and self-propelled guns of the artillery which bear a very close resemblance to tanks. Nevertheless their true function becomes apparent in their tactical employment; for in general infantry fight as infantry, and artillery as artillery, whatever their method of progress.

The mounted arm has to perform two very different roles; so different in fact that often throughout its history two separate branches of cavalry have been formed to undertake them. The first role comprises the complementary tasks of reconnaissance, or the obtaining of information, and protection, that is the provision of a screen to prevent enemy interference with the main body of a force. In the second role mounted troops are used for attack and exploitation in the main battle. The first role is traditionally the task of light cavalry, and the second that of heavy cavalry.

The extent to which mounted troops have been of importance on the battlefield has waxed and waned in accordance with a number of factors, including weapons, tactics, ground and the type of mount used. The three former govern the effectiveness of the last: the animal or vehicle which carries the mounted soldier into action.

11

Introduction

The primary purpose of this work is to deal with modern armoured battle and the development of the tank. But to understand the ideas behind the design and use of tanks, it is necessary to have some knowledge of the history of earlier mounted battle. The first two chapters are therefore devoted to a brief resume of heavy cavalry action during the many centuries which preceded the appearance of the tank in the First World War.

CHAPTER I

From the Hyksos to Charlemagne

THE heading of this chapter covers a far longer period than the rest of the book, for it ranges over some two thousand five hundred years from the invasion of Egypt by the Hyksos till the age of Charlemagne.

Probably the first mounted troops to be used in the main battle were carried in chariots drawn by horses, and the first people known to have fought in war chariots were the Hyksos. Little is known about this warrior race; the name literally means "Princes of the Lands", a title applied by the Egyptians to the rulers of Asiatic districts. Probably they were Hurrites, a people who, coming from the mountains in what is now Kurdistan, had settled in the basin of the Tigris and the Euphrates, and became skilled in the rearing of horses. Horses appear to have been introduced into this country in about 2100 B.C., probably from the southern Arabian deserts where there is a very ancient tradition of horse breeding. Certainly on Egyptian monuments dating from about the time of the Hyksos invasions there are depicted horses of typically Arab type.

The Hyksos overran Upper Egypt in about 1700 B.C. and established a dynasty which lasted some three hundred or four hundred years. Their success was probably due to their mobile hard hitting force of chariots.

When eventually the Hyksos had been driven out of the country a chariot force was retained as the principal arm of the Egyptian army. It was the great chariot charge led by the Pharoah Thutmose III which destroyed the army of the King of Kadesh at the battle of Megiddo in 1479 B.C.; and the disaster which overcame the Egyptian chariots in pursuit of the Israelites is one of the best known of Bible stories. This latter event was commemorated by a canticle sung by Moses and the Israelites, in which the fate of the Egyptian mounted arm is recorded: "Let us sing to the Lord: for he is gloriously magnified, the horse and the chariot he hath thrown into the sea. . . .

Pharaoh's chariots and his army he hath cast into the sea: his chosen captains are drowned in the Red Sea".

It was a long time before the Israelites themselves used war chariots, but they formed an important part of the army of King Solomon (*c.* 972–931 B.C.). In the tenth chapter of the Third Book of Kings (or First in the Authorised Version) it is stated that: "And Solomon gathered together chariots and horsemen, and he had a thousand four hundred chariots and twelve thousand horsemen. . . . And horses were brought for Solomon out of Egypt and Coa [*i.e.* E. Cilicia, which is that part of the present Turkey lying to the north of Cyprus]: for the king's merchants brought them out of Coa, and bought them at the current price. And a chariot for four horses was exported from Egypt for six hundred shekels of silver, and a horse for a hundred and fifty".

Chariots, too, formed the mobile arm of the formidable Assyrian army in the ninth century B.C.

The army of Cyrus, king of Persia in the sixth century B.C., was probably the first in which there was an efficient force of horsed cavalry. The development of cavalry was slow, and it may be that until this period horses were so small that they could be used more effectively in draught than ridden.

According to Xenophon, commander of the famous Greek "Ten Thousand", it was Cyrus who was responsible for the development of the chariot into a really good fighting vehicle. It was considerably stronger than its predecessors and its axles were made long to prevent it being overturned. Long scythes protruded from the axles and from beneath the chariot, and the horses were protected by armour. This fast light chariot had a crew of two, but there was also a very much more cumbersome affair which was drawn by eight yoke of oxen and which could carry twenty men. Its principal feature was a wooden tower from which was operated a field battering ram. It seems to have been used as a form of infantry tank, leading the Persian foot soldiers and breaking the enemy line. Of this machine Xenophon wrote, "Cyrus felt that if he had a series of such towers brought into the field at a fair pace they would be of immense service to him".

Persian cavalry were much superior to any mounted troops that the Greeks were able to bring against them. The Greeks had chariots from very early times (as readers of Homer will be aware), but they were only used to bring warriors into battle, and not for actual fighting. There was no real mounted tradition in the Greek armies. The only effective cavalry at the time of the Persian invasions was provided by the Thessalonians, and it was no match for the Persian horse.

Nevertheless, the Persians, who were accustomed to the wide plains of Asia Minor, did not, in their first encounters with the Greeks, appreciate the extent to which unfavourable ground would limit the effectiveness of their cavalry.

At the action of Erythrae, in 479 B.C., which preceded the battle of Plataea, the whole of the Persian cavalry attacked over broken hilly ground against the serried ranks of the Greek phalanx. The result was a disastrous repulse; and the Persians learned as did so many later commanders of mounted troops, that one cannot charge prepared and unshaken infantry on ground of their own choosing.

Primarily, however, Persian cavalry were mounted bowmen, and in the battle of Plataea they used their mobility to choose their position and to attack with missiles at long range. These tactics were so effective that the Athenians and the allies were cut off from their water supply; a major factor in causing their withdrawal. The Spartans, withdrawing in their turn, were caught by the Persian cavalry before they could occupy their new position, and were pinned to the ground by arrows. The Persian use of mounted troops in this battle was a precursor rather of armoured tactics in the Second World War than of the prevalent shock action of the centuries in between.

A revolutionary and effective combination of infantry and cavalry was achieved in the army of Philip of Macedon in the fourth century B.C. The task of the infantry was to close with and hold the enemy, whilst the cavalry was used in rapid manoeuvre for the decisive attack. Under Alexander the Great this army was the most formidable of its time.

The order of battle of the Macedonian army was unique. On the left of the line was the heavy infantry phalanx; next to it, in the centre, were the light infantry units, keeping elastic touch with the heavy cavalry which formed the right of the line. Reconnaissance, protection and general mounted duties were carried out by a force of light cavalry.

The heavy cavalry wore protective armour of metal corselets and helmets and were armed with sword and lance. Although the lance was the weapon used in the charge it could not be couched because the rider had no stirrups with which to take the shock of the impact. The Macedonian lance was, therefore, light and short and used for thrusting. The horses were probably very small by later heavy cavalry standards. Those depicted on the Parthenon seem to have been only about thirteen hands in height, and this impression is supported by Xenophon's contemporary descriptions.

It was with this army that in 331 B.C. Alexander the Great encountered the Persians under Darius III at the battle of Arbela. As compared with the Macedonians, the Persians had mustered an enormous host, and the mounted arm included not only two hundred chariots with long scythes fixed to their axles, but also a number of war elephants. This, in fact, was the first recorded appearance of elephants in battle outside India. In later battles they were to prove a formidable weapon; but at Arbela, possibly because they were mishandled, they seem to have contributed little to the struggle.

Alexander wished to attack the left flank of the long line of Persians, in order that he could use his mobile right wing; and his approach march was therefore something of a right incline.

Darius, observing Alexander's intention, moved his own army to the left to avoid having his flank turned. The position which Darius had chosen had been well prepared, and all obstacles in front of it which would interfere with the movement of his chariots had been removed. But if he moved too far to the left his chariots, susceptible as they were to the ground, would be unable to operate efficiently. To bring Alexander to a halt, therefore, the Persian heavy cavalry was launched in an attack on the Macedonain right wing. It had some initial success, and Darius took advantage of this to use his principal weapon, the chariots, in a violent attack on the Persian phalanx. But as the long line of chariots with yelling drivers, galloping horses and vicious scythes whirling on the wheel axles, approached the Macedonian line they were broken up by showers of arrows and javelins from the light infantry on their left flank.

At this juncture Alexander led his heavy cavalry in a charge on the position of Darius in the hostile line; and the whole Persian host dissolved in flight.

Although elephants had been ineffective at Arbela, Alexander learned more about this formidable animal when he invaded India in 327 B.C., and, after crossing the Jhelum, encountered the army of Porus. There were two hundred elephants in the Indian line of battle, spaced at intervals of about a 100 feet to cover the whole front of the infantry. To make them more terrible they probably had swords attached to their trunks and lances on either side of their bodies. The howdah, or fighting top, probably carried a crew of about four. Cavalry were useless against them, for the mere sight and smell of elephants upset the horses.

Elephants had their disadvantages, however, for if they panicked they were liable to break through the troops of their own side in an effort to escape. And Porus's elephants did in fact misbehave themselves in this fashion when Alexander's infantry phalanx got to close quarters. Nevertheless Alexander is said to have testified to the courage which was required to face elephants, and he eventually collected a considerable number for his own army. After his death elephants were prominent in the rival armies of his erstwhile generals, and Seleucas valued them so much that he acquired five hundred in exchange for a large part of his eastern territories. These elephants may well have justified their cost for they played a decisive part in the defeat of Antigonas by Seleucas and Lysimachus at the battle of Ipsus. Elephants in these campaigns, however, were not used defensively, as in the army of Porus, but rather as "infantry tanks" to punch a hole in the enemy's line for the supporting cavalry to pour through. At Ipsus they played a most novel role. Antigonus's cavalry defeated that of his opponents and drove the vanquished horsemen headlong from the field. But Antigonus, too, was deprived of his cavalry at the very moment of the battle when he was most in need of mounted troops, for the elephants were deployed across the path of the returning squadrons and foiled the intended decisive flank attack.

Seleucas's successor, Antiochus I, defeated the Gallic invasion of 275 B.C. with his elephants. He had only sixteen of these invaluable beasts, and he kept them in reserve for counter-attack. At the critical moment of the battle they were thrown into the fight in a massive surprise attack, and turned potential defeat into victory.

The odd thing about the Romans is that never, until the latter part of their history, were they anything but an infantry army. Cavalry they used as an auxiliary arm, and only in its light role. The fighting value of the legion was, of course, very high, and it may be that the Romans did not for most of their military history feel the need for a mounted assaulting arm; though for some time they made a limited use of elephants.

Hannibal's appreciation of the use and value of mounted troops in battle gave him a considerable advantage over the Romans. His mounted arm comprised not only heavy and light cavalry but also elephants. At the battle of the Trebia in 218 B.C. Hannibal's defeat of Sempronius was due mainly to his use of his Numidian cavalry. Half of these fierce warriors, who rode without saddle or bridle, he swung wide round the Roman flank for a decisive attack on the rear.

At the later battle of the Metaurus, Hasdrubal broke up the ranks of the legions with a frontal assault by his powerful elephant force. The supporting infantry followed up closely and completed the defeat of the Roman army. Nevertheless the battle showed that weakness of elephants in the excitement of battle which had cost Porus so dear. The noise of the fighting and the confusion of the battlefield eventually bewildered the elephants so that they got out of control and became an equal menace to both sides. The Carthaginians were well aware of this danger, and each mahout was equipped with a long knife and a mallet to drive it into the elephant's spinal cord. Many of the valuable beasts had eventually to be killed by this means.

At Hannibal's last battle in 202 B.C. at Zama, his body of elephants was the main strength of his army. Eighty of them were formed up in imposing and terrifying array along the front of his infantry. His cavalry, marshalled on either flank, were few in numbers, and it was his intention to break the Roman centre with a massive elephant charge.

Unfortunately for Hannibal his great Roman opponent, Scipio, was prepared for just such tactics. Normally the Roman infantry was drawn up so that the maniples of the second line covered off the intervals in the first line, and those of the third covered the intervals in the second. Scipio ordered the maniples of the second and third lines to cover off those of the first line, so that there should be lanes from front to rear.

As the assaulting elephants reached the Roman line they were greeted with an appalling din of horns and trumpets. Terrified, the elephants on the flanks broke back towards their own wings and threw Hannibal's Numidian cavalry into confusion. Those in the centre tore down the lanes which had been left for them, driving away the light infantry but leaving the heavily armoured legions undisturbed.

Nevertheless, the Romans, like Alexander, had been so impressed with the moral effect of elephants that they used them in their own army for the next 200 years. There were never many of them, because the Indian elephants were hard to obtain, and it was difficult to train the African variety for war. Roman appreciation of their value was shown after their defeat of Antiochus in 189 B.C.; for their vanquished enemy was made to surrender all his elephants.

Over 100 years later a Roman army encountered a new type of mounted warfare and was all but annihilated. In 53 B.C. the incompetent Crassus led forty thousand legionaries into Asia Minor and met a much inferior force of Parthians at the battle of Carrhae. Of his troops half were killed and half of the remainder were captured.

The Parthian army was composed almost entirely of mounted archers. There were some ten thousand of them in the force which defeated Crassus, and they were accompanied by a thousand ammunition camels loaded with arrows. The Romans never got anywhere near their mobile opponents, who surrounded them, chose their distance, and went on shooting until the Roman army was destroyed. These tactics foreshadowed similar types of armoured operations in the distant future.

The answer to the Parthian form of warfare was evolved by Mark Anthony. The army which he took with him on his Parthian campaign of 36 B.C. included a strong force of slingers, and these kept the Parthians at such a distance that their fire was largely ineffective. Other commanders some nineteen hundred years after Anthony arrived at the same solution.

In 55 B.C., 2 years before Crassus' disaster, Julius Caesar was being discomforted in Britain by the earliest of mounted arms; for chariots formed the principal arm of the British forces. Caesar himself gives a vivid description of the way the chariots were used. When they were launched to the attack they drove over the battlefield at great speed, hurling javelins at their enemies from a distance. As soon as the opposing infantry was disorganised they leaped from their chariots and attacked on foot; the chariots being taken by their drivers some little distance away, where they were halted with the horses facing away from the enemy. The fighting men could thus retreat rapidly if the necessity arose by running away and jumping into the chariots. The Roman troops were very shaken by these chariot attacks, and the effect on their morale could well have been the real reason for Caesar's withdrawal from Britain.

The horses which drew the British chariots may have been

19

the ancestors of some of the wild ponies in England to-day. Chariot horses shown on pre-Roman coins certainly appear small, and their size may have been the reason why they were used in draught for war rather than ridden.

In the twilight of Imperial Rome cavalry superseded the infantry legions as the principal arm. In A.D. 351 the Emperor Constantine defeated Sapor II, King of Persia, at the battle of Mursa; and it was the charge of the Roman heavy cavalry which finally broke the Persian army and drove it from the field.

Rather strangely it was the improvement in infantry weapons which gave cavalry increased opportunities to charge effectively. Whilst infantry were only armed with shock weapons and maintained a steady front, a cavalry charge had little chance of success. But the adoption of missile weapons, such as the bow, entailed a looser organisation in the ranks; and if cavalry could penetrate the hail of arrows (and on a wet day bow strings could be fairly ineffective) the unfortunate archers had no shields to parry the horsemens' swords.

It is not suggested, however, that the charge was the most effective way of using cavalry. The Huns, who burst into central Europe in about A.D. 450, were an entirely mounted force; but, like the Parthians, they used missile and not shock tactics. Indeed the stocky ponies which they rode would have been far too light to charge, and they would certainly have been no match for the big Roman horses. The Huns were archers, organised in small bands which concentrated quickly for action and dispersed as rapidly when the need arose.

The Gothic horsemen, unlike the Huns, were armed only with spears and swords, and relied on shock action. Their aggressive mounted tactics led to their defeat by the Romans at the battle of Taginae in A.D. 552. The Romans took up a defensive position with their heavy infantry forming an armoured phalanx in the centre, and foot archers supported by cavalry on the wings. The two wings were inclined forward, so that the position as it faced the enemy was concave. The area between the two wings formed what a much later generation of soldiers was to call a "tank-killing ground". The Gothic horse charged the phalanx, against which they could make no impression, and were mown down by the archers on either flank.

The age of Charlemagne, in the latter part of the eighth century A.D., marks a transitional period between the mass armies of the Empire and the armoured chivalry of the Middle

Ages. Charlemange's army was a force of moderate size, but well trained and equipped, as compared with vast numbers of untrained or partly trained men which formed the bulk of the armed forces of his predecessors. This new army was composed of a nucleus of heavily armoured cavalry backed up by an efficient body of infantry.

The cavalry had now become a corps d'elite, and, as a result, war was revolutionised—but for rather an odd reason. Armour and the horses to carry the armoured man were expensive, and the cavalry were therefore recruited mainly from the aristocracy. Whenever this happens the profession of arms is governed by certain codes of conduct and war is invested with an aura of glamour. (Democracy, unfortunately, has the opposite tendency, and democratic wars are all too often marked by a dreary brutal beastliness.) Until the end of the mediaeval period the armoured knight, with his attendant men-at-arms, was the dominant factor on the battlefield; and because the armoured horseman was well protected against the weapons of the day, casualties were much reduced and military operations became the pastime of the gentleman.

Eventually there arose the feudal society which spread all over Western Europe, and which was based on the castle or stronghold and the chivalry of horse and armour. This transformation did not take place in England, however, until after the Norman Conquest. Constant attacks by the Viking freebooters led to concentration on a fleet rather than cavalry, and the Anglo-Saxon army was an infantry force.

CHAPTER II

From the Age of Chivalry to the Age of the Rifle

THE English, it was stated in the last chapter, had invested in warships rather than armoured cavalry. In 1066 the ships let them down; for after defeating one invading army in the north, Harold and his incomparable foot soldiers had to march against another invader in the south. The Norman army at the battle of Hastings, however, was a vastly different force to that of either Harold of England or Harald Hardrada of Norway. It was a formidable example of the feudal military order in Europe, consisting primarily of a mounted body of armoured knights and men-at-arms, backed up by foot archers.

Nevertheless the Normans had yet to learn that the mounted charge cannot succeed against the unbroken phalanx, and it was not till the English infantry broke ranks to follow a feigned withdrawal that the Norman cavalry, counter-attacking under a high angle barrage of arrows, were able to break the stubborn resistance of their opponents.

Hastings confirmed cavalry as the dominant arm on the battlefield, and for the next 250 years tactics were based on the armoured mounted attack. Infantry had only a subsidiary role; a role rated so low in some West European armies, including the English, that in about 1300 the infantry levies were little better than an undisciplined rabble.

Then in the early part of the fourteenth century there appeared a disciplined English infantry armed with a revolutionary weapon: the powerful long bow, which Edward I had adopted from the Welsh. New tactics were devised to co-ordinate the action of the armoured mounted troops and the foot archers, and these new tactics were first seen at the battle of Dupplin Muir in 1332. Edward Baliol, accompanied by Henry Beaumont and others, crossed the border into Scotland with a small force. There they encountered the Scottish Regent, Donald Earl of Mar, who was in greatly superior strength, but nevertheless launched a night attack. The attack was repulsed,

22

and Baliol withdrew to a defensive position on the forward slope of a hill.

The order of battle of Baliol's little army was somewhat reminiscent of that of the Romans at Taginae. He dismounted all but forty of his cavalry and formed them up in a solid armoured line. On each flank were the archers, their lines inclined forward so that the whole front formed an angular crescent. Like the Goths, Mar charged bull-headed at the armoured centre, and the archers, wheeling further inwards, all but destroyed the Scottish horse. Baliol's own cavalry then re-mounted and completed the rout.

In the following year, using practically the same tactics, Edward III again beat the Scots at Halidon Hill.

These tactics, slightly modified, were employed against the French at the battle of Crecy. The English army of Edward III was normally organised in three "battles", of which two were in the front line and the third in reserve. In a defensive position the knights and men-at-arms of the two leading battles were dismounted, whilst those of the reserve were either mounted or prepared to mount. At Crecy the two forward battles were drawn up side by side, each with a phalanx of dismounted armour and their archers thrown forward on the flanks. The whole line thus resembled a form of "W", with the lower portion consisting of two broad bases instead of points. The outside tops of the "W", as usual in this formation, each rested on a natural obstacle of the ground to protect the archers from an attack in flank. Along the front of the lines of archers holes were dug, and stakes, iron-shod at the top, were driven into the ground slanting forward so that a metal pointed barrier faced any attack by the enemy horse.

As at Taginae and in Scotland, the enemy armour charged and was diverted by the arrows and stake barrier against the two phalanxes at the base of the "W". The French horsemen were already somewhat disorganised, because the range of the long bow had enabled the archers to engage them before they had been properly marshalled for the attack, and those who survived the devastating flights of arrows strove ineffectively against the steel wall of the English chivalry. The destruction wrought by these long bows up to a range of 200 yards forecast cavalry's ultimate impotence against rifle and machine-gun fire some six hundred years later.

The long bow was a weapon which could only be mastered

if training had been carried out from youth onwards; and it was only in the hands of the skilled English and Welsh infantry that it was a threat to the armoured knight. The smoothbore firearm was a far less accurate weapon with a slower rate of fire and a much shorter effective range; but anybody could use it after an hour or two of instruction. Hence it was the widespread use of firearms which finally ended the domination of the battlefield by the mounted armoured man.

The introduction of the pike and the combination of pikemen and musketeers in the infantry unit made it still more difficult for cavalry to charge home with sword or lance. As a result, horsemen themselves were armed with firearms. The matchlock, as used by the infantry, was a difficult weapon to operate on horseback; but the invention of the wheel-lock pistol, which could be fired with one hand, provided a solution. Instead of the ponderous business with a lighted match, pressure on the trigger released a spring, and a spinning wheel struck sparks from a fragment of pyrites.

The infantry pike and the cavalry wheel-lock pistol led to new cavalry tactics in the Spanish army in the early years of the seventeenth century. The troopers wore a heavy armour as a partial protection against musket balls, and they formed up for action in close massed squadrons each about ten ranks deep. An attack against infantry was a comparatively leisurely affair: the cavalry trotted forward by ranks in turn, fired their pistols, and then wheeled and filed to the rear of the squadron to reload.

In the Thirty Years War, Gustavus Adolphus, King of Sweden, had two kinds of mounted troops in his army, cuirassiers and dragoons. The former were a partially armoured heavy cavalry, and the latter were (as the name originally implied) mounted infantry. But Gustavus Adolphus made a great change in cavalry tactics. His cuirassiers charged at the gallop and with the sword. The pistol was only used in the subsequent melée. The attack was carried out in column of squadrons (*i.e.* one behind the other and each in line), each squadron being only three ranks deep. The rear squadron, however, was kept under close control and used as a reserve. The deployment of the Swedish cavalry, too, was unorthodox. In battle the cuirassiers were marshalled, not only on either wing of the infantry line, but also behind it. Musketeers were often posted in groups amongst the cavalry, to engage attacking enemy cavalry by fire and thus assist the mounted shock action of the

Swedish horse. For his own cavalry attack Gustavus generally tried to obtain some initial surprise by covering its advance with the smoke of an artillery bombardment.

The superiority of the Swedish cavalry was shown at the battle of Breitenfeld in 1631. Tilly's horse of the Imperial army, attacking in the methodical Spanish way, easily disposed of the indifferent Saxon troops who formed Gustavus's left wing. But Swedish cuirassiers on the other wing, charging at the gallop, broke Tilly's left and centre into such utter ruin that Gustavus gained a decisive victory.

The tactics of Gustavus Adolphus were brought to England by Prince Rupert, and the Royalist cavalry were trained in them. Unfortunately the conditions at the start of the Civil War were such that proper training could not be carried out before troops had to be used in action. As a result, whilst the charge of the Cavalier horse swept all before it, it was impossible to control or rally the headstrong young riders. Rupert, therefore, had to suit his tactics accordingly. He could drive his opponents from the field, but his force was a "one-shot" weapon, and once launched to the attack it left the battlefield at the gallop and never returned. This failing probably cost the Royalists the war.

A far more effective mounted force was produced for Parliament by Oliver Cromwell in the cavalry regiments of the "New Model". These well trained and disciplined troops were ready for the field in 1645, and were formed in eleven regiments of horse and one of dragoons. Each horse regiment consisted of six troops each of a hundred troopers, equipped with light cuirasses, helmets (known as pots), swords, and two pistols apiece. The capacity of this new cavalry was demonstrated at the battle of Naseby. On the Royalist right wing Rupert's horsemen broke Ireton's cavalry and pursued them from the field. As usual, however, the Cavaliers got quite out of control, and by the time they could be rallied and brought back the battle was over and the King's army beaten. On the other wing Cromwell's cavalry had charged and defeated Langdale's. The Parliamentary horse, however, had attacked at the trot and were well in hand. Ordering three regiments to follow Langdale, Cromwell wheeled left with the remainder and rode at the flank of the Royalist infantry. This action was decisive.

Some sixty years later Cromwell was followed by an even greater English commander, the Duke of Marlborough, and a genius in the use of the cavalry arm. Marlborough's usual tactics were to pin the hostile infantry to the ground by attacking with his own infantry, and then to break through by a cavalry charge. Starting at a trot, the final onslaught was carried out sword in hand at the gallop. The use of firearms was strictly forbidden, except for the protection of horses at grass.

The battle of Blenheim provides a notable illustration of Marlborough's tactics. On the right wing Prince Eugene had the task of engaging the Franco-Bavarian left to distract attention from the main attack which was to be delivered by Marlborough against the enemy's right. Marlborough's attack was itself split into two: powerful infantry assaults were planned against the French strong points of Oberglau and Blenheim on either flank of his front, so that the bulk of the French infantry should be pinned to the ground when he launched his decisive attack in the centre.

For this decisive attack the Allied troops were drawn up in four lines. The first, of infantry, was to seize and hold the right bank of the Nebel, which ran right along the hostile front; the second and third lines, of cavalry, were the main assaulting force; the fourth line, again of infantry, was to follow the cavalry, hold the ground beyond the Nebel, and provide a defensive front through which the cavalry could withdraw should the assault prove unsuccessful. This method of employing mounted troops resembles a set-piece armoured battle of the Second World War, and was practicable because Marlborough's cavalry were no more vulnerable to the defensive fire of the period than the tanks of the armoured regiments.

The attack, in fact, was a brilliant success. The long lines of steel and the thundering hooves of the approaching squadrons were too much for the French horse: they broke and fled, and the battle was over.

Cavalry was again the decisive arm at the battle of Rossbach in 1757. Here, however, it was used first in a surprise attack, and later to complete a discomfiture which had been started by the fire of artillery and infantry. Seydlitz, commander of Frederick the Great's four thousand Prussian cavalry, watched the measured approach of the unsuspecting Allied columns. His troops were concealed behind a hill, and, judging his moment, Seydlitz led his squadrons forward. As they cantered into view of the enemy, he threw his pipe into the air to signal the charge, and the Austrian cavalry, taken by surprise and in column, were driven from the field. The Prussian artillery now opened on the disorganised enemy, and the infantry advanced in support of the cavalry. Shaken by the flight of their cavalry and with great gaps torn in their ranks by the Prussian fire, the Allied infantry reeled back in confusion. Seydlitz charged again and completed the victory.

For cavalry to charge unbroken infantry formed in square, however, was generally a fruitless operation. The Prussians relearned this lesson at the battle of Auerstadt in 1806. The King of Prussia tried to stop the advance of Morand's division by massed cavalry attacks, but the French infantry deployed into squares, and the Prussian cavalry swept impotently round the hedgehogs of bayonets.

Napoleon's tactics were based on a very close co-ordination of cavalry, infantry and artillery. The attack was normally prepared by the artillery which forced the enemy to deploy from columns into the less vulnerable line formation. Under cover of the artillery fire the French infantry advanced, and, as they approached the enemy position, the cavalry threatened attack. This made the enemy infantry form into squares. These close packed targets were then assailed by both infantry and artillery fire. At the appropriate moment the infantry attacked the shaken squares and the cavalry exploited the infantry success.

At the start of the Leipzig campaign Napoleon was very short of cavalry, for most of his old cavalry had been lost in the disastrous Russian campaign of the previous year. The raising of new cavalry units was a far more difficult task than forming new infantry battalions. The training of junior officers and other ranks took longer, the country was short of horses suitable as chargers, and the new and hurriedly produced saddlery did not fit.

The lack of cavalry played havoc with Napoleon's tactics. The infantry advanced as before under cover of artillery fire, but since they were now liable to be attacked by the superior enemy cavalry they had to be prepared to form square at a moment's notice. This not only delayed the advance but enabled the enemy to break off the battle and withdraw under cover of the cavalry threat.

By the time the battle of Leipzig took place Napoleon had a total of some fifteen thousand cavalry commanded by Murat. The bulk of this force was employed in a massive attack at the hostile centre, and it was intended that heavy infantry columns should follow close behind. The cavalry attack was successful, but, as after the tank break through at Cambrai in 1917, there were no infantry close enough to follow up and consolidate the success of the mounted troops. If Napoleon's orders had been obeyed and the infantry had supported the cavalry, he would probably have won the battle. As it was, Murat's exhausted horsemen had to meet a counter-attack in flank by the enemy cavalry without support, and were driven back.

In his last battle, at Waterloo, Napoleon's cavalry formed a very high proportion of his army: amounting, indeed, to a quarter of his infantry strength. This fine mounted force was so mishandled by Ney, however, that Napoleon was deprived of a probable victory and lost his throne as well. The great French cavalry charges were carried out against unbroken infantry squares, and without that artillery and close infantry support which could have taken advantage of the targets presented by the squares. When the French Grenadiers of the Guard were launched to the final attack there were no cavalry left fit to fight. Maitland's British Guards Brigade was able, therefore, to meet the attack in line; and good and unshaken troops in that formation could produce a volume of fire that no infantry advancing in close columns could face successfully. For the first time the Grenadiers of the Old Guard turned their back on their enemy.

The Napoleonic wars were the last in which horsed cavalry were used as the principal assaulting troops on a battlefield. But the tradition of the cavalry charge was well established and, partly on account of a few striking successes, it was over 100 years before it was generally realised that the horse was no longer a suitable mount for the main battle.

In the Crimean War the infantry were already equipped with rifles and the cavalry, in consequence, played little part on the battlefield; but their lesser importance was obscured by the two great charges of the Heavy and Light Brigades. The first, however, was against cavalry and the second was a disaster.

In the American Civil War it was soon discovered that the extent to which cavalry could be employed on the battlefield was severely limited by the fire power of the infantry rifle. Perhaps this limitation was accepted more readily than in the later Franco-Prussian War because there was no large body of professional cavalry with its tradition of shock action and the *arme blanche*. However, the practical exclusion of cavalry from the main battle had the peculiar result that, instead of being used in their invaluable role of reconnaissance and protection, the mounted troops on both sides were often sent on long distance raids, the success of which did not compensate a commander for their absence on the eve of a battle.

There was no instance in this war of a great cavalry charge against infantry in position. Nevertheless, under favourable circumstances they could still be used with effect. Major General J. H. Wilson of the United States Army made the following fair assessment:

"To make a proper use of cavalry, you must get it into such a position that it can assail the flank or rear of an enemy, or operate upon his communications with effect. If I were called upon to command a force of 60,000 men, with authority to organise it as I pleased, I would have at least 20,000 on horseback. By using the mounted force to assail the flank and rear of the enemy, I should expect to conduct a more successful campaign than could be done by any other possible means in these days."

The effect of modern weapons on cavalry movement in the American Civil War was not appreciated in the armies of Western Europe, and at the start of the Franco-Prussian War of 1870 both sides still believed that the cavalry charge could be used as in the days of the smooth-bore musket.

The first shocks to the exponents of the cavalry charge came at the battle of Froeschwiller. On the right of the French line a brigade of cavalry charged the advancing German infantry in order to cover the withdrawal of their own infantry. But the French horsemen never got within sabre's reach of their opponents. Their line of attack took them into an area enclosed and broken up with hedges, walls, vineyards and trees; and beyond this obstacle were the scattered houses of the village with German soldiers firing from the windows. Nine squadrons of French cavalry were destroyed in this charge, at a probable cost to the Germans of nothing except their ammunition expenditure.

There was a similar occurrence on the French left, where one brigade of a division of cuirassiers was ordered to charge. Here also the country was enclosed, and repeated gallant charges broke down in face of the devastating rifles of the well posted German infantry.

The one successful cavalry charge of the war occurred at the

29

battle of Vionville, when von Bredow's brigade, in a Balaclava-like attack, overran the French artillery which was disrupting the German advance. A depression in the ground enabled the six squadrons of the brigade to get within two or three hundred yards of the French guns. The short charge which followed took the French completely by surprise. The Germans swept on over the slope behind the gun lines, but they were then checked by French cavalry attacking them in flank. The ultimate fate of von Bredow's brigade was somewhat similar to that of the Light Brigade, for out of a total strength of eight hundred all ranks, only four hundred and twenty returned. But the effects of the charge were far greater, for the guns of the 6th French Corps were silenced, and they were unable to fire again for the remainder of the action. The long distance results were even more impressive; for the charge was cited repeatedly, in the period leading up to the First World War, as proof that the cavalry charge was still a factor on the battlefield.

At the disaster of Sedan, French cavalry were ordered to try and break through the German line to open an avenue of retreat to the west. Three charges were made with great heroism and enormous casualties, but all failed in face of the German fire; though General de Gallifet, commanding the 7th Corps cavalry, followed by a few of his *chasseurs*, got as far as the German reserve infantry. As these few returned exhausted to the French lines they passed in front of a Prussian infantry battalion; but the battalion commander ordered the cease fire and he and his officers saluted their very gallant enemy. And so, effectively, horsed cavalry passed out of the main battle and into history.

CHAPTER III

Towards the Tank

To many soldiers, after the Franco-Prussian War, it was clear that in face of the fire from rifled weapons the cavalry charge was unlikely to succeed. But, perhaps from wishful thinking, the majority remembered the one successful charge by von Bredow and forgot the many disastrous failures. In the Boer War the great distances and wide open spaces of South Africa resulted in such a demand for mounted troops that units of mounted infantry were formed to supplement the cavalry. But mounted troops were needed only in their light role, for the war had soon shown how limited were the opportunities for a successful charge. Nevertheless, and in spite of the subsequent experiences of the Russo-Japanese and the Balkan Wars, there were still many officers who regarded the massed charge as the proper employment of cavalry. One of the notable exceptions was the late Commander-in-Chief in South Africa. Ten years before that war Lord Roberts had stated that the cavalry of the future would have to be employed far more as mounted infantry, and after the Boer War he commented on the way that quite small parties of Boers had been able to keep off whole brigades of cavalry.

Another officer who appreciated the effect of modern weapons of war was a student at the Staff College. Captain (later Major-General) J. F. C. Fuller wrote a paper in 1914 pointing out that the attack in a future war would have to contend with trenches protected by barbed wire. His solution was a vast increase in artillery fire.

Before relating the steps which led to the tracked and armoured fighting vehicle, it is worth while going back into history to consider earlier war vehicles conceived either as an alternative or as supplementary to contemporary mounted troops.

Apart from chariots, the earliest fighting vehicles were the *ribaudequins*, or war carts. The designation covers a very numerous family of carts which were either drawn or pushed into action by horses. Froissart describes some which were in use by the men of Ghent in 1382. He says that they were "high wheel-barrows reinforced with iron and long pointed spikes in front". The main armament was probably a large siege crossbow. A later version is shown in a fifteenth century engraving by Nicholas Glockendun of Nuremberg. It has sword blades in the yokes and is armed with guns. Many of these vehicles were merely carts loaded with men and weapons; others were more formidable and included, for instance, a covered vehicle with a gun in front which was pushed into action by a team of horses and pulled out again.

Jan Jiska, commander of the Hussite forces in the early fifteenth century, was the most successful user of war carts. They were manufactured in numbers by the simple method of putting armour round the supply wagons and mounting weapons in them. Jiska's tactics were to advance till he was in contact with his enemy and then to halt and induce him to attack. The attack was then broken up by fire power, and a counter-attack by cavalry and war carts was launched against the enemy's flanks.

There was another type of vehicle, however, which was a truer predecessor of the tank, and which might be described as an assault car. Designs for some of these vehicles were far ahead of their time, but it does not appear that they were ever used in battle, and it is uncertain even whether they were ever built.

The most notable of these assault cars was invented by Leonardo da Vinci in about 1500. There is a drawing of it in the British Museum which shows an armoured vehicle of almost incredibly modern appearance. The bottom half is shaped in the form of a shallow bowl, with slits cut in the bottom to take the lower parts of four wheels. The wheels are operated by gears and cranks from inside the vehicle, and, according to Leonardo da Vinci, eight men were required to operate the cranks. Over this bowl is fitted a tent-like armoured cover with loopholes for firearms. Leonardo da Vinci described his invention as follows: "I am building secure and covered chariots which are invulnerable, and when they advance with their guns in the midst of the enemy, even the largest enemy masses are bound to retreat; and behind them the infantry can follow in safety and without opposition. . . . These take the place of elephants and one may hold bellows in them to terrify horses or one may put carabiniers in them . . . . This is good to break up the ranks of the enemy but it must be followed up". This is a remarkable forecast of the tank idea, both in its mechanical design and in its tactical use. It is not clear whether the bellows were intended to make alarming noises or to emit unpleasant vapours.

John Napier, a distinguished mathematician, designed another remarkable assault car in 1596. Napier described it as a "round chariot of metal", and it was fully armoured with a metal twice the thickness required to withstand the musket fire of the time. He stated its motive power as being, "by those that be within, the same more easie and more spedie than so many armed men would be otherwise". Whether "those within" would agree the motion to be "more easie" is, perhaps, doubtful. Napier's idea of the employment of his machine was as follows: "The use thereof in moving serveth to break the array of the enemies battle . . . by continual discharge of harquebussiers through small holes, the enemy being abashed and uncertain as to what defence or pursuit to use against a moving mouth of metal". This is a fairly apt description of the modern use of armoured forces.

The above quotations come from Mark Napier's book of 1834, "Memoirs of John Napier"; and, of his ancestor, Mark Napier says further: "He had the skill to frame an engine which by virtue of some secret springs . . . which with other implements . . . enclosed within the bowels thereof had the power . . . to clear a field of 4 miles circumference of all the living creatures exceeding a foot of height, . . . he made it appear that he was able with the help of this machine alone to kill thirty thousand Turks without the hazard of a Christian. It is said that he gave proof upon a large plain in Scotland, "to the destruction of a great many herds of cattel and flocks of sheep whereof some were distant from other half a mile . . . and some a whole mile".

Almost a hundred years later J. Austen and F. Ball patented, "A Machine or chariot of Artillery which is Musket Proofe and soe contrived as to hold two falkonetts or small field pieces and two hand mortars to be used by the party sitting in the chariot and may be conveyed many miles a day with great ease and expedition which hath been seen and approved and thought very useful in our Armies here and elsewhere".

In 1855, during the Crimean War, steam was used to provide the motive power for an assault car. A wealthy man, known oddly as a philanthropist, took out a patent for a formidable machine described as a "Locomotive Battery for a Field of Battle with steam engine". The shape of the vehicle was very similar to that of Leonardo da Vinci, but the cover was of hardened steel with a serrated, instead of glancing, surface, which was intended to shatter the shot instead of throwing it off. It had four wheels and the armament consisted of fourteen-pounder carronades firing through loopholes. For shock action scythes were fixed to the framing and so hinged that they could be folded down when not required. Palmerston, it is said, refused to have anything to do with this machine as being too brutal for civilised use.

That armour was going to be necessary in a future war was foreseen in 1877 by Colonel C. B. Brackenbury. He had followed the Russo-Turkish struggle at Plevna and had made three deductions: firstly, that troops under cover were practically impregnable against frontal assault; secondly, that the shorter the range the greater the effect of artillery fire; and thirdly, that at close quarters artillery fire practically annihilates. It followed that artillery was the arm which should take over the traditional function of mounted troops in the attack. Brackenbury embodied these views in an article entitled *Ironclad Field Artillery* which was published in the *Nineteenth Century Review* of July 1878. He pointed out that owing to the immense increase in the fire power of infantry, gun crews were too exposed for close action; and he suggested that, to provide adequate protection, bullet proof shields should be mounted on the guns.

Brackenbury then proceeded to the revolutionary idea that artillery should be used as an assault weapon; that protected by its armour it should advance continually towards the enemy, combining in itself fire, movement and protection. He maintained that the moral effect of such an advance would achieve far greater results than the casualties which the artillery fire itself caused to the enemy.

Brackenbury's idea was very close to that of the armoured mechanised mount—the tank. Its weakness was that the guns had to be pushed forward by men under cover of the armoured shields, and that their cross-country capacity in such a movement was very limited.

At the time Brackenbury wrote steam operated railways were

already 50 years old, and steam power was established in road traction. But the effect of the existing road laws was that traction engines were the only mechanically propelled vehicles which could use the highways. This naturally restricted development, and there was no suitable engine which could have been used to power an armoured fighting vehicle.

Nevertheless the internal combustion engine, which was to provide the means for military mechanised movement, had been invented, and was being developed in several countries in the eighteen eighties. The greatest success was obtained by two Germans, Gottlieb Daimler and Karl Benz, and they, more than any were the founders of the motor age.

The first effective British motor car was designed by J. H. Turner, and it was exhibited at the Crystal Palace in 1896, the year in which motor cars were at last allowed unrestricted passage on British roads. Four years later an armoured car with a 16 h.p. engine was manufactured in England, and was known as the "Pennington". The armour consisted of a ¼-inch thick steel "skirt" round the entire chassis, and as armament there were two Maxim machine-guns with armoured shields. The car was manned by two machine-gunners and the driver.

In 1902 a somewhat similar armoured car was built for experimental purposes by Frederick Simms. The armour protection again consisted of ¼-inch thick plate as a skirt to the hull. This skirt reached to within 18 inches of the ground, but to give further cover over the tyres a fringe of chain mail was attached to its bottom edge. The car was armed with two Maxim machine-guns and a pom-pom (an automatic one-pounder cannon).

The following year an improved version of the car was exhibited by Simms at the Crystal Palace. The two machine-guns were mounted in turrets and the driver sat in the centre of the car and steered with the aid of a periscope. It was not a success, partly because the 16 h.p. Daimler engine was inadequate for the weight of the vehicle when fully loaded. Nevertheless it was notable as being the first armoured fighting vehicle to have rotating turrets.

The Pennington and Simms armoured cars were confined to roads and so offered no alternative to heavy cavalry in the main battle. To take the place of the horse, a mechanical assault mount would need the same ability to move across country combined with the protection which it was not possible to give the horse and its rider. The means for cross-country mechanical movement, in point of fact, already existed; but it was a long time before those who were battling with the military problem became aware of it. In the early years of the twentieth century Richard Hornsby & Sons developed tracks, primarily for use on oil-engined tractors. Results were successful, and in 1905 a steam driven Hornsby tractor fitted with tracks was purchased, for experiment, by the War Office. Hornsby failed to arouse any other British interest in the invention, and the War Office were unwilling to provide financial support. The American and Canadian patent rights were sold therefore to the Holt Caterpillar Company of New York. The Holt Company developed the track considerably, and by the start of the First World War it was being extensively used on agricultural vehicles.

There were now available the two essential ingredients of the tank: a reliable internal combustion engine and a track to take the place of wheels. It was to be some years yet before the appearance of an armoured cross-country fighting vehicle, but in 1912 an Australian, L. E. Mole submitted a remarkable design to the War Office which was not only very similar to the tanks actually produced but was, as it was later officially admitted, a better design than the tank which went into battle at the Somme in 1916. The design was pigeon-holed and a great opportunity lost. Mr. Mole, then serving in the 10th Battalion, Australian Imperial Force, submitted his idea again to the War Office in 1915. But although work was now proceeding on the production of a tracked fighting vehicle the design once more foundered on a War Office desk.

CHAPTER IV

The Birth of the Tank

FOR its immediate origins the tank probably owes more to the Royal Navy than it does to the Army. In 1914, after the defeat of the German Army at the battle of the Marne, a force consisting of a Naval Brigade and a squadron of the Royal Naval Air Service was despatched from England for the defence of Antwerp. To provide protection for the air base at Dunkirk and to rescue pilots who had been shot down the Admiralty Air Department decided to provide armoured cars. To this end they purchased a hundred Rolls Royce cars which were to be armed and armoured. To save time some of them were sent straight over to France without alteration, and were there fitted with a temporary armour of mild steel boiler plates at a Dunkirk steel works. The armouring comprised an open box body enclosing the rear wheels, triangular boxes covering the front wheels, a small raised box above the head of the driver, and flat plates over the engine and radiator. The armament consisted of one Maxim machine-gun on a pedestal mounting over the driver's compartment.

The remaining cars were converted in England under arrangements made by Commodore M. Sueter of the Air Division of the Admiralty. The first two were delivered in September 1914, and another thirteen in October. They were of great value on the open flank of the Army during the "Race to the Sea" in the autumn of 1914. This was a role far removed from the purpose for which they had been supplied, but the flat Flanders countryside was ideal for the employment of mobile machine-guns on the roads. The cars, however, had no top protection and their crews were very vulnerable to sniping from trees or the upper stories of houses. As a result a new design was produced with overhead armour and the machine-gun mounted in a rotating turret.

The first three of these improved armoured cars were landed in France in December 1914, but they were too late to be as

37

effective as had been hoped. Movement on the northern flank of the battle had ceased, and the opposing sides were facing each other across the barrier of trenches and barbed wire which was to be the predominant feature of the war on the Western Front for nearly the next 4 years.

These new turretted cars were built not only on Rolls-Royce chassis, but also on those of Lanchester, Delaunay-Belleville and Wolseley. They were all very similar in appearance, with the same armament of one Maxim machine-gun and 0·3-inch thick armour.

It was soon apparent that the armoured car force had little scope left for action. The first results of the use of mechanised armour had been encouraging, but a wheeled vehicle could not traverse wire and trenches.

To apportion credit for the introduction of the tank is difficult. The assault car, as we have seen in the last chapter, was a very old idea, and the tracks to replace its wheels and carry it across country were already in use for mechanical movement over rough ground and obstacles. Nevertheless it appears to have been Lieutenant-Colonel E. D. Swinton (later Major-General Sir E. D. Swinton, K.B.E., C.B.) who first appreciated that the solution to the problem posed by barbed wire, trenches and machine-guns was an armed and armoured vehicle moving on tracks.

Swinton went out to France in the peculiar capacity, for a serving soldier, of official war correspondent. He was thus in a position to take a broader and more detached view than officers who were actually concerned in the fighting. He had already acquired a reputation in the Army due to his amusing little military classic, *The Defence of Duffer's Drift*. To Swinton, then, it appeared that if armoured cars could be fitted with tracks they could cross both wire and trenches and defy the efforts of machine-guns to stop them. Before the War Swinton had received a report on the development of the Hornsby tracks, and here seemed the promise of a solution to the problem. In October 1914, therefore, Swinton pressed his idea on the Secretary of the Committee of Imperial Defence, Lieutenant-Colonel Hankey, under whom he had previously been serving.

The eventual result was that a Holt tractor was obtained and given the impossible task of hauling a truck loaded to about two and a half tons (the equivalent of the proposed weight of armour and armament) over a rain-sodden cross country course in February 1915. The War Office representatives, as a result of this demonstration, came to the conclusion that the idea was impracticable. Swinton, however, knowing that the test had been carried out under the most disadvantageous conditions, was not discouraged.

Nevertheless the War Office had lost interest, and the initiative now, rather oddly, passed to the Admiralty. At the instance of the First Lord, the then Mr. Winston Churchill, a Landships Committee was formed on 20th February 1915 under the presidency of Mr. (later Sir Eustace) Tennyson d'Eyncourt.

Some months were spent exploring various technical avenues, and then another type of American tracked vehicle was acquired, a Killen-Stuart Caterpillar Tractor. To enable it to overcome wire obstacles it was fitted at the R.N.A.S. Armoured Car Centre with a naval net cutter, and arrangements were put in hand for another demonstration.

The Admiralty, however, were now tiring of the project, and in July 1915 the decision was taken to disband the Armoured Car Force and to turn over the cars to the Army. The immediate future of the tank was in danger, but Sueter begged successfully for the temporary retention of No. 20 Armoured Car Squadron, which had been conducting the experiments with tracked vehicles. The War Office, too, suddenly displayed a renewed interest and further trials were thus assured.

The War Office interest was due to promptings from G.H.Q. in France, due in turn to Swinton's activities. He had submitted a memorandum giving his ideas and, in its support, had drawn attention to the performance of some caterpillar tractors which he had discovered hauling heavy howitzers. On 15th June he presented another memorandum suggesting specifications for an armoured fighting vehicle. These related to its climbing and gap-crossing ability, its armament, and its crew, and were all accepted by a G.H.Q. committee.

The Naval Landships Committee was now converted into a joint naval and military affair, and for the special benefit of the newer members a demonstration was staged with the Killen-Stuart tractor. Its performance over the trial course was a great success, and this time the War Office representatives as well as the Ministers who watched were impressed.

Subsequent technical progress was due primarily to two men: Lieutenant W. G. Wilson R.N.A.S. (later Major W. G. Wilson, C.M.G.) and Mr. W. Tritton (later Sir William Tritton), managing director of Messrs William Foster & Co. Wilson, a naval officer, transferred in due course to the Army; Tritton's firm were already making tracked vehicles under the trade name of "Centipede".

The contract for the first experimental machine was given to Foster's on 24th July 1915, the design being worked out by Tritton with Wilson's assistance. The result was very much of a "mock-up", the body being constructed of boiler plate with a dummy turret on top. The vehicle was driven by a 105 h.p. Daimler engine, giving a speed of about 2 m.p.h., and it was steered by throwing one track out of gear. A pair of tail wheels were fitted to give increased stability and to provide supplementary steering for minor deviations from the straight.

Tritton and Wilson now started on two fresh designs, working independently. Tritton's machine was similar to the first model but with various improvements in detail. Wilson's was entirely different. The body of the Tritton vehicle rested on the tracks. Wilson carried the tracks right round the body, which in shape was a rhomboid with upturned nose and a slope down at the rear.

The "Tritton" was completed quickly, and trials took place in September 1915 on Thetford Heath watched by King George V. Tritton had made valuable use of his firm's previous experience, and the engine, gearbox and differential had been adapted from those of a Daimler tractor built by Foster's before the War. The engine was a six-cylinder 105 h.p. sleeve valve type, sufficient for a speed of 3·7 m.p.h. It was completely enclosed with a door at the rear of the hull. For a slight turn the wheels on the steering tail were turned by wire ropes operated by the driver. For sharp turns the tail was lifted hydraulically and the vehicle steered by controlling the tracks through the secondary gear-boxes. The trials were only a moderate success, the balance being rather defective.

The "Wilson" was not ready at this time, but a "mock-up" was produced, and its appearance and dimensions suggested to visitors that it was more likely to meet the conditions specified of crossing an 8-foot trench and climbing a 4-foot 6-inch parapet.

At the end of September a meeting was held at Swinton's suggestion to consider what speed, armament and thickness of armour were required. Advised by Swinton, it was agreed that the armour should provide protection against a reversed bullet fired at a range of 10 yards. This seemingly odd choice of a reversed bullet as a standard of measurement was due to a recent discovery that if a bullet was reversed its armour-piercing qualities were greater: the hard outer casing was stopped by a comparatively thin armour plate, but the lead core of a reversed bullet was driven on and could penetrate considerably further. It was agreed that the armour should be 10 mm. thick in front, 8 mm. at the sides and 6 mm. on top. (The frontal thickness was subsequently increased to 12 mm.) The speed, it was felt, should if possible be 4 m.p.h. Tritton had designed his machine to carry two guns, one a 2-pounder and the other, for comparison, a 2·95-inch Q.F. mountain gun. It was decided that the 2-pounder was too light and, since there was some doubt as to whether adequate quantities of the 2·95-inch could be found, the naval 6-pounder was selected as the most suitable available weapon.

Following this meeting Tritton was requested to build a machine of a new type embodying these proposals and also to produce an improved model of his existing vehicle. The second task was completed by the beginning of December 1915. The turret had been removed to lower the centre of gravity, and a new type of track had been fitted to try and improve the rather limited cross-country performance. A trial on 3rd December showed a considerable improvement in performance and steadiness. However, no further development of this vehicle was undertaken, and it was subsequently used for training.

The reason for the cessation of work on the re-designed "Tritton" was the appearance of Wilson's machine. This was so vastly the better of the two that it was decided to put all the effort into its development and production.

This, the first mechanically driven battle vehicle, was a most remarkable machine. Although its prime designer was Wilson, Tritton had contributed a lot to it, and there were many elements in the design which were common to both the "Tritton" and the "Wilson".

The shape of the new vehicle was, as already stated, a rhomboid, with the tracks carried right round its perimeter on either side. At the rear there was a wheel-tail, similar to that of the "Tritton"; the wheels being kept in contact with the ground by springs. The two 6-pounder guns were mounted, one on each side of the hull, in large sponsons. On the top of the hull were two fixed turrets, one at the front and one at the back. The front turret accommodated the commander and the driver, sitting side by side with a machine-gun between them. The commander sat on the left and operated the brakes. In the rear turret there was another machine-gun and outside it were semaphore arms for communication between tanks. There were four doors, one at the back of each sponson, one at the rear of the hull, and a manhole in the top. The remainder of the crew consisted of four gunners and two gearsmen.

The vehicle was of considerable size. From the ground to the top of the hull was 8 feet, and the overall length without the steering tail was 26 feet 5 inches. The weight fully stowed was 28 tons.

The steering procedure was the same as for the "Tritton". To steer on the tracks it was usual to lock the differential and put the gearbox on the side to which it was desired to turn in the neutral position, and the gearbox on the other side to "High" or "Low" ratio. A very sharp turn could be made by braking the track on the neutral side. Turning on the tracks was carried out by the gearsmen under the directions of the driver. To attract their attention the driver banged on the engine cover and signalled his instructions with his fingers according to a standard code.

The engine was identical with that used in the "Tritton", giving the same road speed. The total armament comprised the two 6-pounder Q.F. Hotchkiss guns in the sponsons and four Hotchkiss machine-guns. The armour was of maximum and minimum thicknesses of 12 mm. and 6 mm. respectively, as agreed at the September meeting.

The first run took place on 16th January 1916, and 10 days later the machine was sent to Hatfield Park where a trial course had been laid out.

The name by which the vehicle was to be known presented some difficulty. Some designation was required which would not divulge its nature, and yet would be sufficiently reasonable not to arouse curiosity in anyone seeing this object covered with a tarpaulin on a railway truck. Swinton discussed the problem with Lieutenant-Colonel W. Dalby Jones. After rejecting such names as "cistern" and "container", they decided on "tank". Swinton told a friend of the writer's that the name was suggested to them by the very similar shapes of the new vehicle and the petrol tank of a popular make of motor-cycle.

The trial took place on 2nd February 1916 and was very successful, the tank demonstrating its ability to cross a 10-foot

wide trench and surmount a 4-foot 6-inch vertical obstacle.
The distinguished audience was very enthusiastic (though Lord
Kitchener remained somewhat sceptical as to its battle value).
On 8th February the King rode in the tank and considered that
a large number would be a great asset to the Army.

And so the first tank in the world entered the arena and
ushered in a new era in military history. To modern eyes this
ancestor of all tracked fighting vehicles appears somewhat
cumbersome and unwieldy; but it was a mechanical marvel and
it was not ugly. When Major-General J. F. C. Fuller first saw
it, it appeared to him as, "not a monster, but a very graceful
machine, with beautiful lines, lozenge-shaped, but with two
clumsy-looking wheels behind it".

It was perhaps General Fuller who first grasped its historical
significance, for in a paper he wrote in 1917 on tank tactics he
said of the tank, "it is, in fact, an armoured mechanical horse".

CHAPTER V

The Tanks Entry into War

THE tank which entered the war as the Mark I was identical with Wilson's masterpiece described in the last chapter. But there were two different types, classified respectively as "Male" and "Female". The male tank had the same armament as the prototype, whilst the female was armed with machine-guns only—five Vickers and one Hotchkiss. The addition of the female tank was due to Swinton who foresaw the necessity of the gun tank being supported by a machine-gun tank to give close protection against infantry. Four Vickers guns were mounted two in each sponson.

G.H.Q. in France originally asked for only forty tanks, and it was at Swinton's urging that the War Office increased the order to a hundred. Of these hundred machines, twenty-five were ordered from Foster's and the remainder from the Metropolitan Carriage, Wagon & Finance Co. The Metropolitan had larger works than Foster's, and the former firm subsequently built about 70 per cent of all the British tanks built in the war. The initial order was increased by another fifty after the decision had been taken to build tanks of two different types, and after Lloyd George had undertaken to make the additional engines available.

Command of the new arm was fittingly given to Swinton, who had been so largely responsible for its foundation. However, his function was limited to the formation and training of tank units, and like many another soldier before and since, he was denied the chance of leading into battle the troops he had trained. It was decided that command in France should be exercised by an officer with experience of warfare in France. Swinton suggested Lieutenant-Colonel H. J. Elles, R.E., who had been G.H.Q.'s representative for tank development and policy. Elles (later General Sir Hugh Elles, K.C.M.G., C.B., D.S.O.) was appointed to the command on 29th September 1916.

The results of Swinton's thinking over the months of development and trial were embodied in his *Notes on the Employment of Tanks*. This document contained a remarkable forecast of the correct tactics both for individual tanks and sub-units, and of the place of the new arm in the major battle. For all his foresight, however, Swinton missed the historical significance of a tank force. He first argued that "The tanks cannot win battles by themselves. They are purely auxiliary to the infantry . . .", and ultimately concluded, "It seems, as the tanks are an auxiliary to the infantry, that they must be counted as infantry and in operation be under the same command". But the tanks were *not* infantry. This new force was a reincarnation of the massive cavalry arm which broke the French centre at Blenheim and of Hasdrubal's elephants which shattered the Roman legions at the Metaurus.

The need for secrecy led to some curious titles being given to the new corps. The original title of Tank Detachment was rapidly changed to that of Armoured Car Section of the Motor Machine Gun Service. This cumbrous title was, however, too near the truth and the unit soon became the Heavy Section, Machine-Gun Corps. Some months later, in a tribute presumably to its rising strength, it was re-titled the Heavy Branch, Machine-Gun Corps; and, when the need to safeguard its existence ceased, it became in June 1917 the Tank Corps. The designation "Royal" was granted after the War.

The total first establishment of the Tank Corps (then still the Heavy Section) comprised 184 officers and 1,610 other ranks. The tactical unit was the company and there were six of these, each organised into four six-tank sections (three "male" and three "female" tanks). Each section had a seventh tank in mechanical reserve.

A major problem which still had to be solved was the provision of communications for the control of tanks in battle, and for liaison between tanks and with the infantry with whom they were operating. A small spark wireless transmitter, working on 200 metres with a range of 3 miles, had been designed by the R.E. Experimental Wireless Establishment, but it was useless whilst the tank was on the move owing to the vibration and the noise of the machinery. Communication between tanks was carried out by displaying metal discs, by semaphore with metal arms, and by morse flag signalling out of the roof manhole. For short distances telephone cable was laid from drums mounted on the tank. None of these methods, however, was an unqualified success.

The great battle of the Somme had opened on 1st July 1916, and some 6 weeks later the first thirteen tanks reached France. Others followed in batches until by 30th August the whole of the two companies which were destined to take part in the battle of 15th September were concentrated at the training centre at Yvrench. There were fifty operational tanks and ten spare. By 10th September these two companies, C and D, had moved up to the forward area. By this time A Company had also arrived in France, but it could not join the other two in time for the battle.

No clear idea had been formulated as to how the tanks were to be used. G.H.Q. wanted them quickly, with the result that they inevitably fought in small parties and the crews had no time for adequate training. Not only was the training of the crews in the operation of individual tanks below battle standard, but there had been no training at all in co-operation between tanks and infantry. There was some doubt, indeed, as to when the tank should start its attack: if it started too soon the enemy barrage, it was thought, would come down and catch the infantry; and if it started too late there appeared to be a danger that the infantry would reach the objective first. It was finally decided that the start of the tank should be so timed that it reached the first objective 5 minutes ahead of the infantry. It was also agreed that the primary object of a tank should be to destroy those strong points which were holding up the advance of the infantry.

The list of items which were to be carried in the tank was formidable. Rations for this first tank battle consisted of sixteen loaves of bread and about thirty tins of foodstuffs. The various types of stores included four spare Vickers machine-gun barrels, one spare Vickers machine-gun, one spare Hotchkiss machine-gun barrel, two boxes of revolver ammunition, thirty-three thousand rounds of ammunition for the machine-guns, a telephone instrument and a 100 yards of cable on a drum, a signalling lamp, three signalling flags, two wire cutters, one spare drum of engine oil, one spare drum of gear oil, two small drums of grease, and three water cans. Added to this miscellaneous collection was all the equipment which was stripped off the eight inhabitants of the tank, so that there was not very much room to move about.

The first action was very much an affair of individual tanks, for they were widely distributed amongst a number of infantry divisions. Forty-nine tanks were allotted for the operation, but only thirty-two managed to reach their starting points. Of these thirty-two, nine broke down, five got ditched, nine were well behind the infantry but did some useful clearing up, and the remaining nine achieved the intention of being ahead of the infantry on the objective and causing severe loss to the enemy.

This was not an impressive result, but those tanks which did make contact with the enemy had an enormous psychological effect. Some of the Germans lost their nerve and bolted before the tanks even arrived within gunshot.

Most noteworthy was the feat performed by three tanks of D Company which led the assault of an English and a New Zealand division on the strong point of Flers. One of them drove straight through the village followed by parties of infantry; an event which, according to a colourful press rendering, was reported from the air as, "A tank is walking up the High Street of Flers with the British Army cheering behind". The press were, in fact, right in portraying this as a dramatic event, but it is probable that few soldiers realised that they were witnessing the opening scene of a revolution in warfare.

Since the tanks in this their first action, and in the few remaining operations of 1916, were used in small detachments of three or less, the company organisation virtually disappeared except for administration. Nevertheless on 20th October a notification was received from the War Office that not only was the Tank force to be considerably expanded but that the companies were to be formed into battalions. The four companies in France were to be augmented to twelve and grouped into four battalions. The two companies in England were to form the nucleus of five more battalions. Each battalion was to be organised into three companies comprising four fighting five-tank sections and a headquarters four-tank section. The company organisation was changed again at the beginning of 1917. The fighting sections were reduced from four to three, and the number of tanks in each section became four instead of five. The original fourth fighting section became a spare section. The technical work necessary to keep the tanks in the fighting line was recognised by the addition of a Workshops company to each battalion.

The battalion organisation was soon followed by the formation of brigades. On 30th January 1917 C and D Battalions were grouped as the 1st Brigade, and on 15th February A and B Battalions became the 2nd Brigade. On 27th April Headquarters 3rd Brigade was formed in the expectation of the arrival of two new battalions from the Training Centre at Wool in Dorsetshire.

At the end of December 1916 the Tank force in France received a most important reinforcement in the person of perhaps its most brilliant soldier, for Major (later Major-General) J. F. C. Fuller reported to its headquarters as G.S.O. 2. (General Staff Officer, Grade 2).

As a result of the tank actions of 1916 some modifications were made to the Mark I tank. The most important of these were the abolition of the wheeled tail and the replacement of the Hotchkiss machine-guns by the Lewis type. The wheeled tail had proved very vulnerable to shell fire and the tank could be steered quite adequately by the tracks. It had been intended that the Mark I should be followed by a new type having heavier armour and wider tracks, but tanks were required so urgently that the time could not be spared for these modifications to be put into production. Fifty each of a Mark II and a Mark III were built, but they were practically the same as the modified Mark I.

More extensive modifications were incorporated in the very successful Mark IV, of which the first reached France on 22nd April 1917 after the battle of Arras. It had been designed by Major Wilson late in 1916.

The sponsons of the Mark I had to be removed (a very lengthy operation) before the tank would fit the railway loading gauge. On the Mark IV the sponsons could be swung inboard in a very short time. The sponsons were also smaller; considerably so on the "female" Mark IV. The tracks, rollers and links were of a new design and heavier. Petrol was carried in an armoured sixty-gallon tank mounted on the outside and at the back of the tank: a very much more secure arrangement than the Mark I's two petrol tanks installed inside the driver's compartment. The distribution and quality of the armour was vastly improved; a special type of steel being used which resisted the German armour piercing bullet. Steel plates with pinhole perforations were provided for the driver's vision, in place of the Mark I's attractive but dangerous glass prisms, which splintered into the driver's eyes when hit.

Plate 1   'MOTHER', THE PROTOTYPE MARK I TANK, ON TEST IN BURTON PARK, LINCOLN, 21ST JANUARY, 1916.

Plate 2. MARK I (MALE) TANK CROSSING A BRITISH TRENCH ON ITS WAY TO ATTACK THIEPVAL, 25TH SEPTEMBER, 1916.

Considerable trouble had been experienced through tanks "ditching", that is getting stuck in a trench or soft ground. Various devices were tried, but the most successful was produced in the summer of 1917. A single squared wooden beam, rather longer than the width of the tank, was fixed across both tracks. The moving tracks carried it down under the belly and it generally gave sufficient purchase to pull the tank out. When not in use it was carried on top of the tank clipped to a pair of rails.

The campaigning season proper of 1917 opened with the battle of Arras on 9th April. The ambitious intention was to break the German front and pour the Cavalry Corps through the gap.

The standard Western Front plan for a major attack at this stage of the war was to blast the enemy position with an avalanche of fire for days on end with shells from dumps which had been weeks in the forming. At the end of this softening up process the infantry advanced under the protection of more artillery fire. Without artillery fire the infantry could not move, and when they had reached the extreme range of the guns they had to halt until the artillery could be moved forward. This could be a lengthy process as the artillery had destroyed all the roads over which the guns could move. By the time the guns were in their new position the enemy had reinforced their front and the process began all over again. It was a gunners' war.

With the advent of the tank it became possible to advance without this massive artillery preparation: indeed such a bombardment, far from helping the tanks, actually hindered the advance for it frequently made the ground impassable. There was, of course, the additional disadvantage that the enemy had many days notice of the intention.

Nevertheless the battle of Arras followed the usual pattern. The tanks in small packets struggled forward over the shell-torn ground, and, after an initial success, the tired infantry outran the artillery support and the attack gradually slowed to a halt. Subsequent renewals of the offensive were no more successful.

The Germans were fortunate enough to capture two tanks complete, for they discovered how effective their armour-piercing bullet was against the Mark I. As a result a German order directed that every man should carry five rounds of K (armour-piercing) ammunition, and that every machine-gun should be supplied with several hundred rounds. Henceforth the crews of Mark I tanks were to suffer very heavy casualties. Fortunately it was a long time before the Germans discovered that K ammunition was of little use against a Mark IV.

On 16th April 1917 French tanks went into action for the first time. Colonel (later General) J. E. Estienne was primarily responsible for the adoption of tanks by the French Army. He, like Swinton, saw the need for an armoured vehicle with ability to cross country. Seeing some Holt caterpillar tractors of the British Army at work, he suggested that if such a machine was armoured and provided with a gun the result would be the type of fighting vehicle which was required. Estienne had great difficulty in getting any attention paid to his ideas, but he eventually obtained permission from G.Q.G. to work out a design. Estienne consulted M. Brille of the Schneider Creusot works and prepared a detailed design. On 25th February 1916 G.Q.G. was persuaded to order four hundred tanks from the Schneider Creusot works before work had got any further than the drawing board. Soon afterwards M. Breton, Under-Secretary of the Inventions Committee, succeeded in getting an order placed for another four hundred tanks to an entirely different design prepared by the firm of Saint Chamond.

Both the Schneider and St. Chamond tanks were in fact armoured boxes mounted on copies of the Holt tractor. The Schneider CA1 (M16) was armed with a 75 mm. Schneider gun on the right forward side of the hull and a 8 mm. Hotchkiss on the left forward side. The traverse of the Schneider gun was very limited. The vehicle was powered by a Schneider four-cylinder 70 h.p. engine, giving a road speed of 5 m.p.h. The thickness of the armour varied between 6 mm. and 25 mm. The nosepiece or stem of the tank also acted as wirecutter, and there was a tailpiece for balance and steering. The weight was 14·6 tons. The crew consisted of a commander, a driver and five gunners. Entry to the tank was by a double door at the rear. The Schneider tank was not a success. It was very hot inside, with poor ventilation and observation; it caught fire easily from shell-fire; the tracks were too narrow for soft going; and the vertical armour would not keep out the German "K" bullet.

The St. Chamond was an unwieldy looking vehicle with a heavy overhanging nose, protruding from the front of which was a 75 mm. field gun. As subsidiary armament there were four Hotchkiss machine-guns, one on either side of the field gun and one mounted at each side of the tank. It had a Panhard four-cylinder engine which operated a dynamo supplying current to an electric motor for each track. The road speed of 5 m.p.h. was similar to that of the Schneider. The electric transmission added considerably to the weight, which was 25·3 tons. It was a better tank than the Schneider, but its cross-country performance was poor and its tracks too narrow.

The Schneider tanks, 132 of them, first went into action on 16th April 1917, but with only limited success. The St. Chamonds made their appearance on 5th May, and failed in their first attack. A number of the St. Chamonds were later sent to Russia and were used by the Russian Army until its collapse. In October it was decided to stop building medium tanks for the French Army and to concentrate all further effort on the new Renault light tank.

In June, Fuller, then a Lieutenant-Colonel, wrote an extremely important paper on how he considered tanks should be employed the following year. He drew attention to the slight depth of the entrenched fronts in comparison with their length, and pointed out that more favourable opportunities for a decisive attack had seldom occurred in the history of war. All that was necessary was to maintain an infantry advance of a few thousand yards. But, as he continued, gun-fire could no longer do this on account of the increasing depth of entrenchments, and the tank was the only weapon which could.

It is not proposed to follow here the brilliant reasoning of this remarkable paper, which was over 20 years in advance of current military thought. But Fuller came to the very far-sighted conclusion that, "The one thing to realise is, that mechanical warfare is going to supersede muscular warfare. That is to say, more and more is war going to depend on the engine than on man's legs. . . . Success in war depends upon mobility and mobility upon time. . . . The Tank is first of all a time-saving machine, secondly a shield—it is, in fact, an armoured mechanical horse".

Considering the method of employing them, tanks had achieved remarkable results in their first year of operation. But there had been little which could be regarded as outstanding. The end of their first year was marked by the Third Battle of Ypres, and the appalling conditions of the ground precluded any chance of their proper employment. The heavy rain and the massive artillery bombardment which destroyed the drainage system turned much of the zone of attack into deep liquid mud. Nevertheless there was a brilliant little action at St. Julien on 19th August 1917 which was a presage of armour's true destiny on the battlefield.

After the initial attack the infantry of 18th Corps were held up by a nest of pill-box strongholds north-east of St. Julien. They were well sited, built of reinforced concrete at least 3 feet thick, and so well concealed as to present extremely difficult targets for the heavy guns. Field guns were useless against them. Three of these strongholds were in the ruins of farm-steads and they had garrisons of from fifty to a hundred men. Their capture was essential, but the brigade commanders concerned estimated that it would cost the attacking troops between six hundred and a thousand casualties.

General Sir Ivor Maxse, G.O.C. 18th Corps, then discussed with Colonel Baker-Carr, commanding the 1st Tank Brigade, the possibility of taking the pill-boxes with tanks. Baker-Carr guaranteed to do so at half the estimated cost to the infantry, but asked that there should be no artillery preparation and that the advance of the tanks should be concealed by a smoke barrage. These conditions were agreed and the attack was arranged.

The plan was that two tanks should be used against each pill-box, attacking them from the rear, and that each pair of tanks should be supported by an infantry platoon. A total of nine tanks were to be employed, formed into a composite com-pany. Tanks and their supporting infantry were to use roads as far as these served them, since they offered the only firm surface. At the suggestion of Fuller, GSO 1 of the Tank force, platoons were to move in file behind their tanks. To this novel tactical formation the success of the operation was largely due.

At 4.45 a.m. on 19th August the artillery isolated the German pill-boxes with smoke. Just before 6.0 a.m. the tanks had completed their envelopment of the enemy positions. Shortly afterwards the first pill-box, Hillock Farm, was captured, its garrison fleeing as soon as the tanks started their attack. At 6.15 a.m. two tanks fired forty rounds at the Mont de Hibou stronghold, and those of the garrison who had not fled sur-rendered to the infantry as soon as they arrived. Triangle Farm put up a gallant fight and the garrison was eventually wiped out by the supporting infantry. Of the tanks allotted to the attack of the Cockroft strong point, one became ditched on the way, and the other was ditched within 50 yards of its objective. However the Germans were not aware that the tank was powerless to move further, and they evacuated the pill-box in panic.

The total British casualties were only two killed and twenty-seven wounded.

By this time nearly all the tanks used in action were Mark IV's, and so immune to the German "K" ammunition . A number of Marks I and II were converted into supply carriers to bring up petrol, ammunition and stores for the fighting tanks.

CHAPTER VI

Cambrai

IN his book *Memoirs of an Unconventional Soldier*, General Fuller has called the chapter, in which he deals with the battle of Cambrai, *Knights in Armour*. The title is well chosen, for it was indeed such an armoured charge as those of Crecy and Agincourt, but with the difference that the defenders had no modern equivalent of the long bow with which to defeat the attack.

The origins of the battle of 20th November 1917 had occurred some five months earlier. On 12th June Major-General Sir John Capper, Administrative Commander of the Tank Corps, visited Brigadier-General Elles's Headquarters. Whilst he was there Fuller gave him a copy of his paper on the employment of tanks in 1918, which he had finished the day before. Capper became so interested in Fuller's ideas that he worked out a project of his own based on a force of four thousand tanks and a large number of infantry transporters.

The following day Capper and Fuller roughed out a plan for an attack over the admirable tank country lying to the east of the line St. Quentin-Cambrai. On 14th June Capper went to G.H.Q., taking with him Fuller's paper and their joint scheme.

A month later, on 14th July, a conference was held at G.H.Q. under the chairmanship of General Kiggell, Chief of the General Staff, to consider how tanks should be employed in 1918. Capper discovered that the St. Quentin-Cambrai scheme had not been considered, as the paper had apparently been lost. Everybody present, however, was in favour of Fuller's paper except the chairman. But Kiggell's opposition was sufficient to ensure that the paper was not approved.

On 3rd August Fuller conceived another idea which was to capture St. Quentin by a lightning stroke. The main striking force would consist of two tank brigades backed up by four infantry divisions (two British and two French), with three cavalry divisions for exploitation. Elles thought that this plan

See map page 223

had little chance of acceptance as G.H.Q. would object to co-operating with the French. Fuller then suggested that the attack might be moved to an area immediately south of Cambrai, which was in the British zone of operations. He then drew up an outline plan of a major tank raid which Elles took with him to G.H.Q. He was unable, however, to arouse very much interest. An approach was then made to General Sir Julian Byng, G.O.C.-in-C 3rd Army, since the proposed operation would take place in his sector. Byng liked the idea and sought Haig's approval. But although the Commander-in-Chief was at first in favour, the dismal Kiggell persuaded him that the plan would entail an unacceptable dispersion of effort.

However, in spite of this apparent failure the seed had been sown, and by about 15th October active consideration was being given to a tank attack on the front of 3rd Army. On 19th October Elles told Fuller that a tank attack was to take place on 20th November and that it was to be mounted in the 3rd Army sector in the identical spot south of Cambrai which Fuller had recommended at the beginning of August.

But Fuller had selected this area with a large scale raid in mind and was horrified when the details of the Army plan showed that a decisive battle was planned. The two canals, du Nord and de l'Escaut, would protect the left and right flanks respectively, of a raid, but would hinder any attempts to widen a penetration to achieve a complete break through. Furthermore, and infinitely more important, there were no reserves of infantry to follow up any success: they had all been used up in the long drawn out struggle of Third Ypres.

The area chosen was ideal for tanks. It was mostly open rolling chalk plateau which, as it had lain uncultivated for the past two years, was covered with long grey withered grass matted into a surface ideal for tank tracks. Save for Bourlon's wooded hill to the north-east of the area, there were no prominent features. Low ridges ran across the front from north-west to south-east.

On the reverse slopes of the ridges lay the main German line of resistance, hidden from the eyes of the British observers. The Germans hoped, too, that their trenches here were tank-proof. There were three lines of them, and according to British information they were 12 feet wide and 18 feet deep; in addition there were 2 feet 6 inch high parapets and parados, so sloped as to increase the effective width to some 16 or 18 feet.

To make sure that the defensive system should be proof against infantry as well as tanks, it was covered by a formidable belt of wire which was nowhere less than 50 yards deep. Thicker bulges in the wire made salients into which it was intended that the attacking infantry should be enticed, and these salients were enfiladed by nests of machine-guns. It was estimated that to cut this wire by artillery fire would have taken five weeks and twenty million pounds worth of ammunition. Judging by previous experience, by the time the five weeks of bombardment had finished the Germans would have amassed heavy reinforcements of infantry and artillery to meet the attack, and the subsequent dreary struggle in the shell-pitted ground would have ended in the same fashion as the previous battles. As near as the Germans could make it, therefore, this sector of their front was impregnable.

From the tank point of view the problem was to get the Mark IV tanks, with a gap-crossing ability of 10 feet, over trenches which might be effectively 18 feet wide. It was solved by making fascines out of brushwood. Twenty-one thousand ordinary bundles of the type of fascine used for road repairing were assembled at the Tank Central Workshops. To make a fascine about seventy-five bundles were bound round with heavy chains and then compressed by using specially fitted tanks to pull on the chains in opposite directions. The result was a very strong fascine about 10 feet long and $4\frac{1}{2}$ feet in diameter, weighing about 10 tons. Each tank was to carry one of these fascines mounted on its nose, and a special release gear was fitted inside the tank so that the fascine could be tumbled into the trench which had to be crossed.

Construction of these fascines was not the only work carried out by the Tank Central Workshops in preparation for the battle: a hundred and ten tank sledges were made for carrying supplies and thirty-two tanks were fitted with grapnels and cables to pull away enemy wire from lines selected for the advance of the cavalry.

Fuller, as soon as he knew that the operation was to take place, wrote a note on the tactical employment of tanks in the attack. The following were the salient points:

(*a*) Tanks operating against each separate objective should constitute one tank echelon consisting of a number of tank sections of three tanks each. The three tanks of a section were to be organised in triangular formation—

the leading tank being called the "advanced tank" and the other two the "main body tanks".

(b) The advanced tank was to move slightly ahead of the main body tanks in order to keep down enemy fire, whilst the latter, followed by the infantry, attacked the enemy and trenches. Once this task had been completed the advanced tank would go into reserve, whilst the main body tanks were to place the infantry through the wire, and then to cover and assist them in the capture of the area.

(c) Each main body tank should be followed by a platoon of infantry, with other platoons following up behind.

(d) In the attack the advanced tanks were to cross the enemy wire and then, turning left, to move along the trench close to the parapet. They were not to cross the enemy trench until the main body tanks and their following infantry were over. The main body tanks were to follow each other over the same crossing point so that only one fascine was used. The left-hand tank was then to move left along the trench; the right-hand one was to continue on to the support trench, cross it and then also turn left.

These tactics were approved by Headquarters 3rd Army, but the Commander of the 51st Division was allowed to use other tactics, devised by himself, with unfortunate results.

The intention stated for the attack was to break the German defences between the Canal de l'Escaut on the right and the Canal du Nord on the left, and then, with the assistance of tanks, to pass the Cavalry Corps through the gap to capture Bourlon Wood, Cambrai and the crossings of the River Sensée, and to cut off the German troops holding the line between Havrincourt and the river.

The attack was to be carried out by 3rd and 4th Corps. There was to be no previous artillery bombardment, and artillery fire on the day of the attack was to consist mainly of smoke screens on the front and flanks.

Of the Tank Brigades, 2nd and 3rd were allotted to 3rd Corps, and 1st to 4th Corps. At first a proportion of tank units was held in reserve, but ultimately, to Fuller's disgust, it was decided to have no tank reserve at all.

To bring up the three tank brigades entailed considerable transport organisation. For the sake of security all movement

57

was carried out at night, and thirty-six trains had to be run, each lifting twelve tanks.

A total of three hundred and twenty-four fighting tanks were allocated for the battle, with another fifty-four in mechanical reserve. In addition to the fighting tanks there were eighteen supply tanks, thirty-two wire pulling tanks fitted with grapnels, three wireless tanks, two bridging material tanks, and, at Army Headquarters, one telephone cable tank. From the concentration area this mass of armour moved forward in long columns, dividing into smaller columns at dispersal points, and finally breaking up into detachments of two or three tanks taking up their allotted positions. By 5 a.m., well before the late November dawn, the tanks were in one long 6-mile line. Fortune had favoured them, for the night was very dark with a slight ground mist, and the last stage of the move had been carried out so silently that many of our own infantry did not know that they had arrived.

On the morning of 19th November General Elles wrote the following Special Order:

"Special Order No. 6

(1) To-morrow the Tank Corps will have the chance for which it has been waiting for many months—to operate on good going in the van of the battle.

(2) All that hard work and ingenuity can achieve has been done in the way of preparation.

(3) It remains for unit Commanders and for tank crews to complete the work by judgment and pluck in battle itself.

(4) In the light of past experience I leave the good name of the Corps with great confidence in their hands.

(5) I propose leading the attack of the centre division.

Hugh Elles, B.G.

November 19, 1917   Commanding Tank Corps

Distribution to Tank Commanders—H.E."

Just before the attack started General Elles boarded a tank called *Hilda* of H Battalion, the unit in the centre of the long line with *Hilda* in the middle of its leading tank echelon. He carried an ash stick to which was attached the brown, red and green flag of the Tank Corps; and so in mediaeval style with his distinguishing banner displayed General Elles led his armoured cavalry into action.

Tanks and infantry crossed their start lines at 6.10 a.m., and ten minutes later the artillery barrage came down on the foremost German positions. Before the German infantry had recovered from the avalanche of shells the leading tanks were upon them. Shearing through and flattening the wire, dropping their fascines and lurching over the trenches, the tanks went through the first line with hardly a pause. On they drove, through the second line, and then the Hindenburg line was penetrated, and the German front broken for the first time since trench warfare had paralysed the Western theatre of war.

At German Supreme Headquarters there was a sense of disaster, for there appeared to be nothing to stop the British from advancing as far as they chose. Adequate reinforcements, it was calculated, could not reach the area in less than 3 days. Ludendorff prepared emergency orders for a general retreat.

But there were no British reserves of either infantry or tanks. There was, however, the Cavalry Corps: a great mass of horsemen burning to show what they could do once wire and machine-guns had been swept from their path. Fuller thought that probably for the last time in the history of war cavalry had a fair chance of operating as a mounted arm. But the cavalry divisions were hamstrung by an inept higher command. Elles had shown the true cavalry spirit, riding into action at the head of his troops and even commanding his own tank in the process. Cavalry Corps Headquarters was static and miles in the rear of the battle, and the Corps Commander had made certain that the horse soldiers should be denied their long awaited chance by directing that no action was to be taken without his approval. Since successful mounted action depended upon the ability to take advantage of the fleeting opportunity there was no torrent of hooves to follow the tanks through the gap which they opened to the enemy's rear. The chance of ending the war at a stroke was lost.

Fuller's tank tactics worked brilliantly. The manoeuvre of each section of three tanks had been so well rehearsed that it was performed almost as a drill, and lanes through the forest of wire were so effectively flattened that the infantry could walk through it with no more effort than would be occasioned by marshy ground. As a Highlander put in a letter, ". . . In most places the wire was absolutely down and flat; even at the worst one could pass over in comfort with a little judicious exercise of the "heather step".

The first day's fighting had practically exhausted the tanks. Sixty-five had been knocked out by direct hits, seventy-one had

had mechanical breakdowns, forty-three were immobilised through "ditching" or other causes, and a large number required repairs and re-adjustment after the long distances which had been covered. Even though a considerable number were still mechanically fit for action, their crews were dead tired.

The attack was renewed on the following day, the 21st, but German reserves were now arriving and there was little tank support available for the attacking infantry. On this and succeeding days the impetus of the advance gradually died away in a manner which was all too familiar on the Western Front.

On 30th November the Germans counter-attacked; and, like the British, they did so without any previous preparation. There was a short but heavy bombardment, in which smoke and gas shells were largely used, and under cover of this, German infantry used new infiltrating tactics to penetrate the British positions. The attackers had no tanks, but they were faced by tired troops in improvised positions. On the left the Germans were held at Bourlon Wood, but on the right they succeeded unpleasantly well. A very dangerous situation was saved by the 1st Guards Brigade, and a subsequent counter-attack by the 2nd Tank Brigade.

At the time of this emergency the 2nd Tank Brigade was out of the line at Fins with its tanks dismantled for entraining and the men engaged in clearing up. At 9.55 a.m. the Brigade Commander received information of a heavy German surprise attack. Less than 3 hours later, at 12.40 p.m., the Brigade moved into action. Initially it consisted of twenty-two tanks of B Battalion followed by fourteen of A Battalion; but this strength was gradually increased as other tanks were got ready and hastened towards the scene of action. The Germans were checked, and by the following day the British line was stabilised.

From the very first, successful tank action has depended on adequate communications for command and control. The provision of such communications has never been easy, and at the battle of Cambrai the means available were rudimentary. The normal practice was to establish a Brigade command post as far forward as possible, to which tank commanders reported for orders and to give information. The wireless tanks could not work on the move; they merely carried the wireless equipment which had to be off-loaded and erected before it could work. Wireless communication was supplemented when possible by telephone lines run out to Brigade command posts from a cable head, and laid by cable tanks. Drums of cable were mounted on the rear of a cable tank and poles were slung along its sides. Holes were dug for the poles by fitting jumpers to the tracks. A poled cable route could be constructed quite quickly; for as the tank moved forward cable was paid off from one of the drums and the line detachment, following behind, tied the cable to poles and stuck them into the ground at the requisite intervals.

CHAPTER VII

The Last Year of the First World War

IN February 1918 the then Lieutenant-Colonel Fuller wrote a
paper entitled *Defensive and Offensive Use of Tanks, 1918.* In
dealing with the offensive he proposed that an attack should be
carried out with three echelons of tanks, charged respectively
with the tasks of advanced guard, trench clearing and exploiting;
and that the infantry element of the attacking force, mainly
machine-gunners, should be lifted in both fighting and special
carrier tanks. He listed certain vital needs for tank warfare;
amongst these were tanks which could operate by night, smoke
producers and projectors for installation in tanks, and mortar
tanks for village fighting.

The existing tanks were virtually blinded at night, and were
almost incapable of keeping direction without the aid of marking
tapes or of officers walking in front of them. The proposal
to lift the infantryman in a tank is of particular interest, for this
was a revival of the classic dragoon: the soldier who rides to
battle but normally fights dismounted. The original horse
dragoon had been gradually assimilated into the heavy cavalry.
But since the dragoon fulfils a recurring requirement in war, his
place has often been taken by the mounted infantryman, notably
in the Boer War. With tanks taking the role of the heavy horsed
cavalry, mechanised and armoured mounts for the infantry are
a logical accompaniment. But it was not till a quarter of a
century later that the armoured personnel carrier became a
permanent feature of the Army.

On 2nd March 1918 Fuller attended a conference at G.H.Q.
The discussion centred on defensive plans to meet a German
offensive. This was anticipated owing to the arrival on the
Western Front of divisions released by the collapse of Russia,
and a consequent vast increase of German strength. General
Gough, commanding 5th Army, suggested that the best em-
ployment of tanks in the defensive was as static strong points.
Haig supported this view and proposed to distribute tanks for

the purpose along the entire front. In addition to this appalling method of misusing a mobile arm, there was another proposal which Fuller describes as "slightly less assinine", of excavating a series of large dugouts along the front, each of which would house a tank ready to dart out at the enemy at the appropriate moment: a tactical idea which became known in the Tank Corps as the "Savage Rabbits".

This unfortunate dispersal of tanks was carried out; although, on account of their limited range of action, it was essential for the tanks of that time to remain concentrated. A Mark IV required 5 gallons of petrol for every mile it travelled, and refuelling had consequently to be carried out at frequent intervals. It was not possible to refuel all tanks when they were strung out at wide intervals along the front. By 27th March one hundred and twenty Mark IV tanks had been lost, many of them because they had run out of petrol. This heavy loss in the first week of the German offensive was about 60 per cent of all the tanks engaged in the battle.

At the time of the German attack, on 21st March, there were fourteen tank battalions in France as compared with the nine which fought at Cambrai, and a new 4th Tank Brigade had been formed at the end of 1917. In addition there had been some changes in designation: battalions were now numbered instead of lettered, and companies, which had previously been numbered throughout the Corps, were now given letters inside their battalions.

Whippet tanks went into action for the first time in the March battle. The Whippet, or Medium Mark A, was a new departure. It had been designed by Tritton in December 1916, and was really a development of his original tank. Like the early Tritton models the tracks did not go all round the hull but only round an armour plated chassis. On top of and at the rear of the chassis was mounted the fighting turret. Inside the front of the chassis were two 45 h.p. engines, each driving one track, and giving a speed of 8·3 m.p.h. The radius of action was 80 miles as compared with the Mark IV's 35. The obstacle crossing capacity of the Whippet was much less than that of the Mark IV, since it could only traverse a 7-foot trench or a 2-foot 6-inch vertical wall; but the Whippet was intended for exploitation and the conditions of a more open type of warfare. Its maximum armour thickness was 14 mm. and its armament consisted of four Hotchkiss machine-guns. It was much lighter than the Mark IV, weighing only 14 tons, and it was manned by a small crew of three. Two hundred Whippets were built by the end of 1918.

When the storm broke on 21st March, the 1st, 3rd, and 4th Armies each had one Tank Brigade under command. The remaining Tank Brigade was in G.H.Q. reserve: its Mark IV's were being replaced by Whippets, but only fifty of these had so far arrived.

On 22nd March, the day after the start of the battle, tanks were fighting hard to prevent the threatened collapse of the front. But, fighting in such small detachments, they could do little to seal the wide breaches which had been torn in the British line. German infantry, when they saw the tanks, frequently changed the direction of their advance to avoid them, and the Mark IV's were not fast enough to catch up with them.

On the 3rd Army front the German advance was checked by a successful counter-attack by the 2nd Tank Brigade, though nine of its twenty-five tanks were destroyed by artillery fire.

German tanks made their first appearance in this offensive. The so-called A7V tank was designed in May 1917. It was a very clumsy affair, much larger and heavier than the British heavy tank. It weighed 33 tons and carried the enormous crew of eighteen. The armament consisted of one 57-mm. gun (equivalent to a 6-pounder) mounted forward, and six machine-guns disposed at the sides and rear. The tracks were underhung and the chassis design was somewhat similar to that of the French heavy tanks. Maximum armour thickness was 30 mm., and the front of the tank could resist direct hits from field guns at long range. The armour extended downwards over the tracks giving overall cover, but overhead it was so thin as to provide very little protection. There were numerous crevices and joints in the armour plating which made these tanks very susceptible to bullet splash. Drive was provided by two Daimler sleeve-valve engines of 150 h.p. each. The tracks were sprung and on smooth ground the tank had the comparatively high speed of 8 m.p.h. But the cross-country performance was poor owing to the shape and lack of clearance between ground and body. Under favourable conditions the A7V could cross a 6-foot trench and surmount an 18-inch vertical obstacle. Only fifteen of these tanks were built.

The Germans in fact preferred British Mark IV's to their

Imperial War Museum

Plate 3. MARK II (FEMALE) TANK. NOTE THE SMALLER SPONSONS FOR MACHINE GUNS.

Plate 4. MARK IV (FEMALE). ONE OF THE TANKS WHICH MADE ARMOURED HISTORY AT CAMBRAI.

Plate 5. MARK IV (FEMALE) NEAR PERONNE ON 23RD MARCH, 1918, JUST AFTER THE START OF THE GERMAN OFFENSIVE. NOTE THE UNDITCHING BEAM AND APPARATUS.

Plate 6. FRENCH SCHNEIDER TANK AT MARLY LE ROI IN DECEMBER 1916.

Plate 7. FRENCH ST. CHAMOND TANK.

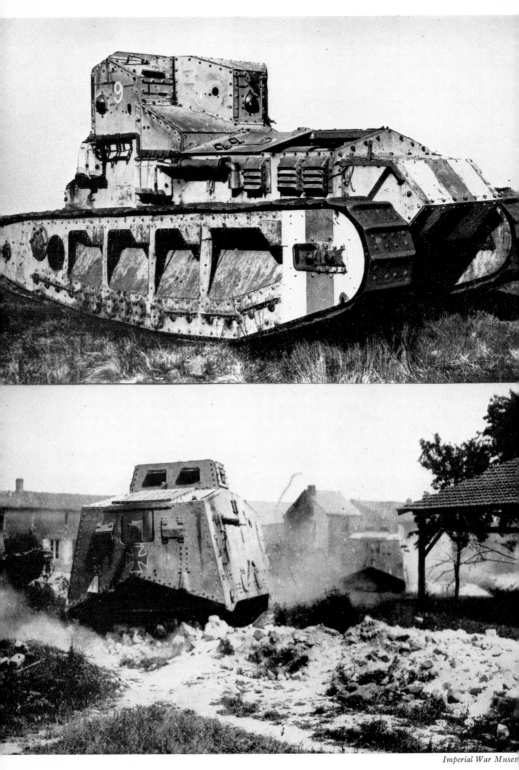

Plate 8.   MEDIUM MARK A, OR 'WHIPPET'. NOTE THE ARMOURED PETROL TANK IN FRONT AND THE FIXED TURRET.

Plate 9.   GERMAN A7V TANKS PASSING THROUGH A VILLAGE ON THE WESTERN FRONT IN JUNE 19

own A7V's, and they eventually designed a model called A7V-U, which was based on the British heavy tank. It had the same lozenge shape with overhead tracks, but it was faster, with thicker armour. Only one was constructed.

On the first day of their attack the Germans used four of their A7V's and five captured Mark IV's. A month later, on 24th April, thirteen A7V's took part in the capture of Villers-Brettoneux. The effect of German tanks on the British infantry was, unfortunately, much the same as that of British tanks on the Germans. The British Official History notes that whenever attacked by German tanks the British line was broken.

The German success at Villers-Brettoneux was immediately followed by the first tank versus tank action. In the neighbourhood was a section of the 1st Tank Battalion consisting of one male and two female Mark IV's. At 8.30 a.m. the G.O.C. 23rd Infantry Brigade, under whom the section was operating, ordered it forward to stem this very dangerous German penetration. The section had suffered from gas shelling and some men of the tank crews were disabled, so it was under some handicap that it moved forward into action. About an hour later the female tanks, which were in the lead, sighted one of the peculiar looking German tanks. Their machine-guns were useless against the A7V armour, and both were put out of action. The male tank then appeared on the scene and, manoeuvring on to the A7V's vulnerable flank, scored a hit, with the result that the German tank ran up on to a steep bank and overturned. Two more A7V's then arrived and were engaged in turn by the Mark IV. One of the German tanks made off, and the crew of the other abandoned their tank and fled. Appropriately, the victorious British tank was No. 1 of No. 1 Section of A Company of the 1st Battalion Tank Corps. Unfortunately it later received a direct hit from German artillery and had to be abandoned.

In spite of the poor performance of the A7V's, the Germans were apparently fascinated by the idea of a moving fortress; for at the end of the war two monster tanks weighing 165 tons were nearly completed. They were designated the "K" type, and were armed with no less than four 77-mm. guns and six machine-guns and manned by a crew of twenty-two. The builders of these colossal machines were the Daimler Motor Company. It would have been interesting to see whether they could have heaved their ponderous bulk across the trenches and shell-pitted wilderness of the Western Front.

The Whippets made their dramatic entry into action for the first time on 26th March. Twelve of them were ordered to clear up the situation east of Cachy. Beyond the village they surprised two battalions of German infantry in the act of deploying to exploit a wide gap in the 3rd Army's front. About four hundred Germans were killed and wounded as a result of this unexpected attack by thirty-six men behind armour on, say, fifteen hundred in the open.

The shape selected for the first tanks, with an upturned nose, proved most satisfactory in enabling them to claw their way into and out of trenches and shell holes, and to climb up and over vertical obstacles. It was so suitable for the man-made obstacles of the Western Front that it was retained throughout the war for heavy tanks. It suffered, however, from one great disadvantage which eventually led to its abandonment. The "all-round" track restricted the disposal of the armament, so that guns had either to be mounted in sponsons on each side, or else between the front horns with a very restricted field of fire.

Medium tanks were not intended to be used in the assault on the main trench system or to struggle through ground torn into a shell pitted morass. In the Whippet, or Medium A, tank, therefore, the armament was disposed in a turret mounted on top of a tracked chassis: a disposition which was destined to be adopted for all the tanks of the future.

A development of the Medium Mark A was the Medium Mark B, which, to the observer, was a cross between the heavy tank and the Whippet. It had a lozenge shaped hull, but of low height and surmounted by a turret with an armament of one 2-pounder gun and four Hotchkiss machine-guns. The primary reason for its introduction was the liability of the Whippet to stall, a failing which was successfully overcome in the Mark B. As regards other differences between the two: the B was slightly the better over obstacles and had the heavier armament, but with a maximum speed of only 6 m.p.h. it was slower, and it was unpopular as it was considerably less accessible than its predecessor. As compared with the Whippet the positions of the engine and the fighting chamber were reversed, the fighting chamber being in front. Only forty-five Medium B's were built owing to the appearance of the much more effective Medium Mark C.

The Medium Mark C was designed by Sir William Tritton in December 1917; for the Tank Corps had already begun looking ahead to the ideal medium tank, and the Mark C was Tritton's interpretation of the specification. The hull was again similar in shape to that of the heavy tanks and surrounded by the tracks. Mounted on top and forward was a large fixed turret, surmounted by a small revolving turret for the commander. The engine, a six-cylinder 150 h.p. Ricardo, was at the rear, but the flywheel and gearbox were forward. The male and female varieties were reintroduced in the Medium C: the male had a 6-pounder gun mounted in the front of the turret and three Hotchkiss machine-guns disposed at the sides and back; whilst the female had four Hotchkiss machine-guns only. The maximum armour thickness was 12 mm. and the minimum 6 mm. The obstacle crossing ability was nearly as good as that of the Mark V and the road speed was 7·9 m.p.h. As a result of experience with the heavy tanks, the arrangements for ventilation and stowage were much improved. The crew consisted of a commander, driver and two gunners. The tank had a radius of action of 120 miles, far greater than any of its predecessors. Thirty-six of these tanks were built, and they formed the main equipment of the Tank Corps after the end of the war.

On 28th April 1918 a conference was held at Tank Corps Headquarters to consider the specification for a still more advanced tank. It was decided that for deep penetration a speed of 20 m.p.h. was required, together with a radius of action of 200 miles. As a result an experimental Medium tank was built as Mark D. It was powered by a 325 h.p. Siddeley-Puma engine which gave it a speed of 18 m.p.h. and it had a wire rope suspension. The hull was lower than that of either the B or the C and it was surrounded by tracks having articulated plates. A revolving turret was mounted on top of the hull at the rear. The Marks C and D were to come into prominence after the end of the war.

In May 1918 the first of the French Renault light tanks went into action. The Renault had been conceived by Colonel Estienne, who visualised the attack as being carried out by armoured skirmishers in open order. As in the days of the armoured chivalry the weight of armour necessitated a mount for each individual. But the motorised mount would require a second man to look after the engine. Renault translated this idea into practice, and the result was the comparatively successful little two-man tank, of which there were still numbers in existence at the start of the Second World War. Compared with the three-man Whippet, however, it was not impressive. The armament was limited to either a 37 mm. gun or a Hotchkiss machine-gun in a revolving turret mounted on top of the forward part of the chassis. It was driven by a 40 h.p. four-cylinder Renault engine, had a road speed of 6 m.p.h., and its radius of action was limited to 15 miles. The armour varied in thickness from 6 to 22 mm. It only weighed 7 tons, and for its size it had a good cross-country performance. Fuller, however, considered these little tanks to be "nothing more than cleverly made mountings for machine-guns". Nevertheless they achieved a striking popularity. Four thousand were eventually built, and they were supplied to the armies of Russia, Italy, Belgium and Poland. The American Army built copies and used them until the early nineteen-thirties.

By the middle of May 1918 the number of British tanks in France was 598. The Mark IV's, totalling 387, were still the most numerous, but there were already 129 of the new Mark V's and they were arriving in France at the rate of about fifty a week. Of Whippets there were now eighty-two.

The Mark V heavy tank was a vast improvement on any of its predecessors. The Mark IV, admirable fighting machine that it was, had many disadvantages. With its clumsy secondary gears turning was a slow and difficult operation, and at least two other men were necessary to assist the driver. In battle the tank was considerably handicapped by the cumbersome controls: the officer had to attend to brakes as well as commanding his tank, and gunners often had to leave their weapons and assist the gearsmen. In addition it had been found that the Mark IV was under-engined for movement over really bad ground.

These defects in the Mark IV had been successfully overcome in the Mark V. With the introduction of a system of epicyclic gears and improved braking the mechanical control of the tank was completely in the hands of the driver. The commander could now give his entire attention to the business of fighting, and, not only could the gunners be assured of being left at their proper task, but the two gearsmen became spare gunners. The engine was more powerful and had been specially designed for the task. It was a 150 h.p. six-cylinder Ricardo and it increased the speed of the tank from the Mark IV's 3·7 to 4·6 m.p.h. The radius of action went up from 35 to 45 miles. Other improvements were incorporated in the light of battle experience. The doors were better designed, there was more orderly stowage, a machine-gun was fitted in the rear plate, and there was much better observation.

But the Mark V suffered from one very serious defect. The engine radiator, for some reason, had been fitted inside the tank, and ventilation was much worse than in the earlier tanks. Sickness from the effects of fumes and carbon monoxide poisoning had been frequent in all the heavy tanks, but in the Mark V's it became so prevalent as to limit seriously the length of time which they could remain in action.

The Mark V was designed in October 1917 and four hundred (two hundred male and two hundred female) were produced by the end of the War. Overall dimensions were the same as the Mark IV, and so (except that Lewis guns were replaced by Hotchkiss) was the armament and the cross-country performance. The maximum armour thickness was slightly increased to 14 mm.

An ingenious development of the Mark V was produced in February 1918 by the Tank Corps Central Workshops. The length of the hull was increased from 26 feet 5 inches to 32 feet 5 inches by the insertion of three extra panels on either side of the hull, and an additional door was provided on each side in the new panels. The greater length enabled the tank to cross 13-feet wide trenches. The modified tank was known as the Mark V One Star. It was a great success and eventually outnumbered the Mark V, 200 male and 432 female being built by the end of the War. As a personnel carrier it could lift twenty to twenty-five men, but having been so lifted they required a considerable time for recovery.

The Mark V's had their first real test in the brilliant battle of Hamel on 4th July 1918. This action was planned as a small scale attack by General Sir Henry Rawlinson, commanding 4th Army. The country in the chosen sector was very open, and it was therefore decided that this should be primarily a tank battle, with as little infantry back up as possible. This section of the front was held by the Australian Corps, and General Rawlinson instructed Lieutenant-General Monash, its commander, to prepare a plan on this basis.

As finally approved, the attack was to be carried out by the 5th Tank Brigade supported by the 4th Australian Division. The actual attacking force comprised sixty fighting tanks (all Mark V's) and ten battalions of infantry. There was to be no preliminary bombardment, but 302 heavy guns and 326 field guns were to put down a terrific barrage and counter-battery bombardment at zero hour. No wire cutting was to be undertaken by the artillery. The barrage was to be supplemented by 111 machine-guns, and another forty-six were to move with the attacking infantry.

Zero hour was at 3.10 a.m. At 2.59 the engines of the tanks were started. At 3.2 they began to move forward towards the infantry, 1,000 yards in front, and at the same time the artillery opened normal harrassing fire to drown the noise of the engines. At 3.10 the barrage opened with a crash, and at 3.14 it lifted from the German front line and moved forward. The tanks had now reached the infantry start line without being heard, and over a front of 6,000 yards surged towards the enemy trenches.

Although the tanks were supposed to follow the first wave of infantry, they soon caught up with them and in most cases went ahead. At 5 a.m. all objectives had been gained and the battle was over.

The Australian losses were only 672 killed and wounded; and of the sixty tanks, fifty-eight reached their objectives and fifty-five returned. The five tank casualties were recovered within 48 hours. Of the tank crews not one officer or other rank was killed, and only thirteen were wounded.

The battle demonstrated the effectiveness and power of manoeuvre of the new tanks. Over two hundred German machine-guns were knocked out by tank attack.

Fuller commented that no battle of the war could compare with Hamel in the rapidity, brevity, and completeness of the success; and he thought that one would have to go back to mediaeval times and the onslaughts of the armoured knights to find a parallel. The comparison is apt, for it was a very similar onslaught, save that the armour was propelled by internal combustion engines instead of horses. Fuller added the further comment that not since the fifteenth century had there been a battle in which the dominant arm had not lost one man killed.

The success of the battle had a far reaching effect. Because it convinced General Rawlinson of the terrific offensive power of armour, it made possible the decisive battle of the war: that of Amiens on 8th August 1918.

On 18th July the French launched, for the first time, an attack based on the Cambrai model. Over two hundred heavy and light tanks, debouching from woods and concealed by the morning mist, assailed the western flank of the 7th German

Army. There had been no preliminary bombardment and the Germans were taken completely by surprise. The tanks broke through the German front followed by infantry. But after a rapid advance of about 4 miles the impetus of the attack faded. The French tanks were incapable of further effort: the little Renaults had a very limited ability and the French heavy tank was described by Fuller as "a kind of kitchen range on tracks—unblushingly useless".

Meanwhile the success of the battle of Hamel had prompted G.H.Q. to consider something similar on a much larger scale, and on 13th July Rawlinson was asked by Haig to draft a plan. The original idea was there should be a limited attack like Hamel, but on a much larger scale. As planning advanced, however, it was decided that the aim should be a decisive battle.

For the operation 4th Army was allotted the Canadian Corps (four divisions), the Australian Corps (four divisions), 3rd Corps (two divisions), and the Tank Corps (420 fighting tanks).

Twelve tank battalions were made available for the battle, of which ten were equipped with heavy tanks and two with medium. The heavy tank battalions each had forty-two Mark V tanks, with the exception of the 1st and 15th Battalions both of which were equipped with 36 Mark V One Star. The two medium tank battalions were each equipped with forty-eight Whippets.

The bulk of the heavy tank strength was massed with the Canadian and Australian Corps, on whose front the major effort was to be made. The Canadians were supported by the 4th Tank Brigade (1st, 4th, 5th, and 14th Battalions) and the Australians by the 5th Tank Brigade (2nd, 8th, 13th, and 15th Battalions). The 3rd Tank Brigade, consisting of the 3rd and 6th Medium Battalions, was allotted to the Cavalry Corps. With the 3rd Corps, which had a rather subsidiary role, there was the 2nd Tank Brigade, but with only one battalion, the 10th. The 9th Battalion was in general reserve. The 1st Tank Brigade took no part in the battle as it was in process of re-equipping and retraining with Mark V's. As a mechanical reserve there were forty-two fighting tanks. A novel feature was the large number of supply tanks. These were Mark IV's with their armament removed, of which no less than 120 had been provided for the battle: fifty-four for tank supply and sixty-six for the infantry.

Superficially the co-operation of the relatively fast Whippet tanks with the horsed cavalry appeared promising. It was hoped that the Whippets would provide the armoured punch to send the horsemen right through the enemy's broken battle line. In actual and depressing fact, close co-operation between horse-men and tanks was found to be impracticable. Over bad going when there was no opposition the tanks could not keep up with the cavalry. But cavalry proved too vulnerable a target to make headway against machine-guns, and when these were encountered the tanks left them behind, instead of helping the cavalry forward. It was not that the tanks were unwilling, but, as soon as they approached, German machine-guns ceased fire. Concealed, as they were, amongst buildings, copses etc., in the open country in which cavalry would be operating, they were extremely difficult to find. Infantry could have wormed their way forward and located the machine-guns under the tanks' covering fire, but cavalry could not have done so without dismounting, and thereby leaving the tanks to undertake the whole of the mobile role.

The general plan of the battle was that the main attack should be delivered by the Canadian Corps on the right and the Australian Corps on the left, both south of the Somme. North of the Somme the 3rd Corps was to make a limited advance with the main object of covering the left flank.

On 8th August 1918 the Battle of Amiens was launched on a front of 13 miles. There were three objectives, entitled in succession, the Green, Red, and Blue lines. Their respective distances from the start line were Green $3\frac{1}{2}$ miles, Red 6 miles in the centre and $4\frac{1}{2}$ on the wings, and Blue 8 miles in the centre and 6 on the wings. Zero hour was fixed at 4.20 a.m., and at 4.8 the tanks were to begin their 1,000 yards move from their assembly areas to the start line.

At zero hour a thick mist added its concealment to the blackness before dawn, and, keeping close behind the barrage, the attacking troops took the Germans completely by surprise and swept over the forward defences.

The Canadian Corps advanced on a front of three divisions, each supported by one tank battalion. On the right the 3rd Division and 5th Tank Battalion had a difficult obstacle in the marshy stream of the Luce. The 5th Tanks lost heavily, fifteen tanks being knocked out before the battalion rolled triumphantly over the Green line. The Red line was gained at the cost of another eleven tanks, leaving only eight still in action.

In the Canadian centre the 4th Tank Battalion, attacking with the 1st Division had an easier task. The ground was firm and open and the tanks swept on ahead of the infantry. The Green line was reached by 8 a.m. and the Red by 11 a.m. But the second objective was gained against formidable opposition from the German artillery, and there were only eleven tanks left to continue the advance to the Blue line.

The 2nd Canadian Division on the left of the Corps was supported to the Green line by half the 14th Tank Battalion, the remaining half battalion taking over for the advance to the Red and Blue lines.

On the Canadian right, where the advance had been the most difficult, the reserve Division, the 4th, passed through the 3rd on the Red line, preceded by the 1st Tank Battalion with thirty Mark V One Star tanks. Each of these tanks was lifting two machine-gun sections which were to disembark and take up positions on the Blue line. Thereafter it had been intended that one half of the battalion should return to help the advance of the following infantry, but one company was caught by the fire of a German artillery battery and was knocked out and the remaining companies reached the objective with only eleven tanks.

The Australian Corps attacked on a two-division front. The two leading divisions, the 2nd and 3rd, were to take the first objective, the Green line, and the 4th and 5th Divisions were then to go through them to the Red and Blue lines. Attacking with each division was one of the battalions of the 5th Tank Brigade. The leading divisions reached the Green line by 7 a.m.; and then the following divisions, taking over, were on the Red line 3 hours later and had taken the Blue line in a further hour. Enemy opposition up to the Red line was eliminated by the tanks, but after that the Australian infantry stormed through the weakened opposition at such a rate that the tanks were unable to keep up. Some unfortunate machine-gun teams were being lifted for deployment on the Blue line; but it was probably just as well that they arrived late, for they were almost unconscious from fumes and carbon monoxide poisoning.

The 3rd Corps got away to a bad start in its somewhat limited role. Two days before the attack, on 6th August, the Germans had themselves launched a local attack; and a counter-attack, which was necessary to restore the situation, had dislocated our own plans. On 8th, therefore, the exact position of the 3rd

73

Corps front line was not known, and a fog added to the confusion. In addition the Corps had few tanks and was unable to make good its initial delay. As a result the left of the Australian Corps was uncovered and could not reach the Blue line.

In places, however, the leading troops were in advance of the third objective and there was now a gap 11 miles wide in the German front. Through this should have passed the Cavalry Corps and the Whippet battalions; but the cavalry could not get going against the surviving German machine-guns and field artillery, and the Whippets were hung up by the cavalry.

Nevertheless a great victory had been won—the decisive victory of the war, though this was not immediately apparent. The major part in this great victory had been played by the tanks, the primary assaulting arm.

The battle now slowed to a halt. The Germans were rushing up reinforcements, many tanks had been knocked out, and in others the crews were exhausted. Only thirty-eight tanks were available for action on 11th August and every one of them badly needed an overhaul. The battle was then rightly broken off.

After some 3 hours in a Mark V tank, closed for action and with its guns firing, most men felt sick and giddy, and frequently suffered, too, from severe headaches, high temperatures and heart disturbance. After the 3 days hard fighting of this battle, most of the tank crews were on the point of collapse.

For the Germans the battle was catastrophic. Their losses in the fighting amounted to 22,000 prisoners and 400 guns; but, of far more dismal import to the German High Command, it was apparent that there could be no further hope of winning the war.

In his diary Admiral Georg Alexander von Muller, of the Kaiser's entourage, recorded under 8th August disastrous news from the Somme and a penetration of the German front to a depth of 12 kilometres. He added that the Kaiser was in very low spirits that evening and had said, "It is very strange that our men cannot get used to tanks".

To quote General Fuller again, "The battle of Amiens was the strategic end of the war, a second Waterloo; the rest was minor tactics".

It is perhaps worth concluding this survey of tanks in the First World War with some mention of the tanks which were built or designed during it but which did not go into action.

The Mark V Two Star was a re-design by Major Wilson in

March 1918 of the Mark V One Star. Three hundred were ordered but only one was completed. On trials in December 1918 it proved very successful. In length and breadth it was identical with the One Star, but there was more curvature in the outline—the flat in the centre being reduced to 6 feet—and the rise forward was fuller. The engine was placed further to the rear so that there was a large central fighting chamber in front of it. This engine, too, was more powerful than in previous tanks, a 225 h.p. Ricardo giving a speed of 6·9 m.p.h.

The lozenge shaped tank did not last long in service after the end of the war, for it was too thinly armoured to be of use as a heavy assault tank against the armour piercing weapons which were coming into production, and it was too slow to compensate for its lack of protection; and, withal, it presented a bulky target.

There were one or two others of the species which were designed. The Mark VI was one of these (conceived by Wilson in December 1916) but it was never built. It had no sponsons and its single 6-pounder gun was mounted in the centre line forward. A year later the Mark VII was designed and three were actually built. Its hull was practically the same as that of the Mark V and its principal feature was a gearbox consisting of two hydraulical pumps. The Mark VIII was intended primarily for the American Army and seven were built by the end of 1918. It was the largest of the "lozenge" tanks with a length of 34 feet and a weight of 37 tons. It was to have been built on a large scale in the United States and fitted with a 300 h.p. Liberty engine. Those built in the United Kingdom were to have Ricardo engines of similar horsepower. An even larger tank, the Mark VIII Star, was designed but never built. There was also a Mark IX, but since this was designed as a personnel and stores carrier it is outside the scope of this work.

The Americans produced three types of tank to their own designs. The Holt Tractor company, in conjunction with the General Electric Company, built the peculiar Holt Gas Electric tank, of which there was one example, constructed in 1918. It had a Holt 90 h.p. four-cylinder engine with an electric generator and an electric motor for each track. Its maximum speed was 6 m.p.h., and the armour thickness varied from 6 to 15 mm. The hull was a rectangular box with sponsons mounted on a tracked chassis. For armament there was a 75-mm. howitzer and two machine-guns.

Another tank which was a solitary example, was the steam tank built in 1918 by the U.S. Army Engineers. It was based on the British Mark IV, but the drive was supplied by two two-cylinder steam engines, one driving each track, with a combined horsepower of 500. There were four machine-guns and a flame-thrower for use against concrete pillboxes, the thickness of the armour was 13 mm., and the maximum road speed was 4 m.p.h

In 1918, in order to make use of the Ford Company's enormous capacity for production, it was decided that a very light tank should be made powered with a standard Ford engine. The result was a two-man tank weighing only 2½ tons, the first of which arrived in France in October 1918. Fifteen thousand were ordered, but all further manufacture was cancelled at the Armistice and only fifteen were actually built. The tank was driven by two Ford "T" engines, totalling 45 h.p., which gave it a speed of 8 m.p.h. It was armed with one machine-gun and its armour was 6–13 mm. thick.

CHAPTER VIII

The Post-War Years

ALMOST as soon as the Armistice had been signed the vast production of British tanks was stopped. On 12th November instructions were issued that no more tanks were to be completed except the new medium types C and D. Of the former, 500 were under construction, but, as stated in the last chapter, only thirty-six were completed. The reason for this lay, as so often, in the reluctance of the Treasury to spend money on defence. It was objected, on 3rd December 1918, that since there was as yet no establishment for a peacetime Tank Corps, there was no justification for spending any further money on tanks. Fuller realised that if he insisted on all the unfinished Medium C's being completed it would be extremely difficult to get financial authority to proceed with the development of the Medium D's. He was faced with a difficult decision; for, whereas the Medium C's promised to be the best of the unsprung tanks, they were far too slow to undertake the tasks envisaged for the Medium D's, and which Fuller rightly foresaw would be required of armoured fighting vehicles in the next major war. Completion of the remaining Medium C's was therefore reluctantly cancelled in order that money should be available for the Medium D's.

The Medium Tank Mark D was designed by a genius, Lieutenant-Colonel P. Johnson, who had been on the engineering staff of the Tank Corps at the Central Workshops in France. In 1919 he was asked to form the first Government Tank Design Department. In the light of existing development the specification for this new tank might well have appeared unrealistic. It was required to cross fairly wide trenches, which inferred a length of about 30 feet; it had to cross most existing bridges, and this imposed a limit in weight of about 20 tons; it had to be able to climb slopes of about one in thirty at 20 m.p.h., a performance for which a much more powerful engine than had been used in previous tanks would be necessary, together with sprung suspension entailing a considerable increase in weight; its armour had to be proof against existing armour piercing bullets, thus again increasing weight and demands on engine power; and, finally, it would need to be able to carry sufficient petrol and oil to supply its powerful engine for 200 miles. To these requirements Fuller had rightly added two more: that the tank should be comfortable and that it should float.

Johnson's solution was revolutionary: a spring suspension was provided, with very little increase in weight, by incorporating a steel wire rope to take the pressure from the tank rollers, and flexible tracks were fitted so that the tank could be turned without stopping one track.

Preliminary trials of Johnson's tank were very successful; it was fast, it could surmount most natural obstacles, and its hull had been made watertight so that it could float. Its most spectacular feats were the repeated crossing of the River Stour near Christchurch. Plunging down one bank into the water, the Medium D swam across the river, using its tracks as paddles, and climbed up the far bank.

The first trials with the new tank had proved so satisfactory that it seemed the specifications had been met, and that the Medium D was well suited for the armoured cavalry of the future. This being the case, it appeared to Fuller that the Army's needs would be satisfied with two other types of tracked armoured vehicle: an infantry tank and a supply tank. On his recommendation, therefore, the Chief of the Imperial General Staff was asked in January 1920 to approve these three categories of tank.

Johnson, in the meantime, had been dispatched to India to find out what kind of tank would best meet the needs of the Indian Army. As a result of his report he was directed to proceed with the design of a light tank of about 7 tons, capable of working with infantry in operations on the North-West Frontier. Johnson thereupon set out to produce a tank which would float, and which would have flexible tracks so that it could be steered by roller bogies with lateral movement. This vehicle, known as the Light Infantry Tank, underwent its first trials in September 1921. It weighed 8 tons, had cable suspension like the Medium D, and was fitted with Johnson's new "snake" tracks. On 19th December further trials were carried out at Aldershot during which it reached a speed of 20 m.p.h. The following

March it covered a distance of 52½ miles in 4 hours, including a maximum speed of no less than 30 m.p.h.   On 20th June 1922 it swam successfully about the Fleet Pond.

But this was the end of an exciting period in British tank development.   In December 1912, before the completion of the Light Infantry Tank trials, Fuller learned that the A5 branch of the Department of the Master General of the Ordnance had, on its own account, ordered a tank from the firm of Vickers without reference to either Fuller or Johnson and without obtaining General Staff agreement to the specification.   Furthermore this tank had now been built, and Fuller was told that it would have to be put into production at once, for otherwise the money which had been voted in the 1921–2 estimates for tank construction would be lost.   The result of this peculiar affair was that the Army was saddled with a tank which, though reliable as a vehicle, was indifferent for fighting.

With two such advanced designs as the Medium D and the Light Infantry Tank there were inevitably a lot of teething troubles, and it was apparent that many months of work would be required to rectify some of them.   Unfortunately this work was not allowed, with the ultimate result that British leadership in tank design was lost, with perhaps some slight bearing on the early disasters of the Second World War.   Johnson's department was closed down and all his inventions scrapped.

Whilst British progress in tank design had come to this sudden end, it did not appear that the French had appreciated that any progress was immediately necessary.   They were satisfied with their own theories of the proper employment of tanks and with their vast number of very indifferent machines which were a legacy of the late war.   After demobilisation by the victorious Powers France was left with the strongest army in the World, and its stock of about 3,000 tanks constituted by far the largest armoured force.   At the end of any major war there is a tendency for the forces of other nations to adopt the ideas, equipment and even uniform of the victors.   The political and economic situation at the time, together with the impressive number of French tanks, resulted in French tank practice being followed in several countries.

The French tank force was made up almost entirely by the ingenious but indifferent little Renault F.T.'s.   Their very numbers were a disadvantage because of the capital cost entailed in scrapping them.   And so, for the next 18 years, there were practically no other types of tanks in the French Army. In fact, some were still left to go into action in the Second World War.

Due probably in part to these little tanks, and to wartime experience with them, French tank theory was the reverse of progressive. For many years after the First World War French tactical doctrine stressed the subordination of tanks to infantry; and in 1920 tanks were designated infantry weapons and were distributed amongst infantry units.

Towards the end of the war the French had designed a new heavy tank for operations in 1919. It was a very large vehicle, weighing nearly 70 tons, and for many years it was the heaviest tank in the world. It had the large crew of twelve, for the tank mounted a considerable armament. There were two turrets, one at the front with a 75-mm. gun and one at the rear with a machine-gun, and there were seven other machine-guns, of which three were mounted in the hull and four were kept in reserve. It was intended as a heavy "break-through" tank under the conditions of trench warfare, and so its armour was 45 mm. thick and it had the low speed of 8 m.p.h. The drive was through one generator and one motor for each track; power being supplied by two Mercedes six-cylinder 250-h.p. engines. A total of 300 of these tanks had been planned, but only ten, which had been under construction at the time of the Armistice, were actually completed—and that was not till 1923! No distinguished career awaited them. Long obsolete, eight were ready to go into action in 1940, but they were all destroyed by bombing whilst they were still loaded on their special railway flat wagons.

French military influence was strong in the United States, and in 1920 the American Tank Corps was abolished and the tank became an infantry fighting vehicle. Nevertheless there was a British element which made the selection of the right type of tank difficult. The American Army was equiped with the heavy Mark VIII and the light Renault F.T. A Caliber Board was set up to consider the matter, and this body, with something of the wisdom of Solomon, decreed that something between the two was the right choice—in other words, a medium tank. The first Caliber Board prototype appeared in 1921 and was designated the Medium A. It weighed 21 tons and its armament consisted of a co-axial 57-mm. gun and machine-gun in the main turret, and a second machine-gun in the subsidiary turret which surmounted the main turret. A second and similar tank was

Imperial War Museum

10. MEDIUM MARK C, OR 'HORNET'. THE LAST TANK TO BE DESIGNED WITH UNSPRUNG TRACKS.

11. MEDIUM MARK D. NOTE THE TRACKS WITH ARTICULATED PLATES AND THE REVOLVING TURRET AT THE REAR.

Plate 12.　FRENCH RENAULT LIGHT TANK IN THE BOIS DE REMS DURING THE BATTLE OF TARDENOIS, 24TH JULY, 1918.

Plate 13. MARK V (MALE) IN MUDDY GROUND ON THE WESTERN FRONT.

Plate 14. MARK V ONE-STAR (FEMALE). NOTE THE LENGTHENED HULL.

Plate 15.   MARK VII (MALE) — THE TANK WITH THE HYDRAULIC GEAR-BOX.

Plate 16.   MARK VIII (MALE). THE BIGGEST OF THE 'MOTHER' TYPE OF TANKS.

produced the following year, and a third in 1925. The Caliber Board's brain-child performed feebly, and American interest in medium tanks lapsed for a period.

In this early post-war period there is no doubt that British tank theory was the most advanced. It was generally appreciated that tanks must be faster, have a much wider range of action than in the past, and be more manoeuvrable. However, some of the deductions drawn from this reasoning were unfortunate. It was suggested that if these requirements were met the tank could be smaller and thus more easily concealed, and that its armour thickness could be reduced with much saving in weight. The new tanks, therefore, had only sufficient armour to protect them from small arms fire, and relied on their small size and speed for protection from shell-fire.

As regards tactics, superficial reasoning led to the argument that a tank force was akin to a fleet at sea, and that the different types of tank should conform to a naval analogy: thus, light or frigate tanks were required for reconnaissance, cruiser tanks for mobile action, and heavy or battle tanks for close co-operation with the infantry and for the assault on defensive positions. It was not appreciated by adherents to this school of thought that naval tactics, designed for fighting at sea, are not applicable to land warfare, and that tanks are not land warships but a revival of the cavalry of the pre-rifle era. That is, an armoured force could be used, like Marlborough's cavalry, both for break through and exploitation.

The first British post-war tank to come into production was that built by Vickers to the order of the M.G.O.'s department, and it was intended to undertake the cruiser role.

Vickers' initial tank, designed and built in 1921, was supplied in response to an order for something similar to the Light Infantry tank. Its innovations included a spring suspension and a turret with an all-round traverse mounting a 3-pr gun. It fulfilled the weight requirements as it was only 8¾ tons, but it was slow, its transmission was poor, and there were other unsatisfactory features. But although this particular model was rejected, the basic design was sufficiently promising for a production order to be given to the firm.

Vickers' second tank was designed in 1922, and the first production models were delivered to the Army in 1924. It was originally entitled the Light Tank Mark I, but it was soon decided that it was required to fulfil a medium role and the

F   81

designation was altered accordingly. To the Army it was popularly known as the "Vickers Medium". Together with succeeding marks, this tank was destined to be the Army's principal armoured fighting vehicle until 1938, and it was still being used for training in 1941. As a vehicle it was very reliable, and the standard of gunnery which its steadiness made possible has never been equalled in any other tank.

The Mark I weighed about 12 tons, which was light for its size; but its armour was only 18 mm. thick and would not even stop small arms ammunition at all ranges. It was powered by an Armstrong-Siddeley 90 h.p. air-cooled V-8 engine, which was intended to give it a maximum speed of 15 m.p.h., and which actually could propel it at about 20 m.p.h. Fuel supplies were sufficient for a 150-mile radius of action. The hull, or fighting body, was mounted above the tracked chassis, and was surmounted by a rotating turret with a 3-pr gun. Close defence was provided by four Hotchkiss machine-guns mounted in the sides of the hull. The crew consisted of a commander, a driver, a wireless operator, and two gunners.

The Mark I was followed by the Mark Ia and the Mark Ia Star, both of which embodied minor improvements. The latter had a Vickers machine gun mounted co-axially in the turret, and it was, indeed, the first tank in which co-axial mountings were fitted.

The Mark II was a much better tank. The armour was thicker and armoured skirting plates were added to protect the suspension. As a result of these and other modifications the weight was increased to 16 tons.

The Vickers Medium was particularly noteworthy as being the first fast tank to be issued to any army in the world.

CHAPTER IX

The Years of Lost Opportunity

Now that the British Army had a medium tank, attention was directed to the need for an assault or heavy tank. This, it was felt, should be able to penetrate strong defences which were backed up by large numbers of anti-tank guns. It should, for this role, be long enough to cross the widest trench which was likely to be built, and its armour should be proof against all anti-tank weapons of a calibre up to and including field guns. Experimental work on such a tank started in secret and a design was produced by Vickers-Armstrong in 1925. In October 1926 Vickers-Armstrong delivered the pilot model of the new tank. Known as the "Independent", its weight of $31\frac{1}{2}$ tons was a good deal less than some of the protagonists of the heavy tank would have liked. Nevertheless in tank design the "Independent" was the greatest advance that had been made up to that date. Unfortunately, in the financial climate of the time, it was apparent that the purchase of any large number of such expensive vehicles would never be approved. Other people were not so bothered about considerations of finance, and an unpleasant omen of the future was the interest which the German General Staff took in the tank—an interest which was revealed in documents captured after the end of the Second World War. It was this tank which figured in the Baillie-Stewart case.

The "Independent" had a fine fighting body protected by 25 mm. armour. Its armament consisted of one 3-pr gun in a main turret and a Vickers machine-gun in each of four subsidiary turrets. The engine was an Armstrong-Siddeley V-12 of 398 h.p., giving a maximum speed of 17 m.p.h.

On the debit side there was a very high oil consumption of $4\frac{1}{2}$ gallons per hour.

The pilot model was the only one ever constructed. Government reluctance to spend adequate money on defence resulted in a loss of British lead in tank design which was never regained;

a perhaps contributory factor to sundry disasters in the Second World War.

Unknown to Great Britain and its allies of the First World War, disturbing events were taking place in Russia. There the Germans, prohibited from possessing tanks, had negotiated a secret testing station and had started tank experiments in 1926. By 1928 they had completed ten tanks of two basic types: a medium tank of about 20 tons with a short 75-mm. gun mounted in a turret and a light tank of about 10 tons armed with a 37-mm. gun.

The Russians themselves did not start building any tanks until about 1925, though they had some British and French tanks of the 1914–18 War, which they had captured from the White Russians. The first Russian tank, the T-18, appeared in about 1927 and was based on the French Renault FT. It weighed 7½ tons, was armed with a 37-mm. gun and a machine-gun, and had a crew of two. It was soon followed by a medium tank, the T-14. Neither was a success.

The French started a somewhat leisurely approach to more modern tank designs with the development in 1926 of a medium tank armed with a 75-mm. gun and weighing about 20 tons. It appeared some years later as the B-1 heavy tank, of which, however, only three were ever built.

The idea of the fast light tank really originated with Major (later Lieutenant-General Sir Giffard) Martel. In 1925 Martel built at his home a little one-man tank of his own design and at his own expense. His demonstration of its capabilities was so successful that the War Office asked the motor manufacturing firm of Morris to build four machines of the same basic design but properly finished. Two of these were completed in 1926, but one was enlarged to take a crew of two. The next two were both built as two-man tanks and were modified as a result of experience with the first two.

Another design for a small tank was produced by Mr. John Carden, who had no connection with the Army at all. He was in charge of a large London garage owned by a Mr. Loyd, and the subsequent conjunction of these two names became as well known in the Army as Rolls-Royce. Carden built both a one-man and a two-man tank, and then followed them with other models which incorporated various modifications as a result of experience. His "Mark IV" weighing only 1¼ tons was sufficiently impressive to be selected for trial by the Army.

The preliminary trials led to the formation of a company of "tankettes" consisting of eight Morris-Martels and eight Carden-Loyds which was incorporated in the Experimental Mechanised Force of 1927. The two types of tankette had 2 years hard testing with the Mechanised Force. They were both very successful, the Morris-Martel proving slightly the more reliable. However the Morris firm were unable to take on further development of the tankette owing to other commitments. Carden, therefore, had the field to himself, and when he produced his "Mark VI" it was adopted as the standard machine-gun carrier. Carden now turned his attention to the design of a real light tank, with the result that his "Mark VIII" of 1929 became the Army's Light Tank Mark I—forerunner of a long line of British light tanks. In the meantime the Carden-Loyd Company had been absorbed in the previous year by the new combine of Vickers-Armstrong, and it was that firm which built all subsequent Carden designed light tanks. The Mark I was a two-man machine armed with a Vickers machine-gun mounted in a rotating turret. Its armour thickness varied between 4 and 14 mm. and it had a 58 h.p. Meadows engine giving it a speed of 32 m.p.h. Subsequent Mark II to IV were very similar but embodied various modifications.

Some of these tanks were sent out to India. In this same year of 1929 Major-General (later Field-Marshal Lord) Ironside, recently arrived in India to take command of the Meerut Division, paid a visit to the Khyber Pass. I was detailed by the Brigade Commander to accompany him round some of the local country. "Tiny" Ironside looked at the forbidding rocky hills which were our training area (or battlefield with the Pathans—depending on the way one liked to look at it). "What you want up here", he said, "are tanks". I, ignorant young officer that I was, thought he was talking nonsense. My actual comment was, "Yes, sir." He was right, of course, and in time I saw light tanks operating over hills that I thought were only accessible to infantry and mules. The Pathans were indignant at this lack of sportmanship, and sent an emissary to tell us so.

The British Experimental Mechanised Force of 1927 was something of a landmark in armoured history, for it was the first armoured formation in the world which was designed for independent operation—the forerunner of the armoured division. The force included two tank battalions: the 5th, composed of three companies of Vickers Mediums Mark II; and the 3rd, which had two companies of armoured cars and the company of "tankettes". The other fighting elements of the force were a motorised machine-gun battalion, and a motorised artillery regiment, some of the guns of which were self-propelled. The name was shortly changed to Armoured Force, but in the following year this promising formation was disbanded.

The Americans also at this period were feeling the need for a light tank, and the first specification called for a vehicle which should not exceed 5 tons in weight in order that it should be transportable on a standard 5-ton truck. The result was the T1 built in 1927, which had its engine in front and a rotating turret at the rear. Its weight was rather over the specification, being 6·7 tons. Its armament consisted of a 37-mm. gun and a machine-gun, and armour thickness varied between 6 and 16 mm. It was very slow for a light tank, having a maximum speed of only 18 m.p.h., in spite of its comparatively powerful Cunningham eight-cylinder V-type 105 h.p. engine. It was strongly built and reliable, but its performance as a fighting vehicle was poor. Only four T1's were built, but these were later modified, but almost equally indifferent models, designated T1–E1 to T1–E3.

At about this time J. Walter Christie appeared on the American scene—a mechanical genius whose ideas were destined to have far more influence in Great Britain and Russia than in his native land. As early as 1919 he had designed a medium tank to meet the specification of the Caliber Board, which embodied his idea of being able to run on either wheels or tracks. It aroused some not very enthusiastic interest but got no further. In 1928 Christie produced a much more revolutionary design. It was again a convertible tank which could run on either tracks or wheels, but Christie had evolved a system of independent springing which resulted in an outstanding performance. There were four large wheels on each side fitted with dual rubber tyres, and each wheel was mounted on a pivoted arm attached to a long adjustable coil spring, which allowed a movement of about 14 inches. It was powered by a Liberty twelve-cylinder V-type engine of 338 h.p. and, since the vehicle only weighed about 8 tons, it was very fast. On its tracks it had a maximum speed of 42½ m.p.h. and with its tracks removed it could run at over 70 m.p.h. on its wheels. Two years later the U.S. Army was still trying to make up its mind about it.

In 1928, too, a noteworthy British medium tank was produced

by Vickers-Armstrong to their own design. It was intended as the successor to the existing Vickers Medium, and so was tentatively designated the Medium Mark III. It was popularly known in the Army as the "Sixteen-Tonner", though its actual weight was 17½ tons. Its armour was thin, being only 14 mm., but its 180 h.p. engine gave it the useful maximum speed of 28 m.p.h. Three machines only were built, and of these two had Armstrong-Siddeley V-engines and the third a Ricardo compression-ignition engine. A 3-pr gun was mounted co-axially with a Vickers machine-gun in the main turret, and there were two forward subsidiary turrets in each of which was a Vickers machine-gun. The tank had a crew of six. The "Sixteen-Tonner" was an immediate success, but it cost £16,000 and owing to the financial crisis of 1931 development was stopped and no more were built. It owed many of its best features to the "Independent" tank, it was very steady, and its forward centre of gravity gave it a very good performance on hills.

In an effort to provide a vehicle which would be cheap enough to be acceptable, Vickers-Armstrong produced as a private venture in 1938 the so-called "Six-Ton" tank. Two models were built; the first had two machine-gun turrets mounted side by side and the second had a single two-man turret in which were mounted a 3-pr gun and a machine-gun. Both had 14-mm. armour and a speed of 22 m.p.h. But again further development was precluded by lack of money.

In 1929 a further series of British experimental tanks were designed classed as A7. They were armed with two co-axial machine-guns in a turret and another machine-gun in a gimbal in the hull. The first two weighed 14 tons and the third 18¼ tons. The armour again was 14 mm. The first two had Armstrong-Siddeley V-8 air-cooled engines of 120 h.p. The third had a very much more powerful twin AEC diesel engine developing 252 h.p. which drove it at 25 m.p.h. Development was slow and the third tank did not appear till 1936. No more were built, but from the A7 were developed the tanks of the Second World War.

In the first year of the decade which was to end in the Second World War the Germans, as a result of their early trials, produced a medium tank called the Nb.Fz (Neubaufahrzeug or New Model Vehicle). It weighed 23 tons and was armed with a 75-mm. gun and co-axially mounted 37-mm. gun in the main turret, and a machine-gun in each of two subsidiary turrets.

The British "Independent" tank appears to have had some influence on the design.

Now that they had started on tanks, the Germans wanted lots of them as quickly as possible. The development of a suitable medium tank promised to be a lengthy task, and as a temporary measure, therefore, they turned their attention to light tanks armed with machine-guns. Of the designs submitted by various firms that of Krupp's was selected. The prototype was ready early in 1934, and by the end of the year acceptance trials had been completed and delivery to the troops had begun. This year, then, was a significant turning point in military history, for it witnessed the birth of the German armoured weapon which within 6 years was to destroy in succession the armies of Poland and France. This first German tank of the new era was Pz.Kpfw. I, Model A. It weighed 5·3 tons, had a crew of two, was armed with two turret mounted machine-guns, had armour 8–15 mm. thick, and could run at 24 m.p.h.

There was no such sense of urgency amongst the other tank-owning nations. The United States Army had no tanks of any fighting value, and in 1931 had not even decided what it wanted. In that year it acquired a Vickers-Armstrong "Six-Ton" tank for a 30-day trial, and this machine soon demonstrated its marked superiority over any existing American light tank. As a result many features of the "Six-Ton" tank were embodied in a new American light tank called the T1–E4. Like previous light tanks in the T1 series, it had a 37-mm. gun and a co-axial machine-gun and armour of 6–16 mm. thickness; but it was far superior to any previous American light tank.

There was still no American medium tank. A very poor vehicle entitled T2 had appeared in the previous year. The design was cramped owing to the necessity of keeping within the 14-ton weight limit dictated by the Army's bridging equipment. However, in 1931 it was at last decided that it was worth giving Christie's invention a trial. Five Christie tanks were accordingly ordered and they were completed in the same year by the Wheel Track Layer Corporation. They were powered by the same 338 h.p. engine as Christie's prototype, but, with an increased weight of 10 tons, they had the slower speeds of 27 m.p.h. on tracks and 47 m.p.h. on wheels. The armament consisted of one 37-mm. gun and a machine-gun and the armour was similar to that of the light tanks. Subsequently two further vehicles, which had been built for the Polish Army, were taken over.

Of these seven Christie tanks, three were allotted to the infantry and designated T3 Medium tanks, and four were given to the cavalry under the entirely different title of T1 Combat cars. The reason for this was that a tank was officially an infantry vehicle, and therefore anything used by the cavalry could not possibly be a tank.

In 1932 five modified versions of the Christie T3, entitled T3-E2, were ordered for the infantry. The following year the Ordnance Department developed a new tank, the T4, based on the Christie, and recommended its adoption for both cavalry and infantry as combat car and medium tank respectively. Sixteen were ultimately built but further construction stopped owing to lack of funds. The U.S. Army then dropped Christie tanks.

At the same time as the first American order was placed for Christies, the Russians also ordered two. At this time the Russian Army was engaged in absorbing ideas from abroad. A number of armoured fighting vehicles were purchased from Vickers-Armstrong between 1930 and 1932, including Vickers Mediums, "Six-Ton" tanks, and Vickers Carden Loyd Mark VI. The two latter were copied extensively: the T-27 two-man turretless tankette being based on the Carden-Loyd, and the T-26 light tank on the "Six-Tonner". Of the latter there were three versions: T-26A with two turrets each with a machine-gun; and T-26B and C, each with a single turret in which were mounted a 45-mm. gun and co-axial machine-gun.

From the Christie tanks the Russians derived the BT (Bystrokhodnii) tank which was produced in large numbers from 1932. It had a 500-h.p. V-12 engine which gave it a maximum speed of 37 m.p.h. on its tracks and 69 m.p.h. on wheels. The first models were armed with a 37-mm. gun and two 7·62-mm. machine-guns. A few years later a 45-mm. gun replaced the 37-mm., and the final version had a short 76·2-mm. gun. The armour was 8–15 mm. thick. Both the BT's and the T-26's formed part of the standard equipment of the Russian Army until the end of 1941, and for some years they together were far the most numerous of Russian tanks.

Two heavier types of tank were developed by the Russians in the early nineteen-thirties: the T-28 medium and the T-35 heavy. The T-28 weighed 29 tons and was armed with a short 76·2-mm. gun and a machine-gun in its main turret, and there was also a machine-gun in each of two subsidiary turrets.

The T-35 weighed 45 tons and had no less than five turrets. In the main turret were a short 76·2-mm. gun and a machine-gun, two of the subsidiary turrets each had a 45-mm. gun, and in each of the other two subsidiary turrets was a machine-gun.

The French Army at last had a new light tank in 1931, but it was a development of the Renault FT and of no particular distinction. Its speed was low; its four-cylinder 100-h.p. Renault engine driving it at only 12 m.p.h., and its radius of action was limited to 60 miles. It was armed with a 47-mm. gun and co-axially mounted 7·5-mm. Reibel machine-gun in a turret, and with another machine-gun mounted in the front of the hull. It had unusually thick armour for the period with a maximum of 30 mm., and weighed 14 tons. Some 160 of these machines were manufactured.

In 1931, after a lapse of 3 years, a British armoured force was again created by the formation of the 1st Tank Brigade. It was, however, an all tank force and consisted of the four existing tank battalions: one light and three mixed, the latter comprising both light and medium tanks. Development of this continued until 1934, when the Brigade was made permanent. But there were still only four tank battalions, and their medium tanks were now ageing and obsolescent.

CHAPTER X

Approach to the Second World War

THE years 1934–39 are noteworthy for the large number of new and modern tank designs produced by nations which were soon to be engaged in war. But amongst these nations only in Germany was there a clear conception as to how these tanks were to be used. Only in the German Army was it appreciated that cavalry were back in business—and the cavalry of the pre-rifle era; not that of the latter nineteenth century. General Fuller realised this, but his country showed little disposition to make use of the wisdom and knowledge of the greatest armoured soldier of the time.

Since the Germans knew what they wanted to do with tanks, they wanted large numbers of a few standard designs. In consequence they selected adequate types and stuck to them. They were not the best in the world, but properly used they were good enough as the instruments of the new armoured cavalry division.

The German Pz.Kpfw. I was mentioned in the last chapter, and at the start of the war it was still a very important element of the German armour. It was followed by another light tank, the Pz.Kpfw. II, and these two types of light tank were preponderant in the German armoured divisions during the European campaigns of 1939 and 1940. The Pz. II was designed in 1934. It had a crew of three and was armed with a 20-mm. gun and a 7·92-mm. machine-gun. The first production models were lightly armoured and weighed 7½ tons, but in 1937 the armour was increased to 20–35 mm. and the weight went up to 10¼ tons. Its top speed was 30 m.p.h. and it was powered by a Maybach six-cylinder 130-h.p. engine. A total of 1,900 Pz.II's were built, and there were eventually thirteen different marks. After it had been superseded in the fighting line it was used for reconnaissance until its withdrawal from service in 1943.

Next in order of power was the Pz.Kpfw. III, though the date of its order, 1936, was a year later than that of the Pz.Kpfw. IV.

It was originally intended that the Pz. III should be a powerful 15-ton light tank armed with a 37-mm. gun, with the role of fighting companion to the medium tank. As developed, however, it became a more heavily armed and armoured vehicle and was more properly a cruiser tank. Eventually, except for its smaller gun, it was very similar to the Pz. IV. It was armed at first with the 37-mm. gun, but this was soon changed to the short 50-mm., and ultimately about half the Pz. III's in a Panzer regiment had the long 50-mm. and the remainder the short 75-mm. The secondary armament consisted of two 7·92-mm. machine-guns. The armour thickness varied from 10 to 30 mm., but additional 20-mm. plates were later added to some tanks. The engine was a twelve-cylinder 300-h.p. Maybach, and this gave the tank a speed of 25 m.p.h. Its weight varied according to armour and armament, but an average weight was 22 tons. It was manned by a crew of five. In 1939, of the German Armoured Division's 416 tanks, seventy-two were Pz. III's. During the next 4 years 5,644 Pz. III's were built and there were twelve different marks.

The Pz.Kpfw. IV remained a formidable fighting tank and an important element in the armoured divisions throughout the War. Total production was greater than that of any other German tank: some 9,000 Pz. IV's being built of ten different marks. It has the same engine as the Pz. III and the same speed. The armour was thicker, eventually reaching 10–85 mm., and it was slightly heavier. The gun was initially a short-barrelled low velocity 75-mm. gun. In 1942 this was replaced by the long-barrelled high velocity 75-mm. gun.

Before all these basic types of tanks were ready the Germans were producing an armoured force with remarkable rapidity. In 1934 the first German tank battalion was formed. By October 1935 there were three armoured divisions, relying mainly it is true on the Pz. I. Each division had one tank brigade consisting of two two-battalion regiments, a motorised infantry brigade, a motorised artillery regiment and an anti-tank battalion.

In September 1937 Field Marshal Sir Cyril Deverell, Chief of the Imperial General Staff, accompanied by General Sir Edmund Ironside, G.O.C.-in-C. Eastern Command, visited the German Army manoeuvres. The show piece of these manoeuvres was an attack by 800 tanks and 400 aircraft. In his diary Ironside recorded how impressed he was with the force that the Germans had managed to create in such a short period. In August the following year he noted that the German Army now consisted of forty-eight divisions of which five were armoured, three were mountain and two were light. Besides these there were twenty reserve divisions and thirty-six Landwehr divisions.

During 1938–39 three more armoured divisions were formed, making a total of six. In 1937 there appeared a smaller formation with an element of armour called a light brigade. In 1938 it was increased in size and re-named a light division, and in the same year another three light divisions were formed. The light divisions varied considerably in strength and organisation, but they were all built up round a core of one tank battalion and four motorised infantry battalions.

Whilst the Germans were pressing on with the production of tanks and their rapid incorporation into armoured divisions, the French too were hurriedly equipping their army with modern tanks. In many ways the new French tanks were better than those of the Germans. But the French still thought of tanks as primarily mobile artillery and failed to appreciate that they were acquiring the means which would have made the tragic cavalry charges of 1870 a success. And so most of these new tanks were intended to be used in the ancillary role of infantry support. In the manufacture of tanks the French effort equalled that of the Germans, for although only forty tanks were produced in 1936, a total of 2,200 had been issued to the Army by the outbreak of war, and this number had increased to 3,500 by the time the Germans launched their attack in the West in May 1940. In fact, the French had more tanks than the Germans.

In 1934 a number of standard types of tanks were ordered for the French Army; most of them being built by the firms of Renault, Hotchkiss and Somua. By 1939 the most numerous of the new tanks was the R-35 (Renault 1935), about 2,000 being built. It became the standard French infantry tank, and for this role it was provided with a 37-mm. gun co-axially mounted with a 7·5-mm. Reibel machine-gun, and armour 20–40-mm. thick. It had a 83-h.p. four-cylinder engine which drove it at the low speed of 12½ m.p.h., and it had a radius of action of 52 miles. It weighed 11 tons and had a crew of two. Like all French tanks of the period it suffered from only having a one-man turret, with the result that the tank commander had to load and fire the gun in addition to commanding his tank, or section of tanks. Another drawback of French tanks was the general lack of comfort which tired the crews and impaired their efficiency; interiors were cramped, springing was hard and observation was very poor. There was a later and modified version of the R-35, the R-40, which had an improved suspension and the long-barrelled 37-mm. gun.

The firm of Hotchkiss built a somewhat similar tank, the H-35, for the cavalry. Its armament was the same as that of the R-35, but it was faster (its six-cylinder Hotchkiss 75-h.p. engine giving it a speed of 17½ m.p.h.), and it had the greater radius of action of 80 miles. A later and modified version, the H-39/40, had a more powerful 110-h.p. engine which increased the speed to 25 m.p.h. It also was armed with the long-barrelled 37-mm. gun.

The most noteworthy cavalry tank was the Somua medium S-35, which at the time of its production was probably the finest of all armoured fighting vehicles, and it was armed with the best anti-tank gun. The armament consisted of a 47-mm. gun with a co-axially mounted 7·5-mm. Reibel machine-gun, and the maximum armour thickness was 40 mm. The Somua eight-cylinder 190-h.p. engine gave it a speed of 29 m.p.h., and it had a radius of action of 143 miles. It weighed 19½ tons and it was manned by a crew of three. During 1936–39 about 500 of these tanks were built. The S-35 performed well in both France and Tunisia. In 1940 a modified version was produced which had a 220-h.p. engine and was designated S-40.

The French heavy tank had a somewhat ancient history. In 1921 there had been a specification for a tank of some 15–20 tons with a powerful gun, and in the course of years three prototypes had been produced to meet this specification. The rather belated result was the B-1 of 1936. It had a short 75-mm. gun in the front of the hull and a short 47-mm. gun mounted in the turret. Its armour had a maximum thickness of 40 mm., and it weighed 30 tons. Only a few B-1's were built, but there was an improved version, the B-1 Bis, of which the firm of Renault had completed some 500 by the time of the German onslaught in 1940. The armament was the same as in the B-1, except that in the turret a machine-gun was mounted co-axially with the 47-mm. The maximum thickness of the armour was increased to 60 mm. The B-1 Bis was the main tank of the *Divisions Cuirassées* and it was also issued to infantry units as the main infantry support tank. It weighed 31 tons, had a six-cylinder 307-h.p. engine, with a resulting speed of 18 m.p.h., and a radius of 130 miles. The B-1 Bis had some influence on British tank history, for its track and suspension were adopted for the Churchill tank.

The foregoing are the most important of French tank designs, but there were a few other non-standard types which were produced in fairly limited quantities.

In 1934 the French Army formed the first mechanised division to be retained as a permanent organisation; and it was such an accurate prototype of the armoured formations of the Second World War that it is a tragedy that its potentialities were not recognised by the French Army command. The *Division Légère Mécanique* (DCM) included a reconnaissance regiment of armoured cars and motor cycles, a tank brigade of two tank regiments, a motorised rifle brigade of three battalions of dragoons each with an organic company of light tanks, and an artillery regiment. Unfortunately the role of this admirable formation was limited to that played by cavalry divisions of the rifle era.

Another type of French armoured formation, the *Division Cuirassée*, has been mentioned above. This was intended for the concentrated use of heavy tanks in direct support of infantry along the main line of attack. The first was only formed in the month of the outbreak of war. It included four battalions of B-1 Bis tanks formed into two *demi-brigades*, together with two battalions of motorised infantry. This organisation was later modified with reduced striking power.

In Great Britain 1934 was the year when replacement of the multi-purpose Vickers Medium really made a concrete start. The tank position was indeed gloomy, for the British lead in tanks had been lost and inferiority in both the quality and quantity of tanks was destined to get far worse. The Vickers Medium was obsolete, and in the following year all except fourteen of the light tanks were obsolescent. These fourteen were the new Vickers-Armstrong Mark V, in which the main improvement on the Mark IV was in the provision of a two-man instead of a one-man turret. There were two Vickers machine-guns mounted co-axially, a ·5-inch and a ·303-inch. The Mark V was quite a successful tank, but rather too sensitive in the steering. It was soon superseded by the Mark VI, which was the pre-dominant light tank in the early campaigns of the war. It had a number of improvements and was a good little tank for its intended role as a reconnaissance vehicle. Owing to the shortage of cruiser tanks, however, the Mark VI's provided a large proportion of the available armour at the start of the war.

In 1934 the replacement for the existing medium tank had still not been decided. Carden, however, was asked to design a medium tank which should be cheaper than the "Sixteen-Tonner", round about 10 tons in weight, and powered by a commercial engine (specification A9).

In the meantime some thought had been given to the types of tanks required. The eventual decision from the number of different views expressed was that, instead of a medium tank, with the dual role of providing close support for the infantry and forming the striking element of a mobile force, separate tanks should be designed for each of these roles. Close support of the infantry was to be undertaken by a heavily armoured and rather slow "Infantry" tank—a revival of the heavy tank conception of 1916–18. The main tank of the mobile armoured force, in development of the old "Whippet" idea, was to be fast with armament equal to that of the infantry tank but with much lighter armour, and it was to be called a "Cruiser"—a naval term considered appropriate to its intended task, armour and armament. Of infantry tanks, it was decided at the War Office that there should be one battalion for every infantry division. This again was somewhat akin to the allotment of Mark V's in 1918.

The first result of these decisions was that Vickers-Armstrong were asked to provide a modified version of the tank they had under construction, but with armour of 30-mm. maximum thickness instead of the 14-mm. which was being fitted to the former, and without its two auxiliary machine-gun turrets. This new specification was designated A10.

Before the end of 1934, then, there were two tanks under construction by Vickers-Armstrong: A9, now intended to fulfil the cruiser function, and the A10 for the infantry tank role. So far the plans were simple, but they were not destined to remain so. Indeed it is not easy to disentangle the complicated story which follows.

Before the prototypes of either the A9 or A10 appeared they were already obsolescent. In 1934 General Sir Hugh Elles, commander of the Tank Corps in the First World War, became Master General of the Ordnance. Based on his own experience he demanded certain characteristics of an infantry tank. These were primarily that the tank's armour should be sufficient to make it immune to the 37-mm. anti-tank gun, but that its speed

Plate 17. VICKERS MEDIUM MARK IA STAR WITH CO-AXIALLY MOUNTED MACHINE-GUN.

Plate 18. VICKERS MEDIUM MARK II. NOTE THE ADDITION OF SKIRTING PLATES.

Plate 19.   GERMAN PZ II LIGHT TANK CAPTURED IN THE WESTERN DESERT IN 1941

Plate 20.   GERMAN PZ III WITH A LONG 50-MM GUN, CAPTURED AT TEL EL EISA IN THE SUMMER OF 1942

Plate 21. GERMAN PZ IV TANK WITH A LONG 75-MM GUN CAPTURED BY BRITISH TROOPS IN FRANCE IN JULY 1944.

Plate 22. FRENCH H35 TANK, CAPTURED BY BRITISH TROOPS IN SYRIA, BEING EXAMINED BY AMERICAN OFFICERS.

need not be much greater than that of the infantry. The armour requirement disposed of the A10 as an Infantry tank.

The other event which affected these new tanks was a visit by Generals Wavell and Martel to the Russian manoeuvres of September 1936. Martel was particularly impressed by the Christie suspension of the Russian BT light medium tank (from which the very successful T-34 was subsequently developed). Demonstrations by the BT tanks showed that they completely outclassed the British A9 and A10 in their performance. At 30 m.p.h. the BT's shot up a bank which had a 5-foot vertical drop on its far side, leaped into the air, and made a jump of 30 feet without any damage to either tank or crew. Martel returned with the conviction that Great Britain must obtain a Christie tank.

And so, when in 1936 the A9 and A10 made their appearance, they did not do so as Great Britain's triumphant answer to the armoured designs of her foreign rivals, but rather as Cinderella's ugly sisters, whilst Cinderella herself lingered in the womb of time (or perhaps the War Office).

Nevertheless the A9, which made its appearance shortly after Sir John Carden's untimely death, was in many ways a very fine machine. Within the limits which had been imposed on size and weight, Carden had produced a good design. The body was inevitably cramped because not enough money could be spared to allow the crew to fight in comfort; but even so the weight of 12 tons was rather over the specification. The most noteworthy feature was the hydraulically powered traverse of the turret, and, indeed, this was the first turret with a powered traverse to be mounted in any tank. The engine was a A.E.C. six-cylinder of 150 h.p., which provided the required speed of 23 m.p.h. The tank was armed with a 2-pr gun and a co-axially mounted Vickers machine-gun in the turret, and with two other machine-guns—one in each of two smaller turrets in the forward part of the vehicle.

The A9 performed well on trial, but it had an awkward pitching movement over undulating ground. Some 18 months elapsed before this and other teething troubles were overcome; then, as the Cruiser Tank Mark I, it was issued to the Army. It did well in the early actions of the war. The regiments of the 1st Armoured Division went out to France partially equipped with these tanks, and the 7th Armoured Division used them in the Western Desert until 1941.

The A10 weighed 14 tons, 2 tons more than the A9, and with its maximum speed of 16 m.p.h. it was considerably slower. In compensation for a lower speed and the absence of the two subsidiary machine-gun turrets, the A10 was protected against ·5-inch armour-piercing ammunition as compared with the A9's modest immunity from ordinary small arms fire.   This additional protection was given by screwing extra armour plates over the hull: the first use of composite armour.   It was soon apparent, however, that the A10's armour was quite inadequate for the role envisaged for an infantry tank, and it was accordingly re-classified as a heavy cruiser and designated the Cruiser Tank Mark II.   It also served in the 1st and 7th Armoured Divisions, and was a more popular and more reliable tank than the A9.

In the meantime General Elles' specification for an infantry tank resulted in the A11, or Infantry Tank Mark I.   It was designed by Carden and the pilot model was delivered by Vickers-Armstrong in September 1936.   It was by no means ideal, for money, as always, was short.   It was heavily armoured, but under-gunned, cramped in size, and manned by a crew of only two.   Its weight was 11 tons, and it was driven at its modest speed of 8 m.p.h. by a Ford V8 60-h.p. engine.   Its armament was limited to one machine-gun of either ·303 or ·5 calibre, but its armour was thicker than that of any other existing tank: 65 mm. in front and 60 mm. at the sides.   As a vehicle it was extremely reliable.   In all 139 of these machines were eventually built.

With these three new tanks of 1936 it might be thought that British tank construction could have gone ahead rapidly.   But the General Staff was unhappy.   Martel's report on the Russian BT tanks was disquieting, and he was authorised to ask the firm of Nuffield Mechanisation Ltd. to try and purchase a tank from Christie.   The outcome was comic.   Christie had only one tank left and this was mortgaged.   However he agreed over the telephone to sell it for £8,000, and the mortgage was duly repaid by the War Office.   A major difficulty now arose as the United States Government learned of the sale and promptly refused an export licence on the grounds that the export of war material was prohibited.   It would seem that the War Office then suggested or connived at smuggling; and in due course a crated "tractor" arrived in England together with a number of cases labelled "grape fruit".   The final hurdle of an irritatingly inquisitive

British customs having been overcome, the contents of crate and packages were assembled as a Christie tank.

It was now arranged that Lord Nuffield should purchase the patent rights from Christie and develop a cruiser tank to a specification, A13, embodying the Christie suspension. The prototype of this tank was completed in September 1937, 10 months after work had started. It weighed 14 tons, had a 2-pr gun and Vickers machine-gun mounted co-axially, and armour of 14-mm. thickness. Power was provided by a Nuffield 340-h.p. twelve-cylinder engine, giving the high maximum speed of 30 m.p.h. The radius of action was between 80 and 100 miles. The first version of the A13 was officially entitled Cruiser Mark III, but a later edition, with the armour thickness increased to 30 mm. and with additional skirting plates fitted to the turret, was called Cruiser Mark IV. The A13 was the third of the types of cruiser tank which fought with the 1st and 7th Armoured Divisions.

But tank inspiration had not ceased to flow from the General Staff. In the latter part of 1937, before the appearance of the A13 prototype, it was decided that medium tanks might well be required and two different specifications entitled A14 and A15 were accordingly prepared. The limitations of the Infantry Tank Mark I was, too, causing concern, and a new specification, A12, was drawn up for an Infantry Tank Mark II. The design of this new infantry tank was basically derived from the experimental A7 tanks described in the last chapter. In armament and general layout it followed the A10, but with a 75-mm. thickness of steel plate it was the most heavily armoured tank in the world. It was, of course, heavy, weighing 26½ tons, and its maximum speed was limited to 15 m.p.h. It was originally powered by two 87-h.p. A.E.C. diesel engines, but later marks had two 95-h.p. Leyland petrol engines. The armament consisted of a 2-pr gun and a 7.92-mm. Besa machine-gun, but close support tanks had a 3-inch howitzer instead of the 2-pr. The radius of action was 60 miles and there was a crew of five.

The Infantry Tank Mark II was exceedingly popular, but it was "hand made" and too much individual skill was required to allow of rapid production. The Mark II's only started to appear, in fact, in 1939, and there were all too few of them available when war broke out. It is difficult to overestimate the value of these tanks in the campaign in France and Flanders in 1940. It is conceivable that had there been no Infantry Tanks Mark II the Germans would have succeeded in surrounding the

B.E.F. and the evacuation from Dunkirk would not have been possible. The Mark II's also gave invaluable service in the early battles of the Western Desert. Their great asset at this period of the war was their very thick armour which was invulnerable to any gun-fire less than short-range engagement by field artillery. It was not till the Germans were equipped with the 88-mm. gun for anti-tank use that they had a weapon which provided an effective defence against them.

The name "Matilda", by which the Infantry Tank Mark II was affectionately known, had been bestowed originally by General Elles on the Infantry Tank Mark I, owing to its resemblance to a fictitious comic duck.

Certain decisions as to tank development policy were taken at a meeting held by the Chief of the Imperial General Staff in December 1937. The Mark II was selected as the standard infantry tank, but in the meantime there was to be further production of Mark I's. As regards cruiser tanks, fifty of the A13 type were to be built, but with some modifications. In addition the A14 and A15 (the latter now changed to A16) medium tanks were to be developed and, if they were successful, preparations were to be made so that they could be put into production rapidly in the event of a war.

The A14 prototype was built by the London, Midland & Scottish Railway Company. It weighed 18 tons and had a speed of 25 m.p.h. The A16, work on which was sanctioned to begin in February 1938, weighed 21 tons, could run at 30 m.p.h., and had a better suspension than the A14. However, neither machine went into production.

As a result of experience with the A13 it was decided that this should be the basis of further cruiser tank development, and nothing further was heard of medium tanks.

The A13 Mark III, which became the Cruiser Tank Mark V, or "Covenanter", was also built by the London, Midland & Scottish Railway, and the first production models came into service in 1939. It was not a success as it suffered from a series of mechanical faults and its tracks were too narrow for the weight they had to bear. The "Covenanter" never went into action, but it gave invaluable service as a training tank. It weighed 18 tons, had a Meadowes 300-h.p. horizontally opposed engine, and its maximum speed was 31 m.p.h.

The next cruiser tank had a far more distinguished career. This was the A15, later entitled the Cruiser Tank Mark VI or

"Crusader". It was designed by the Mechanisation Board between 1938 and 1940 in conjunction with Nuffield Mechanisation, and incorporated some of the features of the "Covenanter". The first models appeared just before the outbreak of war. The "Crusader" had a Christie suspension, and a twelve-cylinder Nuffield Liberty 340-h.p. engine, which was practically identical to that fitted to the A13 Mark I and which gave it a maximum speed of 27 m.p.h. It had armour of a maximum thickness of 40 mm. and its armament consisted of a 2-pr gun, two Besa machine-guns, and a Bren gun on an anti-aircraft mounting. It weighed 18¾ tons. Close support tanks had 3-inch howitzers instead of 2-prs. As a result of experience in battle a number of modifications were embodied in later marks. In the Mark II the armour thickness was increased to 50 mm., with a consequent increase in weight to 19 tons. The Mark III had 52 mm. of armour and a weight of 19¾ tons. In addition the 2-pr gun was replaced by a 6-pr and there was only one Besa machine-gun instead of two.

The "Crusader" was first used in action in the Western Desert in June 1941, where its speed and excellent suspension were made full use of by the British armoured regiments. However, it was not mechanically very reliable, and practical experience showed it to be under-gunned and even under-armoured. Nevertheless its speed and manoeuvrability impressed and bothered the Germans. It remained the standard tank of the 7th Armoured Division until the battle of El Alamein.

The last British tank to be designed before the war was the "Valentine" infantry tank. It was a Vickers-Armstrong product and had, as might be expected, a family resemblance to the A9's and A10's; it had, indeed, been developed from the latter. It was 1940 before the "Valentine" started to come into service, but it ran into eleven different marks and was used in North Africa until 1943. It was reliable and popular, though tiring to drive. The Mark I weighed 17 tons, had a crew of three, armour with the respectable thickness of 65 mm., and an armament of a 2-pr gun and a 7·92-mm. Besa machine-gun. It had a maximum speed of 15 m.p.h. and was driven by an A.E.C. 135-h.p. engine.

The main modifications in later marks concerned the armament and the engine. Marks VIII to X were armed with a 6-pr gun instead of a 2-pr, and Mark XI had a 75-mm. Marks II and onwards were fitted with diesel engines instead of petrol engines.

The last British light tank was another Vickers-Armstrong design. This vehicle, the "Tetrarch", was built in 1939; but thinly armoured light tanks were already obsolescent by the time it came into service. Nevertheless it was small enough to be used as an airborne tank, and as such it played a notable role in the Airborne Armoured Reconnaissance Regiment on the "D" Day operations of 6th June 1944. It only weighed 7½ tons, but it had a powerful 165-h.p. Meadows engine which gave it the fast speed of 37 m.p.h. It was thinly armoured (16 mm.) but was well armed for a light tank with a 2-pr gun and co-axially mounted 7·92-mm. Besa machine-gun. Suspension was by four independently sprung wheels on each side, and shallow radius turns could be effected by pivoting the front wheels.

The 2-pr gun with which British tanks were equipped at the beginning of the war has been much criticised. But in point of fact there was no apparent reason for them to have anything larger. The 2-pr could penetrate 60 mm. of armour plate at a distance of 500 yards, and no German tank at this time had that amount of protection. Indeed the Germans themselves could hardly claim a formidable tank armament: the Pz. II had a 20-mm. gun, the Pz. III a 37-mm. (equal to a 2-pr), and the Pz. IV a low velocity 75-mm. If a bigger gun were fitted less ammunition could be carried, and a tank could manage 150 rounds of 2-pr ammunition, the figure which was regarded by the War Office as the desirable minimum.

Nevertheless there was· an inexplicable lethargy in the development of a more powerful 6-pr gun, the design for which had been initiated at the beginning of 1938.

In 1938 the organisation of British armour took a belated step forward with the incorporation of the Tank Brigade, together with mechanised cavalry regiments, into the Mobile Division—the formation of which had been suggested in 1935. As formed, the Mobile Division consisted of the Tank Brigade (of one light and two mixed tank battalions) and two mechanised cavalry brigades (each of three light tank regiments). The division had some 600 tanks; but of these far the greater proportion were light, and for the heavier element, the main striking force, there was nothing better than the obsolete Vickers Mediums.

On 29th March 1938 Ironside jotted down in his diary his assessment of the state of the British Army. Amongst the armoured fighting vehicles there were only obsolete medium tanks and there were no cruiser tanks and no infantry tanks. It was a lamentable and depressing situation.

In 1939 the Mobile Division was renamed the Armoured Division, and all its armoured units were called regiments. It now consisted of a Light Armoured Brigade (three light regiments equipped with cruiser tanks and light tanks), a Heavy Armoured Brigade (three heavy regiments equipped with cruiser tanks only), and a Support Group (a motorised rifle battalion, a motorised artillery regiment and an engineer company). But one division was quite inadequate, and it was far too late, for on the outbreak of war the division was not equipped.

Whilst in Western Europe tank design and production was proceeding at a rapidly increasing tempo, in the United States design was unimpressive and production dilatory.

In 1934 two light tanks were built, the 8-ton T.2 for the infantry and the very similar but twin-turreted 5½-ton T.5 combat car for the cavalry. From these was developed in 1936–37 an 8-ton production model which was intended for both infantry and cavalry use, and designated the M.1.A.1 light tank and M.1 combat car respectively. It was very fast; for, powered by a 250-h.p. air-cooled engine, it could run at 50 m.p.h. Its armament consisted of one ·5 machine-gun and three ·30 machine-guns, and it had armour of 6–16-mm. thickness. A short time later the legal obstruction, caused by the Act of Congress which assigned tanks to the infantry, was overcome, and the ridiculous distinction of "combat car" was abandoned.

A new light tank was produced in 1938, the M.2.A.3., the most noteworthy feature of which was a 37-mm. gun; thus reversing a policy of arming tanks only with machine-guns. This was followed in 1939 by a M.2 medium tank, incorporating as far as possible components used in the light tank. The design of this tank owed much to the aged Vickers Medium. Nevertheless its appearance had much historical importance, for on its suspension was based that of the M.3 (Grant) and M.4 (Sherman) medium tanks. The M.2 Medium was armed with a 37-mm. gun and no less than eight ·30 machine-guns. The maximum thickness of the hull armour was 26 mm. but the gun mantlet was 52 mm. The tank weighed 17 tons, was manned by a crew of five, and was driven at 30 m.p.h. by a Wright 350-h.p. engine.

At the time war broke out American progress towards an armoured formation was limited to a mechanised cavalry brigade consisting of 112 light tanks and a motorised artillery regiment.

CHAPTER XI

The Battle of Flanders

IN the months which preceded the outbreak of war there was nothing about British armoured progress which could have impressed the French. In 1938 we had said that two armoured divisions would be included as soon as possible in the Expeditionary Force. In March 1939 we informed the French that these two divisions could not be completed before September 1940. The next month we said that the first of the two divisions would be ready by about the end of the year, but that the second would not be available until much later.

And yet when war came the 1st Armoured Division was still without its Cruiser tanks and only two Army Tank battalions had been equipped with infantry tanks. The office of Master-General of the Ordnance had been swept away by Hore-Belisha, then Secretary of State for War, and his functions had been transferred to the Ministry of Supply. General Ironside, the Chief of the Imperial General Staff, asked the Ministry of Supply what was being done to provide the Army with tanks. He received the astonishing reply that there were two committees each working on a separate design. One committee had as chairman Sir Albert Stern, to whose drive and enthusiasm the production of the original tanks of 1916 had been largely due. The Stern Committee, with eyes on the rival Maginot and Siegfried Lines, were envisaging a battering ram of a heavy tank, similar in many respects to the heavy tank of the First World War, including the lack of a turret with all-round traverse. It was larger with much thicker armour and a more powerful armament, but the engine was much out of date. The other committee was headed by the, from a tank point of view, almost legendary Sir Ernest Swinton. The Swinton Committee had similar views on the need for a heavy tank, but to save time they were advocating the adoption of the French B-1 *Bis*. This, however, was hardly a modern tank. Although the idea of making it was eventually rejected, the design of the track and

See map page 224.

104

suspension was copied and, as stated in the last chapter, incorporated in the Churchill tank.

Unfortunately the Ministry of Supply, in setting up these two committees, had not arranged that the General Staff should be consulted about their requirements. The result was that the committees had the impossible task of designing tanks without having been informed of their intended tactical use.

Ironside considered that the Army's future needs could be met by two types of tank. One of these should be a battle tank, weighing some 60 tons, and the other a cruiser of about 30 tons. A cruiser tank of this weight (the Cromwell) was produced in 1943. The battle tank appeared in a modified form as the 40-ton Churchill infantry tank of 1941.

At Ironside's suggestion the Stern and Swinton Committees were amalgamated, and the new committee included tank experts from the War Office. Before the new committee started work the Stern Committee had produced a specification for a very heavily armoured tank with a high trench-crossing capacity. Construction of a prototype was begun in February 1940 and completed in the following October. It was affectionately christened the T.O.G. in reference to "The Old Gang" who had designed it. In appearance it was very like a First World War heavy tank, with the same all-round unsprung tracks. Instead of the sponsons, however, a gun was mounted in front of the hull and there was a machine-gun in a turret with all-round traverse. A second prototype, TOG Mark II, was ready in March 1941. It was rather more modern in appearance without the overall track and, as finally developed and entitled TOG Mark II Star, it had a 17-pr gun and machine-gun in its turret and weighed 80 tons. A 600-h.p. engine drove it at 8½ m.p.h. This is looking well ahead of the present chapter, but it is worth while completing the story of the TOG's for nothing more was heard of them. They had been designed for the wrong war.

In the meantime the British Expeditionary Force had sailed for France with a grossly inadequate number of tanks. The divisional cavalry regiments had nothing better than the Vickers Mark VI Light tanks, and the Infantry tanks, good in their way as they were, were all too slow for the pace of modern warfare, and there were no transporters for their long-distance movement. The armoured division was still in England and deficient of a very large part of its equipment. Its progress was not helped

by being split up in the winter of 1939–40, and its units despatched to various parts of the country for home defence and
internal security. Reformed in the early part of 1940, it was
proposed that the Division should carry out training on the
Marlborough Downs; but this proposal was turned down on the
grounds that the area was required for gallops by the local
racing stables!

In March 1940, 6 months after the outbreak of war and
3 months after the date by which the French had been told the
Division would be ready, it still had less than half its tanks,
none of its artillery, no bridging equipment, and little of almost
everything that really mattered.

The French Army certainly had the large numbers of modern
tanks which the British lacked, but the value of their tanks was
limited by the pessimistic official assessment of their vulnerability.
For in the view of the French Army command the tank was too
vulnerable to the fire of artillery and anti-tank weapons to
undertake other than an ancillary role. It was intended, therefore, that it should act in close support of infantry and undertake
the protective and reconnaissance tasks of the horsed cavalry
which it had replaced.

In the German Army the more senior generals at first held
views similar to those of their French contemporaries. But
there were a number of younger generals who had been en-
couraged by General von Seckt in both the practical and theore-
tical study of armoured warfare; and it was the organisation
and tactical doctrine which they proposed which was ultimately
accepted in the German Army. The idea of fast moving warfare
with a promise of swift decision was attractive enough to get the
support of Hitler; though any benefit which this may have been
to the German Army was more than offset by his disastrous
interference with military strategy on the Russian front.

For the attack on Poland the German Army could muster
six armoured divisions, equipped predominantly with light
tanks, and four light divisions, each with a comparatively small
armoured element. However, these divisions were sufficient
for the job and they formed the decisive component of the
attacking force. The campaign started on 1st September, and,
after a rapid advance by the German centre, an armoured corps
broke through the Polish defence on 8th September and drove to
Warsaw. On the German left another armoured corps swung
round behind the Polish armies and pushed on southwards in

their rear. By the time the Russians crossed the frontier Polish resistance was collapsing and there were no forces to oppose them.

This rapid campaign, with its demonstration of the striking power of armoured cavalry, came as a severe shock to the Western Allies. On 5th October 1939 General Gamelin, Commander-in-Chief of the French Army, held a conference which was attended by Ironside. Gamelin deduced, truly, that the chief lesson to be learned from the Polish campaign was the power of penetration possessed by the fast and hard-hitting German armoured formations, and the close co-operation of the supporting air force. He then went on to describe the methods which the Allies should use to stop the German thrusts. He considered that armoured columns might penetrate between two forts or strong points, but that, if this should occur, such posts were to hold firm and stop any attempt by infantry and transport to follow up the tank units. The German tanks would then run out of petrol, ammunition and food, and, having been brought to a standstill, could be destroyed. In theory this sounded excellent, but it surrendered the initiative completely to the Germans and assumed that they would be content with such a narrow penetration as to risk separation from their supporting and administrative troops. Gamelin then made the serious error of saying that the only place where the decisive battle could be fought was the plain of Belgium; for only there could the Germans use armour to achieve a decisive result. Ironside, with a more realistic appreciation of the capabilities of armour, maintained that the main German thrust would come through Luxembourg and the Ardennes, and thence along the line of the Franco-Belgian frontier. This was, of course, the plan eventually adopted by the Germans.

At another conference at the French G.H.Q. on 9th November 1939 Gamelin discussed the possibility of an attack through the Ardennes and ruled it out as impracticable. He stated that the Ardennes with its deep valleys and thickly wooded hills was not suitable tank country, and that the River Meuse, which ran through it, with its high steep banks was the best tank obstacle in Europe. And so the French Command, at any rate, settled down in the comfortable conviction that the Ardennes was not suitable for tanks and made their dispositions accordingly.

During the lull between the campaign in Poland and the

opening of the battle in the West, the Germans increased the strength of their armoured formations. The four light divisions were made into armoured divisions, bringing the number up to ten, and many of the indifferent Pz. I's were replaced by tanks of a later type. Of the total of 2,574 tanks in the armoured divisions, 627 were now Pz. III's or IV's and 334 were Czech tanks designated 35 (t) and 38 (t) and armed with 37-mm. guns. This represented a considerable increase in the weight of armour since the Polish campaign. The most numerous tanks then were the Pz. I's, of which there were 1,500, and the Pz. II's came a close second with 1,200. Of heavier tanks there had been only 100 Pz. III's and 200 Pz. IV's. The Czech tanks were issued to the converted light divisions. Most of the Pz. I's were put into reserve as available for reinforcements.

The French had the impressive strength of some 3,500 recently manufactured tanks, of which about 800 were either medium or heavy and all were more heavily armoured than their German equivalents. The French tanks were organised in fifty-six tank battalions, as compared with thirty-five German battalions. But there the French superiority ended, for in the organisation of their armour and in its tactical and strategic deployment they were hopelessly inferior. There were three D.L.M.'s and four low-strength *Divisions Cuirassées*, but most of the tank battalions were distributed in close support of the infantry.

The British armoured strength was slight. In the 1st Army Tank Brigade were the 4th Royal Tank Regiment with Mark I infantry tanks and the 7th Royal Tank Regiment equipped with twenty-seven Mark I and twenty-three Mark II infantry tanks and seven light tanks. The third regiment of the Brigade, the 8th Royal Tank Regiment, was still in the United Kingdom. The regiments intended to carry out the cavalry role of reconnaissance and protection were equipped with Mark VI light tanks. They were the 4th/7th and 5th Dragoon Guards, 13th/18th and 15th/19th Hussars, 1st Lothian and Border Horse, Fife and Forfar Yeomanry, and East Riding Yeomanry.

In April 1940 the German forces on the Western front were disposed in three army groups. Army Group "B" faced Holland and Belgium north of Liege, and had three armoured divisions under command; Army Group "A" faced Luxembourg and the Ardennes, and had seven armoured divisions; and Army Group "C" was drawn up opposite the Maginot Line from Longwy to Switzerland, without any armoured formations or units at its disposal. The disposition of the armoured divisions, had they been known to the Allied staffs, would have shown where the blow was to fall, and shown too the correctness or Ironside's appreciation and the disastrous fallacy of Gamelin's.

If the locations of the German tanks would have given valuable information, those of the French tanks would not have disclosed any likely armoured thrust; for no armoured thrust was contemplated. Each of the eight French armies had a group of from two to seven battalions of light tanks; about half of these battalions being behind that portion of the Maginot Line which stretched between the Rhine and the Ardennes. Most of them had the R-35 tank, but some were equipped with the old 1918 pattern Renault FT: an archaic anachronism on a 1940 battlefield. The heavy B type tanks and H-35's allotted to the infantry were all in the *Divisions Cuirassées* which were in reserve. The three DLM's were equipped with all the S-35's, and the majority of the H-35's and the similar H-39's.

On 10th May 1940 the Germans launched their offensive in the West, and immediately the roads winding through the forested heights of the Ardennes were alive with German tanks hastening onwards nose to tail. French cavalry opposition was brushed aside, and by 13th May the seven armoured divisions of Army Group "A" had covered 70 miles of these roads and were on the banks of the Meuse. The crossing of this formidable tank obstacle started the same day, the defending French troops being paralysed and demoralised by waves of screaming dive-bombers. At Sedan the whole of Guderian's 19th Panzer Corps of three divisions stormed over the river and broke right through the French line on a wide front. Further north Rommel's 7th Panzer Division crashed over the Meuse at Dinant. Within 48 hours the German armour was in open country and driving along virtually undefended roads. Coming into action belatedly and piecemeal, the *Divisions Cuirassées* made ineffectual attempts to halt the German advance. Similar ineffectual attempts to do the same thing where being made by the German High Command who had got nervous. But the German armour had the bit between its teeth and was driving along at 50 miles a day.

On 14th May the War Diary of Field-Marshal von Rundstedt's Headquarters (Army Group "A") recorded a worry over the increasing vulnerability of the southern flank of the breakthrough, and suggested that the armour might be halted on the Oise. On 16th May von Rundstedt himself ordered a temporary halt so that the infantry masses in rear could close up, and gave the Rivers Sambre and Oise as the line which was not to be crossed without his permission.

By this time the *Divisions Cuirassées* were wrecked. The 1st had ceased to exist after being thrown into the gap left by the rout of the French 9th Army; and the 2nd and 3rd were destroyed in detail a few days later as their units were thrown individually into the battle.

By 19th May, after resuming their advance, German tanks had arrived at the Canal du Nord, with only 50 miles between them and the sea. Five armoured divisions formed the spearhead of the attack, the 1st, 2nd, 6th, 7th, and 8th; whilst close behind were two more, the 5th and 10th. On the right was Rommel's 7th Armoured Division, and the next day it ran into unexpected British resistance at Arras. Rommel put in repeated attacks on the 20th, but without any success. In the meantime the other armoured divisions swept forward through the thin screen of gallantly defended localities, which had been hastily manned by the under-strength British 12th and 23rd Infantry Divisions. The 8th Armoured Division reached Montreuil that evening and the 2nd Armoured Division occupied Abbeville during the night. The Allied forces were now cut completely in two, and those to the north of the German thrust were severed from their lines of communication.

Meanwhile in the Arras area the SS *Totenkopf* (Death's Head) Division had come up on the left of the 7th Armoured, with the result that the town was now partly surrounded.

On 21st May the German armoured divisions which had broken through wheeled northwards, but their further progress was soon halted by an order from higher command. At dawn on 22nd the advance was allowed to proceed. Later in the day Boulogne was passed and contained, and on 23rd Calais was sealed off. On 24th the Aa Canal, only 10 miles from Dunkirk, had been crossed at several points. But then, with decisive victory in sight, the German armour was again halted, and orders from Army Group "A" forbade any movement across the Aa. Those units which had crossed the canal were thereupon withdrawn. Headquarters Army Group "A" had had a nasty shock.

The cause of the shock was an attack by a small British force at Arras. On 21st May this force had arrived at Arras with the primary object of preventing British G.H.Q. from being overrun by Rommel's command. It consisted of two tank regiments of the 1st Army Tank Brigade and two tired Territorial battalions of the Durham Light Infantry from the 151st Brigade of the 50th Division. After long moves on their tracks only fifty-eight Mark I infantry tanks and sixteen Mark II's were serviceable. Major-General Martel, commanding 50th Division, formed this force into two columns, each consisting of one tank regiment one infantry battalion, one machine-gun company, one field battery and one anti-tank battery. To make the tank regiment more equal, seven Mark II's from the 7th Royal Tank Regiment were transferred to the 4th Royal Tank Regiment, which was equipped with only Mark I's. Martel's plan was for the two columns to advance southwards on roads about 3 miles apart, cross the River Scarpe west of Arras, and then turn south-eastwards. He gave the River Cojeul as the first objective, and the River Sensée, 3 miles further on, as the second. The 3rd French DLM, with some sixty tanks remaining, was to cover the right flank of the attack.

The attack was timed to start at 2.0 p.m., but by 1 p.m. it was apparent that the weary infantry would be about half an hour behind time on the starting line. It was therefore decided to open the attack with the tanks alone and to follow up with the infantry as soon as possible. The artillery support was also late, and although air support had been promised the aircraft never arrived.

The counter-attack forces were far too small to achieve more than local and temporary success; yet the punch which they delivered had a tremendous immediate tactical effect, and an ultimate strategic effect which was far greater than either of the opposing commanders could have possibly imagined.

As it happened the tanks attacked an hour before a new German attack was to be mounted against Arras. Rommel's 7th Armoured Division was to advance north-westwards round the western flank of Arras with the SS *Totenkopf* Division on its left, and the 5th Armoured Division was directed against the east of the town.

The advancing British armour caught the Germans "on the wrong foot". The first brunt of the attack fell on the motorised infantry of the 7th Armoured Division and on the SS Division. Part of the latter panicked and fled. The Germans found to their dismay that their anti-tank guns were useless against the armour of the British infantry tanks; one Matilda receiving fourteen direct hits from 37-mm. guns without effect. Rommel said that his guns were destroyed by fire or overrun and that their crews were mostly annihilated.

Eventually the British force was brought to a halt, and the remains of the 1st Army Tank Brigade were withdrawn to the Vimy area. They little knew at the time how much they had achieved. Rommel thought that he was being attacked by tanks in superior strength to his own, and referred to "hundreds of enemy tanks and following infantry". This infers that he estimated the British strength to be at least a complete armoured corps. Bad news always gathers strength as it travels and Headquarters Army Group "A" were soon in a state of "jitters". They envisaged a massive British counterstroke which threatened to cut off and immobilise the bulk of their own armour. Hence the advance of the German tanks was checked on 21st August, and the 1st and 2nd Armoured Divisions were pulled back in case of any further threat from the Arras area. The remaining armoured divisions were halted on 24th, first by von Rundstedt, and then by a confirmatory order from Hitler himself, after he had visited von Rundstedt's headquarters. The following day it was decided that the armoured divisions must be kept intact for later operations. On 26th, however, the armoured advance was allowed to proceed. But it was then too late; for the ground was being rapidly flooded and the defence was solidifying.

General Elles had indeed served his country well by his insistence on a heavily armoured tank.

The decisive part played by the German armoured formations in the campaign in France and Flanders of 1940 had a tremendous impact on military thinking throughout the world. As far as the United Kingdom was concerned, however, it did appear that the armoured divisional organisation was proceeding on the right lines; and this impression was endorsed by experience with the 1st Armoured Division in the operations in France which followed the Dunkirk evacuation.

Early in 1940 a second infantry battalion and an anti-tank/anti-aircraft regiment had been included in the support group. In addition the two armoured brigades of the armoured division had been re-organised so that each consisted of three armoured regiments each equipped with cruiser tanks. As a result of the 1940 campaigns an armoured car regiment was added to the

23. THE CAVALRY MOUNT AT THE START OF THE SECOND WORLD WAR—THE LIGHT TANK MARK VI.

Plate 24. THE FIRST BRITISH CRUISER TANK, THE A9.

Plate 25. A10 CRUISER TANK; VERY SIMILAR TO BUT MORE HEAVILY ARMOURED, MORE RELIABLE
SLOWER, AND MORE POPULAR THAN THE A9.

Plate 26. THE FIRST BRITISH TANK WITH A CHRISTIE CHASSIS, THE A13.

Imperial War Museum

Plate 27.   INFANTRY TANK MARK I; THE ORIGINAL INSPIRATION OF GENERAL ELLES'S 'MATILDA',
THE 'COMIC DUCK'.

Plate 28.   THE INFANTRY TANK MARK II, OR 'MATILDA'.

Plate 29. 'CRUSADER' MARK I, ARMED WITH A 2-POUNDER GUN.

Plate 30. 'CRUSADER' MARK III, ARMED WITH THE EXCELLENT 6-POUNDER GUN.

division for reconnaissance and the combined anti-tank/anti-aircraft regiment was split to provide separate regiments for each of these roles. At the same time the short-lived second infantry battalion in the support group was removed; but in compensation an infantry battalion was included in each armoured brigade, so that the total infantry strength in the division was increased by a battalion.

The Germans had no particular need to alter the organisation of their armoured divisions, but a re-organisation was enforced by a shortage of tanks. As a result of the victories in the West the number of armoured divisions was doubled, but there were insufficient tanks to equip all these divisions to the original scale. In consequence the number of tank regiments in each division was reduced from two to one. In six divisions the regiment had three tank battalions, but in the remaining divisions it only had two. On the other hand the fighting power of the tank battalion was increasing owing to the greater number of more powerful tanks which were now coming from the factories. The new pattern battalion had two light companies equipped with Pz. III 50-mm. gun tanks and one medium company with Pz. IV 75-mm. gun tanks. Pz. II's were retained for reconnaissance duties. The infantry brigade of the armoured division was re-organised to comprise two two-battalion motorised rifle regiments and one motor cycle rifle battalion. There was also added a third artillery battalion and an anti-aircraft regiment with 88-mm. guns, which were later to become famous in a devastating anti-tank role.

The 1940 battles had a rapid effect on American military thinking and organisation. In July 1940 the old distinction between infantry and cavalry armour was abolished and two German-type armoured divisions were formed. They each included a reconnaissance battalion, an armoured brigade, an infantry regiment, an artillery battalion, and an engineer battalion. In the armoured brigade were two light tank regiments, each with three battalions of M3 light tanks, one medium tank regiment with two battalions of M3 medium tanks, and an artillery regiment with two battalions of self-propelled 105-mm. howitzers. With a proportion of eight battalions of tanks to two of infantry, however, the division was too overweighted in armour.

CHAPTER XII

The Defeat of Italy in the Western Desert

A T the start of the desperate air conflict known as the Battle of Britain, the possible prelude to a German invasion, General Sir Alan Brooke, Commander-in-Chief Home Forces, was still dangerously short of tanks. During June and July the manufacturers had managed to turn out over 300, but this was not nearly sufficient to equip an armoured counter-stroke against a German invasion.

But British interests, vital to the successful prosecution of the war, were being seriously menaced in another theatre. On 10th August 1940 the Secretary of State for War held a conference which was attended by Brooke and General Sir Archibald Wavell, Commander-in-Chief Middle East. Wavell needed tanks desperately to meet the massive Italian threat to Alexandria, the key to our whole position in Egypt and the Mediterranean. Churchill had decided that the need must be met, and he, together with General Sir John Dill, Chief of the Imperial General Staff, took the very courageous step of directing the despatch to Egypt of three tank regiments drawn from Brooke's anti-invasion forces. These regiments were the 7th Royal Tanks, equipped with Mark II infantry tanks (Matildas), the 2nd Royal Tanks, with A13 cruiser tanks together with a few A9's and A10's, and the 3rd Hussars with Mark VI light tanks. These three regiments arrived in Egypt in September.

The 7th Armoured Division was already in Egypt. Its original organisation had included one heavy and one light armoured brigade each with the modest strength of two regiments. These brigades had now been re-organised so that each comprised one heavy and one light regiment. In the so-called heavy regiments, however, more than half the tanks were light, the remainder being A9 and A10 cruisers. In each of the light regiments one squadron was equipped half with cruiser tanks and half with light tanks. A comparatively small proportion of the Division's tanks, therefore, were armed with 2-pr guns.

Thus the three regiments which arrived from England more than doubled the number of gun-armed tanks.

The armoured regiments in the 7th Armoured Division were the 1st and 6th Royal Tanks and the 7th and 8th Hussars. In accordance with the policy of having cruiser tanks in each unit, one squadron of the 2nd Royal Tanks exchanged tanks with one squadron of the 3rd Hussars. The 2nd Royal Tanks now joined the 7th Hussars and 6th Royal Tanks in the 4th Armoured Brigade, and the 3rd Hussars went to the 7th Armoured Brigade with the 8th Hussars and the 1st Royal Tanks. The 4th Armoured Brigade, with two heavy regiments, was much the more powerful of the two. The 7th Royal Tank Regiment, with Matildas, was retained directly under Headquarters Western Desert Force as Corps troops.

Although in the remarkable campaign which was to follow the British armour played the decisive part in the defeat of the Italian forces, its wide-flung and rapid movement over vast distances was only possible through new techniques in command and control. It is not too much to say that, though the destruction of one of the armoured regiments would not necessarily have resulted in the failure of the operations, heavy personnel and equipment losses in either the 7th Armoured Divisional Signals or the Western Desert Force Signals (the two Royal Signals regiments principally concerned) would have brought the operations to a halt.

The training carried out by the Tank Brigade before the War had shown that it was not possible to control tanks in battle without radio telephony over a minimum range of 10 miles. To meet this requirement a wireless set, the No. 9, was designed and production started in 1935. Rather oddly, in spite of the helplessness of a tank without good communications, the tank designers failed to provide sufficient room in all tanks to accommodate this set; and in none of them, despite signal advice, was space allowed for separate wireless batteries. To save weight and space reliance was placed on one common battery in a tank for all purposes. In infantry and light tanks, which could not take the No. 9, a small infantry set (the No. 11) was installed with a "high power" attachment to give greater range, but the result was not very satisfactory. In fact, distances in the Western Desert were too great for the No. 9 Set when working on ground wave, and aerials had to be improvised by Royal Signals to permit of sky-wave working. The result of the decision to have a common battery was nearly disastrous. When tanks were halted for any length of time the battery ran down, and then neither would the wireless set work nor was their power available to start the engine. 7th Armoured Division had therefore to arrange for spare batteries to be crammed into all tanks and wireless vehicles and for more independent charging equipment to be obtained.

The greatest communication problem was to find a satisfactory method of exercising command from the headquarters of an armoured formation whilst it was on the move. It was solved through the introduction of the armoured command vehicle, equipped with wireless sets and protected by thin armour plate against small arms ammunition. The A.C.V. was divided into two major compartments—a large one for staff officers and a small one for the wireless equipment and operators. A hatchway connected the two compartments so that the wireless operator could deal directly with requests for radio telephone calls and assist in the case of any difficulties. Divisional main headquarters was accommodated in seven or eight A.C.V.'s; the Divisional commander, his G.S.O. 1 and his Commander Royal Signals travelling in A.C.V. No. 1. So that discussions could take place between staff branches on the move, each A.C.V., in addition to its main wireless set, had a short range set for intercommunication with the other A.C.V.'s.

The A.C.V.'s and their crews belonged to the Divisional Signals, and one of their unique and most valuable features was the partnership which arose between commander or staff officer and his wireless operator. Woe betide the Commander Royal Signals who changed the Divisional Commander's wireless operator without good and sufficient reason!

When halted side shelters were put down to provide extra office accommodation by day and sleeping accommodation by night, and from cable drums under each vehicle lines were run to a telephone exchange installed in an A.C.V. reserved exclusively for signal use.

The Italians, though having enormous superiority in numbers of divisions, were much worse off than the British in the number and quality of their tanks. In addition, they had no armoured formations and tank units were used individually in support of the infantry.

In September 1939 the Italians had a total of about 1,500 tanks, but they were practically all L/3-35 light tanks. The

L/3-35 was a 1935 Italian development of the British Carden Loyd Mark VI machine-gun carrier. It was very small with no turret and armed with either one or two machine-guns. It was manned by a crew of two, had armour varying in thickness from 5 to 14 mm., weighed under 4 tons, and had a speed of from 26 to 28 m.p.h. Just coming into production in 1939 was a medium tank, the M/11-39. It was armed with a 37-mm. gun and two machine-guns, but it was badly handicapped by having its gun mounted in the hull, with hardly any traverse, and only machine-guns in the turret. It had a crew of two, armour of from 10 to 30 mm. in thickness, a weight of 11 tons, and a 125-h.p. diesel engine which drove it at a speed of 20 m.p.h. This was the most powerful Italian tank available during the earlier phases of these operations. The latest Italian tank, the M/13-40, did not come into action till the final battle of this first Libyan campaign at Beda Fomm. The M/13 was really an improved version of the M/11. It had a bigger gun of 47 mm. which was mounted in a two-man turret instead of in the hull. A machine-gun was mounted co-axially with the 47-mm. and there were two others in the hull. The speed of the M/13 was the same as the M/11, but its armour was 10 mm. thicker. It was also 3 tons heavier and had a crew of four instead of three. Altogether it was a very much better tank than the M/11, and many of those captured were eventually used to equip the 6th Royal Tank Regiment.

The arrival in Egypt of the three armoured regiments was a great relief to the British command. On 13th September the Italians started rolling slowly forward. There was indeed nothing very venturesome about their movements, for on 17th September this advance of some five divisions came to a halt around Sidi Barrani, having covered about 60 miles from the frontier. Not that the advance had been without opposition, for it had been hampered by a series of vigorous rear guard actions fought by the British covering troops.

The Italians now installed themselves in a number of fortified camps. The main camp was at Sidi Barrani. Fifteen miles to the east of this and on the coast was Maktila. Ten miles south of Sidi Barrani was a string of three camps, Tummar West, Tummar Central and Tummar East. Seven miles south of Tummar West was Nibeiwa, and 20 miles south-west of Nibeiwa was the centre of another group of camps, Rabia, Sofafi East, Sofafi North-West and Sofafi South-West.

Some 70 miles away from the Italian camps, in the neighbourhood of Mersa Matruh was the main body of the British Western Desert Force under Lieutenant-General R. N. O'Connor. This force was considerably smaller than the Italian army opposing it. It consisted of the 7th Armoured Division, the 4th Indian Division (which like all Indian divisions of the regular establishment was composed of about two-thirds Indian and one-third British units), two independent infantry brigades, and the 7th Royal Tank Regiment. Its total strength was 30,000 all ranks and 275 tanks, whereas the Italians in the Sidi Barrani area had 80,000 men and 120 tanks.

The weeks went by without any further Italian advance. Wavell was in a difficult position, for he was not only faced by a powerful Italian force to the west but there was another Italian threat, from the east, to the Sudan. He decided, therefore, to attack the enemy position at Sidi Barrani; not with any hope of inflicting decisive defeat, for that seemed precluded by the disparity in numbers, but with the intention of hitting the enemy sufficiently hard to throw him off balance and so stop any possibility of an immediate advance. If this could be achieved he intended to switch part of O'Connor's command to strike hurriedly at the Italian army on his eastern flank.

To implement the Commander-in-Chief's directive, O'Connor's plan was to capture the camps of Nibeiwa and the Tummars with the 4th Indian Division and the 7th Royal Tank Regiment, whilst using the 7th Armoured division to cover the deployment of the attacking force, by masking the camps at Rabia and the Sofafis and preventing the Italian mobile reserves from reaching the battlefield.

On the evening of 7th December the 7th Armoured Division moved off. Leading its advance was the 4th Armoured Brigade, with its light tank regiment (7th Hussars) in front, followed in turn by the two heavy tank regiments (6th and 2nd Royal Tanks). The brigade moved on a unit frontage and depth of 2,000 yards and 1,300 yards respectively, with 1,000 yards between units. In this formation the speed through the night was 8 m.p.h. The next day it reached a position between Nibeiwa and Rabia.

The 7th Royal Tank Regiment, with its comparatively slow Matildas, started its move on 5th December, and on 7th it was south-east and within 12 miles of Nibeiwa, its first objective. The regiment then lay up for the night of the 7th and during the hours of daylight on 8th December, and carried out maintenance

tasks on its tanks.   On the night of 8th it made its final approach
march, passing about 3½ miles south of Nibeiwa, with aircraft
flying low overhead to drown the noise of the Matildas.

At dawn on 9th December the leading brigade of the 4th
Indian Division, accompanied by the 7th Royal Tank Regiment,
advanced the remaining few miles to the start line, about 1,500
yards from Nibeiwa camp.   At 7.25 a.m. the leading squadron
crossed the start line.   It covered half the distance to the camp
before the surprised Italian artillery opened fire, though with
little effect, for their shells could not penetrate the Matildas'
thick armour.   Just outside the camp were twenty-three M/11
tanks with their startled crews hurriedly pulling on clothes and
attempting to start the engines.   The enemy tanks were an
easy target, and within 10 minutes of the Matildas opening fire
the whole lot were destroyed.   As the 7th Royal Tanks broke
into Nibeiwa, the morale of the Italian infantry collapsed, but
the artillery, with great gallantry, went on firing until the guns
were overrun or the crews shot down.

The tanks were followed by the 11th Indian Infantry Brigade,
but there was little resistance left for them to deal with.   Four
thousand prisoners were taken at a cost to the 7th Royal Tank
Regiment of seven men killed.   Similarly successful attacks were
now launched on camps Tummar Central and Tummar East.

In the meantime, whilst the support group of the 7th
Armoured Division watched the Rabia and Sofafi camps, the
4th Armoured Brigade drove north-westwards in search of
Italian armour which was reported to be at Azzaziya, about
8 miles west of Sidi Barrani.   However, Azzaziya was clear of
the enemy and the brigade pushed on about 2 miles to the coast
road, cutting the main line of retreat from Sidi Barrani.

The next day the 16th (British) Infantry Brigade, which was
under command of Headquarters 4th Indian Division, advanced
northwards from the Tummars but was soon held up by heavy
artillery fire.   After the previous days fighting the 7th Royal
Tank Regiment could only muster ten tanks which were formed
into a composite squadron.   This squadron arrived to help
the brigade and went straight into the Italian battery positions,
knocking out seven of them.

On the following day, 10th December, the main enemy camp
at Sidi Barrani was assaulted.   At 2.30 p.m. the 6th Royal Tank
Regiment from the 4th Armoured Brigade was sent eastwards
to stop enemy troops from Maktila interfering in the battle.

Then at 4 p.m. the 4th Indian Division attacked from the south and the 2nd Royal Tank Regiment, together with the 7th Royal Tank Regiment's seven remaining Matildas, attacked from the west. Italian resistance was short, and some 2,500 prisoners and a 100 guns fell into British hands.

General O'Connor's principal aim now was to exploit his great victory as rapidly and as far as possible. The 7th Armoured Brigade which had been in reserve was despatched immediately to the coast at Buq Buq, 20 miles west of Sidi Barrani. This rapid move resulted in the brigade arriving on the coast road in time to intercept the main body of retreating Italians. Surprise was complete and 14,000 men and sixty-eight guns were captured.

In the meantime, the 4th Armoured Brigade, after refuelling and carrying out maintenance on its tanks, was directed to block the escape routes from the Sofafi camps. However, the camps had already been evacuated, and the brigade, reinforced with armoured cars and artillery, was sent in pursuit.

Further exploitation was hampered by Wavell's removal of the 4th Indian Division to meet the threat to the Sudan. O'Connor was left the 16th Infantry Brigade, but it was of no immediate operational assistance, as it was fully employed in looking after 20,000 prisoners. O'Connor was promised the 6th Australian Division as soon as possible. There were still tasks, however, which the 7th Armoured Division could carry out on its own. The 4th Armoured Brigade with its attached armoured cars and artillery was directed past the fortified positions of Capuzzo and Sollum, at the frontier of Egypt and Cyrenaica, to block the road between Bardia and Tobruk, so again getting across the Italian line of retreat. They reached the road on the morning of 14th December after a journey of about a 100 miles from the battle area.

Bardia was now effectively cut off from assistance but its capture had to await the arrival of the 6th Australian Division.

By 1st January the concentration of the 6th Australian Division had been completed, and at about the same time the strength of the force was further, and formidably, increased by the arrival of the 7th Royal Tank Regiment with twenty-two of its Matildas once more ready for action and formed into a composite squadron of five troops. The title of O'Connor's command was now changed from the Western Desert Force to the 13th Corps.

On 3rd January Bardia was attacked by the 6th Australian Division and the 7th Royal Tank Regiment. One brigade, supported by Matildas, broke through the Italian positions. The other attacking brigade, which had no supporting tanks, was driven back with heavy casualties. On 5th January the Italians gave in and 40,000 men laid down their arms. The other fruits of victory included 127 tanks and 462 guns. The outstanding part played by the 7th Royal Tanks in this action was recognised by the commander of the brigade they were supporting. In his opinion each Matilda was worth a battalion of infantry.

Tobruk, 70 miles further on, was the next objective, and it was isolated by the 7th Armoured Division in the same fashion as Bardia had been. It was attacked by the 6th Australian Division and sixteen tanks of the 7th Royal Tank Regiment on 21st January, and its garrison of 25,000 men surrendered on 22nd January. The booty included eighty-seven tanks and 208 guns. The swift success was again largely due to the tanks.

O'Connor's next target was the desert track centre at Mechili, 100 miles west of Tobruk and 45 miles south of the coast at Derna. The 4th Armoured Brigade was given 48 hours to get there, and set off that night. This move illustrated the dependence of an armoured force on communications, for a wireless silence had been imposed and there was no moon. At daybreak no tank regiment was in sight of brigade headquarters and none of them were within sight of each other. It took 30 hours to assemble and re-organise the brigade.

Nevertheless the 4th Armoured Brigade arrived at Mechili late on 23rd, which was well inside the time limit which it had been given. Mechili was attacked the following morning, but the Italians were in strength with the support of M/11 medium tanks and were able to hold their own.

It was a noteworthy achievement by Royal Signals that, over these large distances, O'Connor should have been kept continuously in touch with the situation and was in a position to issue immediate orders to the 7th Armoured Division to prevent the Italian force at Mechili from withdrawing. However, it was too late. By 27th, when the 7th Armoured Brigade and the Support Group reached Mechili, the Italians had escaped. Shortage of petrol had delayed the arrival of the British reinforcements.

The remarkable achievements of the 7th Armoured Division

had been gained at the cost of a heavy loss in tanks, mostly from mechanical trouble rather than from enemy action. The divisional tank strength had sunk, in fact, to fifty cruiser tanks and ninety-five light tanks. Nevertheless the division was to be called upon for a crowning effort.

The Australians, working along the coast, had bumped into strong Italian defences beyond Derna. O'Connor decided to send the 7th Armoured Division across the desert to the coast to get right behind the Italian forces. But in view of the depleted tank strength he postponed this move until the 5th Royal Tank Regiment, which had recently arrived in Egypt, could join the 7th Armoured Division with its fifty-eight cruiser tanks. The advance was therefore planned for 12th February.

On 3rd February O'Connor received information which caused him to advance the date of his new thrust and to make it far more ambitious. Air reports showed that the enemy was planning to abandon Benghazi and all positions east of it, and that the retreat had already started. If the Italians were to be intercepted there was no time to lose. The 7th Armoured Division was directed to cut the coast road south of Benghazi and 150 miles from Mechili.

At 8.30 a.m. the next day, 4th February, the Division started on its historic journey with only 2 days rations, no great quantity of petrol, and appalling country to cross. A mid-day air report showed the head of the Italian retreat to be already south of Benghazi. It appeared that the original axis of advance directed on Solluch, 30 miles south of Benghazi, was too far to the north if the leading Italian troops were to be intercepted. The direction was therefore changed so that the coast road would be cut some 40-50 miles further south. In addition, to accelerate the advance, a wheeled force of armoured cars, infantry and artillery was pushed into the lead. On 5th February, at about mid-day, the wheeled force reached the coast, and by 3 p.m. it was established in a defensive position and ready for the first Italians. These, artillery and civilian evacuees, were received in the evening.

The 4th Armoured Brigade, moving close behind the wheeled force, were informed by wireless from the armoured car regiment that there were columns of Italian troops moving down the coast road 30 miles ahead of them. The 4th Armoured Brigade immediately sent forward its fast tanks, the "lights" and the A13's, and these went into successful action against artillery and transport at Beda Fomm, 10 miles north of the defensive positions occupied by the wheeled force.

The next morning, the 6th, there was more formidable opposition. Heavy enemy columns, supported by M/13 tanks, started rolling through Beda Fomm. The Italians had vast superiority in gun-tanks, for there were over a hundred M/13's, against which the 7th Armoured Division could only muster twenty-one cruiser tanks. Fortunately the Italian tanks arrived in small packets, presenting magnificent targets to the British tanks shooting from hull-down positions.

The majority of the remaining Italian units were destroyed at Beda Fomm, and over 100 enemy tanks were left on the battlefield. This was the end of the campaign. In 2 months, and in spite of the delay imposed by the withdrawal of the 4th Indian Division, O'Connor had advanced 500 miles and with a loss of less than 2,000 casualties had destroyed an Italian army of ten divisions. With never more than two divisions under his own command, he had captured 130,000 prisoners, 400 tanks and 850 guns. It was one of the greatest feats of arms in the history of war.

CHAPTER XIII

Enter Rommel

THE sequel to the first Libyan campaign was one of the most drastic reversals of fortune in military history. The destruction of the Italian army had been so complete that O'Connor believed that no enemy force was left in the field which could stop the 7th Armoured Division from driving to Tripoli. Subsequent information has shown that this belief was correct. Certainly O'Connor had no intention of giving the enemy any time to prepare a defence, and the battle of Beda Fomm was hardly over before the 11th Hussars were on the move westwards; and by the following day, the 8th February, they had covered the 90 miles to Agheila. But that was the end. A decision had been reached in London that there was to be no further advance in North Africa, and that as many of Wavell's troops as possible were to be sent to the aid of Greece.

The merits of that decision, which resulted in British defeats in both Greece and North Africa, are still being argued, and it is not intended to join in the discussion here. It was singularly unfortunate, however, that the brake should have been applied to the 7th Armoured Division at this juncture, for it enabled Rommel's *Afrika Korps* to disembark at Tripoli. Worse, Rommel was not to be opposed by seasoned and victorious troops, but by formations which were new to the desert and incompletely trained.

The 6th Australian Division went to Greece and the 7th Armoured Division returned to Egypt for rest and refit. In their place came the 9th Australian Division and the 2nd Armoured Division. Neither were ready for battle and both were short of equipment. Of the 2nd Armoured Division, indeed, one of its armoured brigades and part of its support group had been sent to Greece.

The Africa Corps consisted of two armoured divisions, the 5th Light and the 15th Panzer. The difference between "Light" and "Panzer" (or armoured division proper) was, by this time, purely in the nomenclature; organisation, equipment and roles of both were now the same. Such a merging of different types of mobile troops seems to happen frequently in their history. Horse and dragoons, for instance, evolved into similar heavy cavalry, and ultimately both light and heavy cavalry were mounted and equipped for any cavalry task. Similarly, in more recent times the tendency is to build one type of tank for all armoured fighting.

Both the 5th Light and 15th Panzer were on a reduced establishment of two tank battalions and three motor infantry battalions each.

The 2nd Armoured Division was deployed in defence of the Mersa Brega area, just to the east of Agheila. Here the sea on one side and a saltmarsh on the other narrowed the traversible ground to a narrow neck. The 3rd Armoured Brigade of the Division consisted of three regiments; the 3rd Hussars, the 5th Royal Tanks and the 6th Royal Tanks. Of the two heavy regiments, the 5th had only twenty-three tanks left out of their fifty-eight; the remainder were out of action due to mechanical wear they had suffered on the long drive from Egypt and on subsequent exercises. The 6th had been brought hurriedly from Egypt, leaving their tanks behind. On arrival in the area they had been re-equipped with Italian M/13 tanks which had been fitted with No. 11 wireless sets. One squadron of the 3rd Hussars had also been given M/13's.

The first enemy armoured division to land at Tripoli had been the Italian *Ariete*. It was followed closely by the German 5th Light, of which the bulk was ashore by 11th March. Then, without waiting for the 15th Panzer, Rommel was off and on 31st March he was attacking Mersa Brega. That evening the Germans managed to penetrate the British defences on a limited front, and during the night the 2nd Armoured Division's support group began to withdraw. This was fatal, and from that moment the campaign was lost. The withdrawal resulted, or so it would appear, from a too literal interpretation of Wavell's order that if the British forces were attacked they were to fight a delaying action.

Rommel was now through and he followed the retreating British so relentlessly that by the evening of the next day, 1st April, he was hustling them at Antelat, 90 miles from Mersa Brega. On 3rd April the German reconnaissance battalion entered Benghazi, already evacuated by the Australians, and another German column was probing towards Mechili.

In the meantime there was increasing confusion on the British side and orders were issued which did not relate to the actual situation. Much of this was due to wide-scale failures in communications and a consequent lack of information as to the positions of our own forces and those of the enemy. The breakdown in communications was caused by flat wireless batteries, and seldom can the absence of proper charging arrangements have had such disastrous results.

An inaccurate report by the Royal Air Force that 100 tanks were approaching Msus, the 2nd Armoured Division's main petrol and supply dump, led to a panic order for the destruction of the petrol. Fuel was thereby denied, not to the enemy, but to the 3rd Armoured Brigade, whose movements were in consequence drastically curtailed. A further result of this report was that Lieutenant-General Sir Philip Neame, who had relieved O'Connor, ordered a general retreat to the Derna-Mechili line; and hence the burning stores in a rapidly evacuated Benghazi which greeted the German reconnaissance battalion.

On 4th April Rommel directed the bulk of his armour in a rapid thrust towards Mechili. On the British side a muddled groping in the dark led to the 6th Royal Tank Regiment being ordered to attack the mythical enemy occupying Msus. There was of course no enemy—and neither was there any fuel. Since many of the M/13 tanks were now empty of the diesel fuel they required, the least serviceable were destroyed after their remaining fuel had been transferred to the others.

Two days later, on the night of 6th April, a German motor-cycle patrol had a windfall. It captured not only General Neame, but also General O'Connor and Brigadier Combe who had been sent up from Egypt to give him assistance.

On 8th April a German force with a few tanks and a number of special dust raising vehicles surprised Headquarters 2nd Armoured Division together with a large number of the divisional troops. Several parties managed to break out but the remainder were captured.

On 11th April Rommel isolated Tobruk, on 12th he captured Bardia, and on 13th he was in Sollum and Capuzzo. In just 2 weeks Rommel had cleared his opponents out of all Cyrenaica except for Tobruk, which he had invested. This crushing defeat was due largely to the lack of training of the troops, indifferent communications and fumbling in command.

The 9th Australian Division had withdrawn to Tobruk, and

it was joined there by an infantry brigade which had been sent up from Egypt. Also from Egypt came the 1st Royal Tank Regiment (less one of its squadrons). It had been re-equipped in a hurry with a mixture of cruiser and light tanks in Egypt, and acquired some more cruisers from Tobruk workshops. Some of its light tanks were used to form a composite squadron from "dismounted" personnel of the 3rd Hussars and the 5th Royal Tank Regiment. A further very welcome reinforcement was a squadron of the 7th Royal Tank Regiment which came by sea and arrived on 19th April. It brought eight Matildas with it and was issued with four more which had been repaired in the Tobruk workshops. Ten days later another six had been repaired, bringing the squadron total up to eighteen tanks.

Meanwhile the enemy's build-up round Tobruk had been progressing and eventually comprised the 5th Light Division, the *Ariete* Armoured Division, and the *Brescia* and *Trento* Infantry Divisions.

After "feeling" the defences, Rommel attacked on 14th April with the 5th Light Division. He broke through the perimeter but on a very narrow front, and, after an advance of 2 miles, pressure by British tanks and guns on his flanks forced his withdrawal. On 30th April Rommel mounted a more ambitious attack. It started with a night assault by the infantry of the 5th Light Division, who succeeded in making a breach in the British defences on a front of a mile and a half. On the morning of 1st May the tanks continued the advance, but the leading wave ran on to a minefield and seventeen out of their strength of about forty tanks were disabled. The second wave of thirty-four tanks, mostly Pz. II's, crossed the British perimeter behind the first wave and then swung right in an attempt to widen the breach. After an advance of some 3 miles they ran into British cruiser tanks firing from hull down positions and were forced to withdraw. Further efforts by Rommel were equally unsuccessful, and he reluctantly gave up the attempt to take Tobruk for the time being.

News of the disasters in the Western Desert had been received with dismay in the United Kingdom. In view of the urgency the decision was taken to rush out some 300 tanks by the very risky Mediterranean route. Wavell, however, had decided to counter-attack without waiting for the convoy carrying these tanks. The forces which he could muster for the operation were limited and something of a "mixed bag". They comprised the

7th Armoured Division Support Group, the 22nd Guards (motorised) Brigade, the 11th Hussars (armoured cars), the 2nd Royal Tank Regiment with twenty-nine cruiser tanks (mostly A9's and A10's), the 4th Royal Tank Regiment, less one of its squadrons which was in Eritrea, and equipped with twenty-six Matildas, and some artillery regiments. Major-General W. H. E. ("Strafer") Gott was placed in command.

The attack was launched on 15th May, but the attacking troops immediately encountered strong enemy resistance and suffered heavy tank casualties. The Matildas had to cross a number of obstacles, and as they rolled slowly over them they reared up presenting their vulnerable under parts to the waiting guns. The enemy artillery took a heavy toll. Few were damaged beyond repair, but although twenty-four were brought out of the battle only six were immediately ready for action. The 2nd Royal Tank Regiment were in worse shape, as none of the twenty-two cruiser tanks remaining to them were fit to fight. Under these circumstances Gott decided that it was of no use continuing the action and he ordered a withdrawal.

The tank convoy arrived on 12th May. One of the five fast ships of which it had been composed was sunk by a mine with all its tanks. The remaining four ships brought 135 Matildas, eighty-two cruiser tanks, and twenty-one light tanks: a very welcome reinforcement for the hard-pressed armoured units. Amongst these tanks were many of the new Mark VI cruisers, or "Crusaders", which were making their first appearance in action, and there were just sufficient to equip the 6th Royal Tank Regiment. The other cruiser regiment, the 2nd Royal Tanks, had a mixture of partially reconditioned A9's, A10's and A13's. These two regiments were allotted to the 7th Armoured Brigade. The 4th Armoured Brigade also comprised two regiments, the 4th and the 7th, but both these had Matildas.

A new attack was now proposed with the old team of the 7th Armoured Division and the 4th Indian Division under the command of Lieutenant-General N. M. de la P. Beresford-Peirse. In the first phase the fortified area Halfaya-Sollum-Capuzzo was to be captured by the 4th Indian Division with the 4th Armoured Brigade in support, whilst the remainder of the 7th Armoured Division protected the left flank. If this part of the plan was successful, then in the second phase the whole of the 7th Armoured Division was to push right through to Tobruk, and

Plate 31. VALENTINE MARK II, ARMED WITH A 2-POUNDER GUN.

Plate 32. VALENTINE MARK XI, ARMED WITH THE 75-MM GUN.

Plate 33. AMERICAN LIGHT-MEDIUM STUART, OR 'HONEY', TANK, ARMED WITH A 37 MM GUN.

Plate 34. AMERICAN GRANT MEDIUM TANK WITH A 75-MM GUN IN THE HULL AND A 37-MM IN THE TURRET.

Plate 35.   AMERICAN SHERMAN MEDIUM TANK WITH A 75-MM GUN IN THE TURRET.

Plate 36. CHURCHILL INFANTRY TANK MARK V, ARMED WITH A 95-MM HOWITZER.

Plate 37. MARK VII CHURCHILL TANK WITH A 75-MM GUN.

then, reinforced by the Tobruk garrison, it was to exploit to the line Derna Mechili.

To oppose this attack Rommel had a smaller force than the information available to Wavell had led him to believe. Wavell's estimate was that there were 100 enemy tanks in the area of the frontier and another 200 in the neighbourhood of Tobruk. The frontier estimate was reasonably accurate, but there were less than 100 tanks about Tobruk. On the frontier was the tank regiment of the 15th Panzer Division, which had recently arrived, and near Tobruk was the tank regiment of the 5th Light Division. Only about half of the German tanks were mediums. Against these the British could muster about 100 cruiser and 100 infantry tanks. Since no Italian tanks were used, Wavell had a superiority of armour in the coming battle. At the moment of attack, in fact, the British superiority in gun-armed tanks was about four to one.

The British attack was not a success and its failure was mainly due to superior German tactics. Rommel had grasped that tanks and anti-tank guns were complementary arms, which should be used together in much the same fashion as Englishmen of an earlier generation had used men-at-arms and archers. And so, as on many future occasions in the Western Desert, the British armoured weapon was blunted against hidden anti-tank guns. The German tank counter-attack then fell on a staggered and weakened enemy.

The 4th Armoured Brigade attacked with the 4th Royal Tanks on the right and the 7th on the left. The latter, fighting concentrated, were the major factor in the capture of Capuzzo; but the 4th Royal Tanks' C Squadron ran into well-sited German anti-tank guns and lost nearly all its tanks.

In the 7th Armoured Brigade it was hoped that the new Crusader tanks would come as an unpleasant surprise to the Germans, and the 2nd Royal Tank Regiment was put into the lead so that the 6th Royal Tanks could be thrown in at the appropriate moment. The 2nd Royal Tanks had two squadrons equipped with A9's and A10's and one with A13's. The two former squadrons led the way as far as the frontier, and the fast A13 squadron was then pushed ahead to seize the Hafid Ridge a few miles west of Capuzzo. Shortage of wireless sets now again contributed to failure. Vital information was never received at Headquarters 7th Armoured Brigade and some of the reports which came in were completely inaccurate. According to one of these the 2nd Royal Tank Regiment had taken the Hafid Ridge, whereas in fact it had run into German gun positions. The Regiment knocked out one gun area, but it then came under fire from another and withdrew.

After waiting for a long time, unsuccessfully, for information, the 6th Royal Tank Regiment was directed to attack. As the opening performance of a new tank the thing was a "flop". The 6th Royal Tanks ran straight into one of Rommel's anti-tank ambushes and lost a large number of Crusaders.

At the end of the day's fighting less than half the tanks with which the British had entered the battle were fit for action, and the casualties had been caused largely by artillery fire and to a lesser extent by mechanical breakdown. The German tanks had hardly been engaged.

The next morning Rommel threw in his armour; the 15th Panzer Division attacking at Capuzzo and the 5th Light trying to swing round the British left flank. The 15th were repulsed, the 7th Royal Tank Regiment firing from hull down positions and knocking out many of the German tanks. The 5th Light engaged in a bitter struggle with the 7th Armoured Brigade, which had only twenty-five tanks remaining by the end of the day. The next day, in face of a deteriorating situation Beresford-Peirse decided to withdraw.

In desert armoured warfare possession of the battlefield was of tremendous value in making good tank losses. A large proportion of tanks immobilised in battle were only slightly damaged, and could be recovered and repaired in a comparatively short time. On this occasion the British lost ninety-one tanks, many of which could have been recovered had the battlefield not been surrendered to the Germans. The final German loss, on the other hand, was only twelve tanks, for all their other casualties were repaired. It was unpleasantly true, however, that the Germans had had the better of the armoured struggle. This was primarily due to their tactical employment of anti-tank guns, but also because a proportion of the British tank strength had been frittered away in supporting the infantry. In actual tank versus tank fighting British units had shown that they were fully the equal of the Germans, but by the time these tank contests took place the latter, through Rommel's successful tactics, and a superiority in numbers.

The relative position of the two opponents as regards guns at this time was peculiar. The heaviest German tank, the Pz. IV, was armed with a 75-mm. gun, but it was a short-barrelled weapon with a low muzzle velocity and poor powers of armour penetration. This 75 mm. could outrange the British 2-pr, but the latter at its chosen distance was the more effective armour-piercing weapon. The 50-mm. gun, with which Pz. III's were armed, was about equivalent in range and penetration to the 2-pr. In anti-tank guns the Germans were far better off. The mobile gun, which was used offensively, was the long barrelled 50-mm. It was much superior to the tank 50-mm. and also, therefore, to the 2-pr. As a defensive anti-tank gun Rommel used the 88-mm. anti-aircraft gun, and in this improvised role it was one of the most successful anti-tank weapons of the war. To counter these German weapons the greatest British need at this time was a dual purpose tank gun which could take on tanks with armour-piercing ammunition and anti-tank guns with high explosive.

CHAPTER XIV

Operation Crusader

WELL before the start of his great counter-offensive General Sir Claude Auchinleck, the new Commander-in-Chief in the Middle East, had made known his needs in armour. On 4th July 1941 he told Churchill that he would want a minimum of two (and if possible three) armoured divisions to ensure victory. He pointed out that in the open desert country infantry could not be used in offensive action against armoured forces. Their proper role was to hold defended localities, and to capture those belonging to the enemy after the hostile armoured forces had been beaten or neutralised. The main offensive was the task of the armoured divisions with motorised formations in support.

Auchinleck confirmed Churchill's estimate that by the end of July he would have 500 gun-tanks, but pointed out that for any operation it was necessary to have a 50 per cent reserve of tanks, of which half would be in the workshops and the other half ready to replace battle casualties. These figures were supported by the enormous wastage of tanks experienced in battle, both from enemy action and mechanical breakdown.

In fact, when Operation Crusader started the British had 756 gun-tanks, made up of 336 cruisers, 225 infantry, and 195 of the American light-medium Stuarts. Against these the Axis had 320 gun-tanks, of which thirty-five were Pz. IV's, 139 Pz. III's and 146 Italian M/13's. Besides these there were seventy-five light Pz. I's and II's. The British numerical superiority was further increased by the reserves. Immediately available were 259 tanks, and a further ninety-six were on the way out from the United Kingdom. In addition the 1st and 10th Armoured Divisions were under training in the Middle East and they had 231 tanks between them. (These formations were not being used in the forthcoming battle).

As compared with these lavish reserves the Germans could only muster fifty tanks under repair in their workshops. However they had other assets which largely offset the British

See map page 226.

advantage in numbers. Firstly they had a considerable superiority in the number and quality of their anti-tank guns: the long barrelled Pak 38 50-mm. used in a mobile role in both attack and defence, and the 88-mm. anti-aircraft gun which was one of the finest defensive anti-tank weapons of the war. (In fact the British 3·7-inch anti-aircraft was even better than the 88-mm. as an anti-tank gun, and there were three times as many in the theatre; but for some reason, which is still a mystery, its use as such was only belatedly allowed, and then only in very small numbers.) Secondly, the German medium tanks were better than the British Crusaders—the main equipment of the armoured brigades. The Crusader was fast and manoeuvrable but its reliability was poor, and however satisfactory the 2-pr gun had been at the start of the war it was now overdue for replacement. The slow Matildas and their successors the Valentines had lost half their effectiveness when the German 88-mm. gun appeared on the battlefield. On the other hand, the machine-gun armed light tanks had been replaced by the much more effective American Stuart, or "Honey", armed with a 37-mm. gun which had a better armour penetration than the 2-pr. The third German asset lay in their tactics—their co-ordination of tanks and anti-tank guns. For they had realised that tanks were heavy cavalry, whilst in the British Army the idea was all too prevalent that an armoured force approximated to, and should be employed in much the same way as, a fleet at sea.

The American Stuart tank was a modification of the Light Tank M3 of 1941. The first version employed by the British Army, the Mark I, weighed 12½ tons, and had 40-mm. thick armour. Its armament consisted of a 37-mm. gun, with a co-axially mounted ·30-inch Browning machine-gun and another similar machine-gun in the hull. It was powered by a seven-cylinder air-cooled radial 250-h.p. engine, giving it a speed of 36 m.p.h. It was manned by a crew of four. There were eventually six different marks embodying various modifications in structure and engine.

On 29th September Auchinleck gave Churchill a good report on the Stuart tanks, which had been issued to the 8th Hussars. He said that the officers were delighted with their reliability and endurance as compared with the British tanks, and found them manoeuvrable and fast. Some minor alterations had to be made before they could be fitted with British wireless sets.

After a late and slow start in American tank design, the Stuart was indeed a startling advance.

Failure to "tropicalise" tanks before their shipment from the United Kingdom caused considerable trouble. On 11th October Auchinleck reported to the Prime Minister that the tanks of the last armoured brigade to arrive, the 22nd, had not been treated for desert conditions. This failure led to very serious delay, because, although all workshop resources were devoted to the task, it was nearly the end of the month before the tanks were ready. In the meantime the Brigade's training in desert warfare had been held up.

The forces which had been allocated to Lieutenant-General Sir Alan Cunningham, commanding the 8th Army, consisted of the 30th Corps under the command of Lieutenant-General C. W. M. Norrie, the 13th Corps commanded by Lieutenant-General A. R. Godwin-Austen, and the Tobruk garrison commanded by Major-General R. M. Scobie. The 13th Corps was a mainly infantry force and comprised the 2nd New Zealand Division, the 4th Indian Division, and the 1st Army Tank Brigade. The 30th Corps was primarily an armoured formation, consisting of the 7th Armoured Division (7th and 22nd Armoured Brigades), the 4th Armoured Brigade Group, the 22nd Guards (Motor) Brigade, and the 1st South African Division. The 2nd South African Division was in reserve. In the Tobruk garrison were the 70th Infantry Division, the 32nd Army Tank Brigade and the Polish Carpathian Infantry Brigade Group.

In Rommel's army were the Africa Corps and six Italian divisions, of which one (the *Ariete*) was armoured and the remainder infantry. The Africa Corps now consisted of the 15th Panzer Division the 21st Panzer Division (the new title of the 5th Light Division) and the 90th Light Division. The latter had been formed from a number of independent German units in Africa. It had no tanks, and the designation "Light" may have been adopted to mislead the British.

Of Rommel's forces, three Italian divisions were besieging Tobruk, with a fourth in reserve, the *Ariete* Armoured Division and the *Trieste* lorried Infantry Division were about El Gubi, 40 miles south of Tobruk, one Italian division and a German detachment were in the frontier fortress area of Bardia-Sollum-Halfaya, the 90th Light Division was on the coast just east of Tobruk, and the two Panzer divisions were between Bardia and Tobruk, the 15th below the escarpment which borders the coastal fringe and the 21st above it.

On 17th November 1941 the 8th Army started its move into battle positions. Auchinleck had given it as its objectives the destruction of the enemy armoured forces. The Commander-in-Chief had appreciated that if the Africa Corps could be defeated the *Ariete* Armoured Division would present little problem and the collapse of the Italian infantry divisions would follow. The best way to get the Panzer divisions to attack would be to threaten Rommel's vital interests—the frontier defences and the approach to Tobruk. To put these ideas into effect, the 30th Corps was directed towards Tobruk with the object of forcing the German armour to attack. At the appropriate moment the Tobruk garrison was to move out of its defences and threaten the enemy's flank and rear. The task of the 13th Corps at this stage was to pin down the enemy in the Halfaya and Sidi Omar positions and stop any threat to the British advanced base area. Once success had been achieved in the armoured battle, the 13th Corps was to advance westwards.

Cunningham's method of carrying out the Commander-in-Chief's plan was based on the theory already mentioned, that armoured warfare was a land version of naval warfare, and that the tank versus tank battle was therefore an end in itself. That such a theory should even have been propagated by senior soldiers showed a remarkable misreading of military history. It should have been apparent that the handling of mounted troops in the main battle must be based on the same fundamental principles, whether the mount was a horse or a tank. Tactics formed on a naval analogy could take no proper account of the influence of ground and a defence pivoting on well-sited anti-tank guns.

From the Commander-in-Chief's plan stemmed the importance of the dominating Sidi Rezegh ridge, 12 miles from the Tobruk perimeter and connected to it by a motor track dropping down from the escarpment.

Swinging wide on the southern flank a long column of motor transport passed the deserted Italian camps which had been the scene of the fighting of the previous year, and reached the frontier well south of the existing enemy positions. The 30th Corps streamed through the frontier wire and turned northwest in the general direction of Tobruk. That night of the 17th, as the Force halted, a terrific storm swept over the battle area, and men rose in sodden clothing for the advance to battle on the following morning.

On 18th November the 30th Corps continued its advance under cover of a strong force of fighters. By nightfall the 4th Armoured Brigade Group and the 7th Armoured Brigade had reached the Trigh el Abd, a desert track which crossed the frontier 10 miles south of Sidi Omar and ran north-westwards through El Gubi.

On the 19th the attacking wing started to split into several components. On the right the 4th Armoured Brigade Group bore further to the right to protect the left flank of the 13th Corps. In the process it encountered and was severely mauled by the 21st Panzer Division (The brigade's estimate of the number of German tanks destroyed in this engagement contributed to the subsequent misplaced optimism at the Headquarters of both the 30th Corps and the 8th Army). On the left the 22nd Armoured Brigade reached El Gubi and pushed back the *Trieste* and *Ariete* Divisions. It destroyed thirty-four M/13 tanks; but it suffered heavily from the Italian artillery, losing more than forty of its 160 Crusaders. In the centre the 7th Armoured Brigade had little more than skirmishing, and its 6th Royal Tank Regiment pushed rapidly ahead and halted that night on the escarpment at Sidi Rezegh. Early the following morning the remainder of the Brigade arrived together with the 7th Armoured Division Support Group.

By dawn on the 20th, after one day's fighting, the disposition of the 30th Corps was the reverse of what had been intended. There had been no change in the obviously correct plan to keep all the armour in the attacking wing concentrated. And yet, as it happened, that same armour could hardly have been more widely dispersed. The result was nearly disastrous, for it had been Rommel's plan to concentrate his own armour and to try so to manoeuvre as to engage and defeat the British armoured brigades in turn. However the wide distances which now separated these armoured brigades made any such strategical manoeuvre unnecessary.

No reason has been produced for this dispersal; but wireless communications were appalling, and it seems probable that the failure to keep concentrated was due to lack of communications. As so often has happened, the provision of signal equipment suitable for the task and the training of signal personnel had been given inadequate priority. It is conceivable that low-powered wireless sets and poor arrangements for battery-charging had more serious effects on operations than the shortcomings of the 2-pr gun.

At midday on 20th the 22nd Armoured Brigade was ordered to go to the assistance of the 4th Armoured Brigade Group. This involved a move of about 30 miles. Much closer at hand, from 7-12 miles away, were the 1st Army Tank Brigade and the New Zealand Division. Offers of assistance from these two formations were, however, refused by the commander of the 4th Armoured Brigade Group on the grounds, apparently, that an 8th Army instruction forbade the 13th Corps to intervene in the armoured battle. The 22nd Armoured Brigade arrived in the evening by which time the 4th's 165 tanks had been reduced to ninety-seven.

Having disposed of the 4th Armoured Brigade Group for the time being, Rommel issued orders on the night of the 20th for a concentrated attack with all his German armour against the 7th Armoured Brigade and the Support Group. Both Panzer divisions moved north-west before dawn, the 21st Panzer Division withdrawing from contact with the two British brigades. When daylight came they found that the Germans had gone, but they did not, unfortunately follow up immediately. In consequence Rommel was able to attack the Sidi Rezegh position without being harried from his rear.

In the meantime, at Sidi Rezegh, a British attack against the airfield was being prepared: the 7th Armoured Brigade and the Support Group attacking from the Sidi Rezegh Ridge and the 70th Division attacking from Tobruk. But before this operation could get started Rommel attacked himself. As soon as the approach of the two columns of German tanks was observed, two regiments of the 7th Armoured Brigade were sent to oppose them whilst the third supported the attack of the Support Group on the airfield. The Support Group soon had to halt their attack and turn about to face the German tanks with 2-prs which were outranged and 25-prs which were ineffective over 600 yards.

Sidi Rezegh was held, but only just; for when the 22nd Armoured Brigade at last arrived on the scene with some ninety tanks, the 7th Armoured Brigade had only twenty-eight tanks left. But Rommel was reduced to fifty, and so on the arrival of this considerable British reinforcement he withdrew from the battlefield.

From Tobruk the attack had been carried out mainly by the 32nd Army Tank Brigade. They had done well but had lost sixty of their 109 tanks.

Communications were again shocking and none of the higher headquarters knew what was going on at Sidi Rezegh. However, it was assumed that Rommel's armour was now effectively contained, and so the 13th Corps was ordered to move forward. The New Zealand Division, which had been straining at the leash, advanced rapidly and reached Bardia that night after 17 hours on the road.

The morning of the 22nd November passed peacefully for the British forces at Sidi Rezegh, but about noon the 21st Panzer Division put in an attack which was only narrowly repulsed, largely by the fire of the Support Group's guns. Various forces were now hurrying to the scene. On the British side were the 22nd Armoured Brigade, the 5th South African Brigade and the 4th Armoured Brigade Group. On the Axis side the 15th Panzer Division was driving to the sound of the guns. This formation was fortunate enough to fall in with the tail end of the 4th Armoured Brigade Group and captured the whole of its headquarters. This was a major disaster as, without any means of command and control, the 4th Armoured Brigade for the time being ceased to exist as a fighting formation. The disaster was all the greater because at the time this was the only formation remaining to the 30th Corps with a large number of operational tanks. Apart from this episode, the various British brigades suffered again from extremely poor communications, and knew little of the whereabouts either of the enemy or each other. In consequence a planned counter-attack was abandoned, and the day ended in confusion and the recapture by the Germans of both the Sidi Rezegh Ridge and the air field. To complete the day's discomfiture, the 15th Panzer Division arrived as night fell to strike the units of the 4th Armoured Brigade Group in the back.

On the morning of 23rd November the 30th Corps armour was at last concentrated, at least in theory. In practice it was not capable of co-ordinated effective action. The 7th Armoured Brigade had only fifteen tanks left; the 22nd Armoured Brigade was not much better off with thirty-four; and the 4th Armoured Brigade Group with ninety tanks was out of action as a formation.

On the early morning of 23rd there was some recompense for the loss of the Headquarters of the 4th Armoured Brigade

Group, for the advancing New Zealand Division captured Headquarters Africa Corps. Its able commander, General Cruewell, was unfortunately temporarily absent, and he was able with his tactical command post to provide sufficient communications to continue the exercise of control.

Cruewell's continued ability to command was soon shown, for he put in an attack on the battered British in the Sidi Rezegh area with the united German and Italian armour—though the *Ariete* Division was late. The 3rd Royal Tank Regiment arrived accidentally in the path of the attack, giving time for the defence to stiffen up. Field and anti-tank guns put up a terrific fire on the German tanks and at 11.30 a.m. Cruewell drew off with seventy of his 150 tanks out of action.

In the afternoon Cruewell, having managed to collect some 120 German and Italian tanks, attacked again. This time he was more successful. Only fifty British tanks could be brought to oppose him, and at the end of the day the British forces withdrew, leaving the Germans in possession of the field. The 5th South African Brigade had been nearly annihilated, and nearly all the British armour was virtually out of action. The 4th Armoured Brigade had been practically paralysed through lack of command and communications.

Alive at last to the true situation, there was a great deal of despondency at Headquarters 8th Army. However, on this same day of 23rd November Auchinleck arrived at Army Headquarters. He appreciated that, gloomy as the tank situation appeared, it probably seemed as bad or even worse from Rommel's point of view. He therefore ordered an immediate offensive against Sidi Rezegh. The 13th Corps was still pretty well intact, and the New Zealand Division (less one brigade) together with the 1st Army Tank Brigade (eighty-six Matildas) were directed to recapture the Sidi Rezegh Ridge. At the same time the 30th Corps, with about seventy tanks still fit for action, set about the tasks of reorganisation and re-equipment.

Rommel, believing that he had finally disposed of the 30th Corps, took the decision which led to his eventual defeat. This was to drive with all his armoured forces deep into the British rear areas. His primary intention was to so disrupt the British lines of communication as to bring about a general withdrawal, and his secondary to relieve his frontier garrisons.

Rommel's force for this ambitious operation consisted of the two Panzer divisions and the *Ariete* Armoured Division.

With these, on the morning of 24th, he headed rapidly eastwards. As it happened his route, probably unwittingly, took him through an extraordinary number of British headquarters—the 7th Armoured Brigade, the 7th Support Group, the 7th Armoured Division, and the 30th Corps. The progress of the German tanks was constantly heralded by the rapid dispersal into the desert distance of British "soft-skinned" vehicles with their sometimes half-clad occupants. Rommel reached the frontier wire at Sherfezen (10 miles south of Sidi Omar) with the best part of the 21st Panzer Division at 4 p.m., having covered about 60 miles in 5 hours. Rommel's immediate intention now was to bottle up and destroy the 13th Corps, and to that end he ordered a battle group towards the Halfaya Pass. For some distance across the frontier he led this group in his command vehicle, and then turned back without escort to rejoin his tactical headquarters.

A long-distance armoured pentration of this nature is unsettling to all but the stoutest nerves, but Auchinleck appreciated that, dangerous as it might appear, it was of no strategic importance. Indeed, Rommel's expedition was ultimately as damaging to his own side as was General "Jeb" Stuart's spectacular ride round the Federal Army in June 1862.

On his way back Rommel's vehicle broke down. He was rescued from possible capture by the arrival as dusk was falling of a captured British A.C.V., known to the Africa Corps as "Mammoth", in which were General Cruewell and his battle group. Rommel and his chief of staff scrambled thankfully aboard. However, they were not out of trouble, for the A.C.V. hunted unsuccessfully for a gap in the wire, and eventually had to stop on the wrong side of it for the night. It was an anxious night for the occupants, for the A.C.V. was passed by Indian dispatch riders, and British tanks and lorries. Luckily for them a broken down British A.C.V. was not an unfamiliar sight.

The rest of Rommel's forces arrived late. The 15th Panzer Division had started late, and was further delayed by harrassing attacks along its march route by British tanks. In the meantime the further progress of the 21st Panzer Division had been stopped by the 4th Indian Division. The British field artillery of the Division put up a magnificent defence, using their 25-prs with deadly effect against the German medium tanks. The 52nd Battery of the 1st Field Regiment, Royal Artillery, came under fire from twenty-eight German tanks at a range of 2,000 yards. The battery waited until the enemy had approached to within 800 yards and then opened fire, destroying eight Pz. III's and IV's. The remainder withdrew, but by this time more than half of the battery's strength were casualties.

The 15th Panzer Division, when it did arrive with fifty-six medium and light tanks, achieved little and the *Ariete* Armoured Division contributed nothing at all.

Whilst one part of the 13th Corps had defeated Rommel's long range offensive, another part had retaken Sidi Rezegh and joined hands with the Tobruk garrison. This success had been achieved by the 1st Army Tank Brigade and the New Zealand Division.

With the loss of some thirty tanks and after the expenditure of a lot of precious fuel and considerable track mileage, Rommel at last turned back on the night of 26th November to restore the deteriorating situation in his rear.

In the meantime the armoured strength of the 30th Corps was being restored. Fresh tanks were being delivered and some seventy tanks had been recovered on the battlefield. By the 27th the armoured brigades were once more in fighting trim, and when on that same day the 15th Panzer Division was sighted returning westwards the 4th Armoured Brigade and the 22nd Armoured Brigade moved to intercept it, the 4th attacking it in flank and rear and the 22nd hitting it in front. Although the British had a considerable superiority in the number of tanks, this did not offset the formidable German anti-tank artillery which was deployed to meet them. At nightfall the British drew off. The next morning the attack was renewed but was unable to make progress against the anti-tank defence.

On 29th the eighty-five British tanks which remained out of the 120 with which the attack started were all placed under the command of the 4th Armoured Brigade. But this concentration of effort failed to prevent the Germans from reaching the neighbourhood of the Sidi Rezegh Ridge.

That night the strength of the two British brigades was again raised to 120 tanks, and on 30th they attacked again. But again the German anti-tank screen held them off, whilst the 15th Panzer Division overran the 6th New Zealand Brigade and captured the Sidi Rezegh Ridge.

After this serious reverse there was a general British withdrawal and Tobruk was once more cut off. Rommel by his brilliant combination of tanks and anti-tank guns had won this action, despite his considerable inferiority in the number of tanks.

Nevertheless, although it appeared superficially that Rommel was once more in the ascendant, his victory had been only tactical and, strategically, owing to his lack of reserves, his position was extremely precarious. On 3rd December German efforts to regain touch with the frontier posts were unsuccessful, and on 4th December Rommel's wireless intercept service furnished him with British messages which showed that an attack was being mounted against his lines of communication. It was apparent to him that an immediate withdrawal was necessary if his line of retreat was not to be cut off. That night the Africa Corps moved rapidly westwards to the neighbourhood of El Adem.

On 5th December Rommel, having considered an appreciation of the situation prepared by his staff, concluded that he had a chance of inflicting a decisive defeat on the British by throwing all his armour against El Gubi (25 miles south of El Adem). He attacked the next day, and again on 7th December, but without success. There was now no alternative to the evacuation of Cyrenaica. On 8th December, as a first stage in this evacuation, Rommel ordered a withdrawal to a line running south from Gazala, and 40 miles west of Tobruk. Except for those cut off in the frontier garrisons and Bardia, all Axis forces had reached this line by 11th December.

On 13th December the British attack on this line started. After the initial clash, Godwin-Austen, commanding the 13th Corps and all troops immediately opposing Rommel, ordered the 7th Armoured Division to swing right round the Axis southern flank and attack the enemy in the rear whilst the infantry divisions attacked in front. This attempt to destroy the enemy was unsuccessful, due in part to a weakness in the design of the Stuart tank. The 4th Armoured Brigade, the only armoured formation then in 7th Armoured Division, was equipped entirely with Stuarts. They were good little tanks but they had a maximum range under the best conditions of only 70 miles, and they were running out of petrol before the Brigade could complete its approach move.

On the night of 16th December Rommel started the second stage of his withdrawal, right back over the 250 miles to Agheila. The 7th Armoured Division was sent in pursuit. They failed to cut Rommel off, but caught up with him at Agedabia, where an attack by the Guards Brigade was repulsed. Then the re-equipped 22nd Armoured Brigade, trying a turning movement, was caught and badly mauled. After 2 days fighting the remains of the Brigade got away with only about thirty out of its original ninety tanks. The 22nd fought gallantly, but throughout this operation the brigade had suffered through lack of initial training in desert warfare.

On 6th January Rommel completed his withdrawal to Agheila.

It is generally supposed that for success in the attack a superiority of three to one over the defence is none too great. It is perhaps noteworthy that this great British victory was achieved without anything like this proportion. In the number of tanks the British superiority was indeed considerable, but in quality the Germans had the advantage. Rommel was far better off in anti-tank guns, and he had actually the larger number of men—119,000 against 118,000. The casualties, including prisoners, were British 18,000 (of which 10,000 were killed and wounded), Axis 38,000 (including 8,400 killed and wounded). The numbers of killed and wounded were remarkably small when compared with the casualties of some of the great battles of the past—particularly those of the First World War.

One lesson of the battle was the effectiveness of field guns, when properly handled, against tanks. The success of the 4th Indian Division in building their defence round field artillery led Rommel to adopt a new type of battle organisation to compete with it. The attacking tanks were followed by field and medium artillery whilst anti-tank guns and lorried infantry moved forward on the flanks. Against this form of attack the British placed infantry in support of the defending field guns to prevent enemy infantry from entering the gun positions. In addition 2-pr anti-tank guns were deployed for close defence against the enemy tanks, and tanks were held in mobile reserve for counter-attack.

CHAPTER XV

Gazala

F EW could have foretold at the time of his defeat that Rommel's rebound would be so rapid. And yet on 5th January, the day before he completed his withdrawal, the means for a renewed offensive had been placed at his disposal. On that day there arrived in the harbour of Tripoli a convoy of ships loaded with, amongst other material of war, fifty-five tanks, twenty armoured cars, and many anti-tank guns. With these reinforcements the German armoured strength rose to 111 tanks in the forward area and twenty-eight in the rear. The Italian Motorised Corps (*Ariete* and *Trieste* Divisions) had another eighty-nine.

On the British side the armoured regiments were no longer those battle-hardened units which had defeated the Africa Corps, but regiments new to the desert and composed of as yet unseasoned soldiers who had not even finished their training in desert warfare.

It had been the intention of the British Command to start a new offensive in the middle of February to clear the enemy out of the whole of Tripoli. With this in view the 7th Armoured Division was withdrawn to Egypt to rest and refit. It was replaced by the 1st Armoured Division which had recently arrived in Egypt. The Armoured Brigade of this division, the 2nd, was engaged in training at Sannu, some 90 miles behind the forward positions. To hold these positions were two weak motorised infantry formations; the 22nd Guards Brigade and the 1st Support Group, each of two battalions. Near Benghazi was the 4th Indian Division with, under command from 14th January, the 8th Royal Tank Regiment with thirty-eight infantry tanks (Valentines).

These forces composed the 13th Corps, and they were hardly deployed for defence. An attack, however, was not expected; and indeed Auchinleck had said in his despatch that it was unlikely that Rommel could take the field again in the near future.

See map page 227.

Plate 38.   GERMAN TIGER TANK WITH 88-MM GUN. NOTE ITS GREAT WIDTH.

Plate 39.   RUSSIAN T-34 TANK MOVING INTO ACTION.

Plate 40.   RUSSIAN KV-1 HEAVY TANK.

Plate 41.　RUSSIAN JS-III HEAVY TANKS IN THE VICTORY PARADE DOWN THE BERLIN CHARLOTTENBURG CHAUSSÉE, 7TH SEPTEMBER, 1945.

Plate 42.   GERMAN PANTHER TANK CAPTURED AND MANNED BY A CREW OF THE 4TH BATTALION COLDSTREAM GUARDS MOVING INTO ACTION ON 27TH NOVEMBER, 1944.

This would probably have been a safe prediction of any average general, but the aggressive, bustling master tactician of armour who commanded the Axis army was by no means average.

On 21st January, just a fortnight after his defeat, Rommel's forces leaped forward on a drive which was to carry them within 60 miles of Alexandria and the prospect of seizing all Egypt and the Suez Canal.

The country over which the German advance started was very bad going and was extremely difficult to traverse with wheeled vehicles. The Germans, however, had a number of half-tracked vehicles, which gave them considerably more liberty of movement than the British, who had none of them.

The Germans advanced in two groups; one, which included 90th Light Division and which was led by Rommel in person, moved by the coastal road, driving back the 1st Support Group and destroying most of its guns; the other, consisting of the Panzer Divisions of the Africa Corps, moved across the desert to the Wadi El Faragh and then turned north.

The 2nd Armoured Brigade was now ordered forward and given the peculiar instruction to hold the line Agedabia-El Haseiat to the last. The Guards Brigade, with only one battalion (the other was still some distance to the rear) was directed to take position south of Agedabia with the same inflexible orders.

Agedabia fell to the enemy by 11 a.m. on 22nd January; at 3.30 p.m. Antelat was captured; and Sannu fell after a short fight at 7.30 p.m.

On 23rd Rommel tried to surround the 1st Armoured Division, and the 15th Panzer Division became engaged in a fierce battle with the 2nd Armoured Brigade near Antelat. Lacking battle experience, two of the British regiments were very roughly handled by the enemy. By that evening the Brigade had only eighty tanks left out of its original 150. The Germans had made devastating use of their anti-tank guns, pushing them forward in bounds from point to point to give covering fire for the movement of their tanks.

The next day, despite efforts by the 1st Armoured Division and the Guards Brigade, the 15th Panzer Division had seized Msus with its invaluable dumps by 11 a.m. The 1st Armoured Division, with only thirty tanks left, was now hardly an effective fighting force.

On 27th Rommel made a feint probe to the east and then suddenly pounced westwards to capture Benghazi; its vast accummulation of stores set ablaze by the evacuating British.

On 31st January Rommel resumed his eastward advance, though his supply lines were now too tenuous to support more than two small armoured battle groups. But they were not seriously opposed, until on 6th February they reached the line which the 8th Army had established between Gazala and Bir Hacheim. This was too strong for the now weakened impetus of the German offensive.

On 30th January, in a dismal report to the Prime Minister, Auchinleck stated that the British armoured forces as then equipped, organised and led needed a superiority over the enemy of at least two to one for success, and also the close co-operation of infantry and artillery.

The Gazala line, which the 8th Army was now occupying, was by no means ideal for defence. Indeed, it had been sited as a firm foothold from which to launch an attack, rather than a position on which to fight a defensive battle. From the coast, 5 miles west of Gazala, the line ran south for 50 miles to Bir Hacheim, and along the whole of its length it was covered by wide belts of mines. Behind and between these minefields were fortified posts, or "boxes", each occupied by an infantry brigade. Wide shallow depressions were normally selected for these boxes, so that guns could be sited out of view from beyond the rim of the depression.

The 1st South African Division held the right of the line. On its left was the 50th Northumbrian Division. Two of its brigades, the 151st and 69th, were on the right of the divisional front. There then followed a 30-mile stretch, about the centre of which was the remaining 150th Brigade, and at the southerly end the Free French Brigade Group at Bir Hacheim.

There was no depth to this line, and G.H.Q., realising this, had suggested an area defence with a perimeter Gazala-Tobruk-El Gubi-Bir Hacheim. However, instead of adopting this idea the 8th Army chose to establish a refused left flank from Bir Hacheim, with defended localities at Point 171, 3 miles south-east of it, at Retma 15 miles north-east of Point 171, and at El Gubi 12 miles east of Retma. At each of these localities was a brigade group: the first manned by the 3rd Indian Motor Brigade, the second by the 7th Motor Brigade (with some of the new 6-pr anti-tank guns), and the third by the 29th Indian

Infantry Brigade. All three formations were under the command of the 7th Armoured Division.

Inside the forward defences, Commonwealth Keep, Acroma, Knightsbridge, and El Adem were all held as defended localities, or "boxes".

At Belhamed, 15 miles east of El Adem, a big base had been built up for the projected offensive. The existence of this base had an unfortunate influence on the course of the forthcoming battle, as the assumed necessity of denying it to the enemy crippled the free movement of the British armour.

The British forces under the command of Lt.-Gen. Ritchie consisted of the 13th Corps (Lt.-Gen. Gott), which was primarily an infantry force, and the 30th Corps (Lt.-Gen. Norrie), which contained the armoured striking force. In the 13th Corps were the 50th Division (69th, 150th, and 151st Infantry Brigades), the 1st South African Division, the 2nd South African Division (the 3rd brigade of which was the 9th Indian from the 5th Indian Division), and the 1st and 32nd Army Tank Brigades with infantry tanks. The 30th Corps comprised the 1st Armoured Division (with the 2nd and 22nd Armoured Brigade Groups), the 7th Armoured Division (consisting of the 4th Armoured Brigade Group, the 7th Motor Brigade Group, the 3rd Indian Motor Brigade Group, the 29th Indian Infantry Brigade Group, and the 1st Free French Brigade Group), and the 201st Guards Motor Brigade. In addition to these the following remained directly under Headquarters 8th Army: the 5th Indian Division (less 9th and 29th Infantry Brigades), and a small column of all arms and various nationalities called Dencol. The 10th Indian Division and the 1st Armoured Brigade were under orders to join the 8th Army but had not yet arrived.

At this time the brigade group idea was enjoying one of its recurrent periods of popularity in the British Army, and all divisions had been re-organised into three brigade groups with the divisional field and anti-tank artillery divided amongst them.

Auchinleck had given instructions that all British armour should be held concentrated. Rommel fervently hoped that it would not. Headquarters 8th Army elected to favour Rommel's wish rather than Auchinleck's. The 1st Armoured Division was located between Knightsbridge and El Adem, whilst the 7th Armoured Division was east of Bir Hacheim, looking after the southern end of the front. The 1st and 32nd Army Tank Brigades were split up in support of the infantry.

147

In the 4th Armoured Brigade, of the 7th Armoured Division, were the 3rd and 5th Royal Tank Regiments and the 8th Hussars; and each of them had two squadrons equipped with the newly arrived Grant medium tanks and one with Stuart light medium tanks.

The Grant tank was a modified version of the American M3 Medium, or Lee, tank. The M3 derived from a requirement placed in August 1940, when it became known that the Germans had a 75-mm. gun in the Pz. IV. However, as no suitable turret was available for a 75-mm. gun, and time would be required to develop one, the 75-mm. gun had to be placed in a hull mounting, a prototype of which already existed. The successful 37-mm. was installed in the tank's turret. The pilot model was ready in January 1941 and production started the following July. The Grant differed from the Lee mainly in its turret, which was of British design. In all other, except minor, respects the two were similar. The Grant weighed 28 tons, had armour of a maximum thickness of 57 mm., was manned by a crew of six, and had a nine-cylinder 340-b.h.p. radial engine which gave it a speed of 26 m.p.h. and a radius of action of 144 miles.

Any comparison of British and German armour in the Western Desert at this time has evoked wide differences of opinion. Ritchie, reporting the action at Agedabia on 30th December, stated that British tanks were outgunned and were not sufficiently robust, and that the American Stuart was far ahead of the British tanks mechanically but inferior to the German as a fighting machine. Auchinleck agreed with these views, but thought the Stuart inferior to the British cruiser tank for fighting.

Much criticism has been levelled at the British 2-pr (40-mm.) gun. At this period of the war it was indeed obsolescent, but it did not compare badly with the short 50-mm. gun mounted in most of the German Pz. III's. The 2-pr had a muzzle velocity of 2650 and a penetration with ordinary ammunition which was somewhat better than that of the short 50-mm., with its muzzle velocity of 2247. The Germans were also using, however, A.P.C.R. (Armour Piercing Composite Rigid) ammunition, composed of a hard tungsten carbide core enclosed in a soft metal jacket. Because it was lighter than the normal projectile it had a much higher muzzle velocity (3444 in the short 50 mm.), and penetration was easier because it was only the small diameter core which had to be driven through the armour plate. At short and medium ranges this was a very effective ammunition, but its velocity fell off so rapidly that at long ranges it was probably inferior in effect and less accurate than the normal ammunition. The American M6 type 37-mm. mounted in the Stuarts and the Grants had a muzzle velocity of 2900. It was a much more effective gun than the 2-pr because it fired A.P.C.B.C. (Armour Piercing Cap and Ballistic Cap) ammunition which compared well with the German A.P.C.R. Some of the Pz. III's were now armed with the long 50-mm., which was a considerably better gun than the short type. Muzzle velocities for normal and A.P.C.R. ammunition were, respectively, 2700 and 3930. The 75-mm. of the Pz. IV's had the low muzzle velocity of 1263. It had no A.P.C.R. ammunition and its penetration was considerably less than that of the long 50 mm. The Grant M2 type 75 mm. was a much better gun, though it had only a medium muzzle velocity of 1850, and no capped ammunition.

As regards armour, the Pz. III's and IV's had now been fitted with additional plates which made them about equal in armour protection to the Crusaders and Stuarts, but inferior to the new Grants. The Valentines and Matildas had the thickest armour of all.

The practical effect of the rival guns and armour at a normal tank fighting range of 1,000 yards was that only the Grants and the Pz. III's, armed with the long 50 mm., could penetrate the hull front of their opponents. But there were only nineteen of these Pz. III's as compared with 167 Grants. The inferiority of the British built tanks lay mainly in their gunsights (which were not as good as those of either German or American design), their rather poor mechanical reliability, and the comparative ease with which they caught fire. The Grant was gravely handicapped by the position of its 75-mm. gun, which was mounted in a sponson on the right hand side of the hull. Not only had it a very limited traverse, but it could not be used at all when the tank was "hull-down".

The new British 6-pr (57-mm.) anti-tank gun, which was just coming into use, was a very good weapon—even better than the excellent German 50-mm. Pak 38. But there had been insufficient time before the Battle of Gazala to train men properly in its use. The 2-pr guns still formed the bulk of the anti-tank equipment. As a heavy anti-tank gun Rommel had the formidable 88-mm.; but he only had forty-eight of these. On the British side sixty of the 3·7-inch anti-aircraft guns had been modified for anti-tank use, but only about twelve were available for the battle.   Although the 3·7-inch was a better weapon than the 88-mm. it was much inferior in performance due to its defective sights.

In numbers of tanks the British held a significant advantage. There were some 700 present on the battlefield and another 570 either in reserve or with armoured formations still under training. Rommel had a total of 560 tanks available, but only fifty in reserve, including those under repair. Further, of his 560, fifty were light and 230 were the rather inferior Italian M/13's. However, to counter-balance the M/13's, the 250 British infantry tanks (included in the 700) were not really suitable for the armoured battle.

Apart from the armour, the two forces were fairly evenly balanced. As regards fighting spirit and quality the individual British and German units were probably the best in existence. It was likely, therefore, that the issue would be decided by generalship allied with tactical doctrine.

Rommel's plan was bold but simple, aiming at the destruction of the whole of the army opposed to him. The action was to start with a frontal attack by the Italian infantry divisions against the northern part of the British line. This was designed to attract British attention and the orientation of their reserves. In the meantime the whole of the Axis armour was to move south, and, turning round the southern flank of the Gazala defences, sweep north to the sea   The object of this move was twofold; first to cut off the British divisions holding the Gazala line, and secondly to destroy the armoured formations which would certainly oppose it. The 90th Light Division was allotted the subsidiary objective of the El Adem-Belhamed area with the task of stopping the movement of British supplies and of cutting off the Tobruk garrison.   To make up for its shortage of tanks it was allotted a number of vehicles fitted with air-screws as dust raisers to suggest a large body of tanks.

At 2 p.m. on 26th May the infantry of the Italian 21st Corps was launched to the attack against the 1st South African Infantry Division near Gazala, and at the same time the Axis armour began to concentrate east of Segnali.   At 8.30 p.m. the long columns of vehicles started their southward move.   They were spotted and reported by British aircraft, but the scale and extent of this movement were not appreciated and the further progress of Rommel's armada was soon concealed by darkness.

At dawn on 27th May 10,000 tracked and wheeled vehicles

swept round Bir Hacheim and fell like an avalanche on the southern defences. The 3rd Indian Motor Brigade was destroyed, the 7th Motor Brigade was driven away with heavy loss and Headquarters 7th Armoured Division was overrun. The move forward of the 4th Armoured Brigade was delayed, and the regiments were engaged individually by the 15th Panzer Division before they could concentrate in their battle positions. The 8th Hussars ceased to exist as a fighting unit; but the Grant tanks of the 3rd Royal Tank Regiment came as an unpleasant shock to the Germans, the Regiment inflicting such severe losses that the advance of the 15th Panzer Division was held up until three batteries of 88-mm.'s could be rushed to its assistance. In the evening the 4th Armoured Brigade retired towards El Adem, and was then directed to Belhamed.

At 7.30 a.m. the 22nd Armoured Brigade was ordered to move south and engage the enemy, but, unsupported, it suddenly encountered both the 15th and the 21st Panzer Divisions. The 22nd lost thirty tanks and many guns, and was driven back to the north-east. The 2nd Armoured Brigade now came to the assistance of the 22nd, and a counter-attack by the 1st and 32nd Army Tank Brigades was launched by the Commander 1st Armoured Division, causing heavy casualties to the German tanks.

In the meantime the 90th Light Division had reached the cross-roads at El Adem and had captured a number of British supply dumps. General Norrie and his Corps Headquarters, in face of the German advance, withdrew into the El Adem box which already held General Gott and his Corps Headquarters. The 90th Light, however, had had its difficulties. Shortage of fuel had forced it to leave some of its few and valuable tanks on the wayside. They were not all lost, as they should have been, for there was such an astonishing delay in dealing with them that the Germans were able to refuel some of them by air, and these drove off. The remainder were destroyed by the British on 1st June.

Rommel, thinking that he had accounted for most of the British armoured units, moved off with a column to link up with the 90th Light Division. But the 2nd Armoured Brigade, still very much in being, attacked him with Grant tanks and he was forced back.

Further German progress to the north was, according to Rommel, accompanied by heavy fighting with the 1st Armoured

Division which attacked him from the north-east under cover of heavy artillery fire. Most of his lorry columns became separated from his armoured units, with resulting shortages of fuel and ammunition. At the end of the day's fighting he had lost more than a third of his tanks.

On the evening of 27th both Panzer divisions were in the neighbourhood of Knightsbridge, with their forward elements 3 miles north. *Ariete* was coming up behind and on the left flank.

Rommel now admitted that his initial plan had failed, mainly because of the unexpected strength of the British armour with the new Grant tanks. At the same time he commented scathingly, if with considerable relief, at the failure of his opponents to concentrate their armour.

On the morning of 28th the 21st Panzer Division got within 5 miles of the coast road, the main supply route between Tobruk and Gazala. The 15th Panzer Division, almost out of ammunition and with very little fuel left, had halted on the Rigel Ridge, close to Knightsbridge.

The 90th Light Division was now recalled by Rommel from its position at El Adem. On the way it was harried by both ground and air attack, and was even forced to halt for a time. But British attempts to destroy it were far too slow and it eventually rejoined Rommel in the area west of Knightsbridge which was now being called the "Cauldron".

By this time Rommel's armoured force was in a bad way, and he admitted to being uneasy. On the morning of the 29th the "Cauldron" position looked extremely unpleasant. At Rommel's back was the continuous belt of British mines and the box occupied by the 150th Infantry Brigade. In front was the Knightsbridge box manned by the Guards Brigade. Apart from these two fixed bastions he was hemmed in by the British armour.

From the British point of view it would seem that it was only necessary to contain Rommel, whilst delivering a massive armoured blow at the Italians holding the north of the Axis position, for the whole of the enemy army to be rolled up and destroyed. But speed in the execution of such a plan was vital. Nothing happened. At Army and Corps Headquarters the very efficient staffs were engaged in planning.

From 8 a.m. the 15th and 21st Panzer Divisions were fighting their way southward from the Rigel Ridge, where they had leaguered the previous night, whilst Rommel in person was leading a supply column through a gap which he had observed the previous evening. But these supplies were only a fraction of what his force required, and quite insufficient to enable him to renew the offensive. His primary need now was a corridor through the minefield at his back to provide a short and sure line of communications.

Norrie, in the meantime, had decided to concentrate all his armour against the "Cauldron" and smash Rommel against the rear of the 50th Division—to attack the enemy, in fact, at his strongest point. But everything started slowly, and the move of the 2nd Armoured Brigade was hampered by a sharp riposte from the Africa Corps, and both the 4th and 22nd Armoured Brigades were held up by sandstorms.

By the morning of 30th May the *Trieste* Division had succeeded in clearing a narrow gap through the minefield. Rommel now planned to widen this gap and to ensure its security by destroying the 150th Infantry Brigade which flanked it. In a still almost desperate situation he was even planning ahead to follow up this operation with the reduction of Bir Hacheim and the subsequent capture of the divisions in the Gazala line.

On 31st May Rommel launched his attack against the 150th Infantry Brigade, against the advice and even pleading of Bayerlein, his Chief of Staff, and Nehring, commanding the Africa Corps. Indeed, from the German point of view it was incredible that the 8th Army could allow Rommel to destroy the 150th Infantry Brigade and its attached tank regiment, whilst powerful British forces stood by inactive. Yet this is precisely what happened. By midday on 1st June the resistance of the 150th Brigade was finally broken down after a fight of such gallantry that it earned the tribute from Rommel that "as usual the British fought to the end".

It had been a very near thing for Rommel. On 31st May a British officer prisoner had protested to him that if his desperately thirsty men of the 3rd Indian Motor Brigade could not be provided with food and water they should be allowed to go back to the British lines. Rommel told him sympathetically that they were getting the same ration as the Africa Corps and Rommel himself—half a cup. He added (as recorded in *Rommel*, by Desmond Young), "But I quite agree that we cannot go on like this. If we do not get a convoy through to-night I shall have to ask General Ritchie for terms. You can take a letter to him from me".

No adequate reason for the 8th Army's failure to attack on or before 31st May has ever been given. An attack was indeed planned for the night of 31st, but, as stated in Auchinleck's Despatch, both Corps Commanders asked for 24 hours respite in order that they could assemble and prepare their forces. It seems extraordinary that the request should have been made and inexplicable that Ritchie should have granted it. Napoleon was prepared to be asked for anything but time; and on this occasion a failure to appreciate the time factor deprived the 8th Army of its chance to finish the war in North Africa in one decisive stroke.

On 1st June the 150th Brigade had ceased to exist, with the loss of 3,000 prisoners and 101 tanks and armoured cars, a path through the minefields had been secured for the Axis army, and a re-provisioned Rommel was ready for further action. In the evening a British attack was launched against the enemy forces in the "Cauldron". It was too late and it failed. In the meantime the 90th Light and *Trieste* Divisions were already moving south against Bir Hacheim.

The next day Rommel, agressive as always when he had the opportunity, pushed an armoured reconnaissance northwards. Auchinleck had advised an attack against the northern sector, held by the Italian infantry, but this German probe persuaded the 8th Army command that it was not a practicable operation, as the enemy could counter it by an armoured thrust at the flank of the attacking force. For the same reason an attack in the south was ruled out. It is remarkable how Rommel, in his still very uncomfortable position, was able to retain the initiative and make the British commander follow his wishes. The one thing that Rommel wanted was that his opponent should attack his "Cauldron" position. It is unlikely that he imagined his northward reconnaissance would have that effect.

The British plan for the attack on the "Cauldron" consisted of three phases and involved a change of operational command at each phase. The main geographical objectives were the Aslagh and Sidra Ridges. The first phase was to be directed by the 5th Indian Division and was a night assault on the Aslagh Ridge by the 10th Indian Infantry Brigade, supported by the 4th Royal Tank Regiment, and after a bombardment by four artillery regiments. In the second phase, under the direction of the 7th Armoured Division, the 22nd Armoured Brigade was to cross the Aslagh Ridge at first light and, supported by the same four artillery regiments, go through to capture Sidi Muftah some 4 miles further on and in the heart of the Cauldron position. The 9th Indian Infantry Brigade was to follow and establish itself at Sidi Muftah. At the same time as this attack was taking place, the 32nd Army Tank Brigade was to attack south, supported by one artillery regiment, and capture the Sidra Ridge. One lorried infantry battalion was placed under command to take over the position when captured. This phase of the attack, in fact, envisaged and entailed the destruction of the enemy armour in the "Cauldron". In the third phase, which was to follow the successful completion of this task, the 5th Indian Division was to resume command in the "Cauldron", whilst the 22nd Armoured Brigade was to move north and join the 1st Armoured Division in a drive through the Italian infantry defence to complete and exploit the victory.

The attack started at 2.50 a.m. on 5th June, but owing to a miscalculation it was launched too far to the east, and when it halted at daybreak the infantry had only penetrated the outpost line held by units of the *Ariete* Division. The artillery bombardment had barely touched the main enemy position. Thus the 22nd Armoured Brigade had to take the Aslagh Ridge, the first objective, before it could start its attack on the second one. Driving the *Ariete* Division off the ridge, it then stormed on and crashed into a very heavy fire of anti-tank guns and field artillery. Leaving sixty of its 156 tanks behind, the 22nd veered away to the right in the direction of Knightsbridge.

The 32nd Army Tank Brigade was even less fortunate. It attacked with two regiments of Matildas in line, with its lorried infantry battalion following behind. The advance was covered by a thick smoke screen put down by the supporting artillery. But when the brigade emerged from the smoke it ran on to an unreconnoitred minefield and into a storm of fire from the 21st Panzer Division on the Sidra Ridge. The brigade lost fifty-eight of its seventy tanks. The supporting squadron then arrived on the scene with another twelve tanks, only to have all but two of them knocked out.

The British armoured attack had ended in disaster; and now Rommel mounted his counter-blow. As a preliminary, a wave of tanks swept over the Aslagh Ridge, destroyed one of the infantry battalions which had taken part in the night attack, and then engaged part of the 22nd Armoured Brigade. In the early afternoon the 21st Panzer Division attacked south of the

Aslagh Ridge, drove round the southern flank of the 10th Indian Infantry Brigade, and wheeling north, overran the 9th Indian Infantry Brigade and the Headquarters of both the 5th Indian Division and the 7th Armoured Division. The attack by the 21st Panzer Division was held up by the 5th Royal Tank Regiment, but unfortunately the rest of its Brigade, the 4th Armoured, were too far back to defeat this wing of the enemy thrust before night put a stop to the fighting. The 10th Indian Infantry Brigade was now cut off.

That night the 2nd, 4th and 22nd Armoured Brigades were placed under the command of the 7th Armoured Division, with a view to relieving the 10th Indian Infantry Brigade the following day. But through delay and confusion this operation never even started, and by the evening of 6th June the 10th Indian Infantry Brigade and the four regiments of artillery of 5th Indian Division had been completely destroyed.

Auchinleck considered that this day was the turning point of the battle. At its start Ritchie had calculated that he had 400 tanks to oppose the 230 Axis tanks. At its close, through a conduct of operations for which inept is not too strong a word, the British tank strength had fallen to 170, whilst Rommel still had over 200.

On the evening of 6th June Rommel was in a strong enough position to send a battle group to assist in the reduction of Bir Hacheim, and 3 days later he followed this up with another one.

On 10th June the 4th Armoured Brigade attacked south of Knightsbridge, but it failed against the German anti-tank defence, and the Brigade lost sixteen tanks. That evening the French garrison evacuated Bir Hacheim.

On 11th June a wireless intercept gave Rommel the following accurate information of the 8th Army dispositions: on the Rigel Ridge were Headquarters 1st Armoured Division, the 22nd Armoured Brigade, and the 2nd Battalion Scots Guards; in the Knightsbridge box there was the 201st Guards Brigade; the 4th Armoured Brigade was south-east of Knightsbridge; Headquarters 7th Armoured Division was on the ridge to the east of El Adem; and in the El Adem box was the 29th Indian Infantry Brigade. The failure of some British commanders and staff officers to appreciate that the enemy took a keen interest in their wireless communications was of considerable assistance to German operations in the Western Desert.

In the light of this information Rommel ordered the 15th

Panzer, 90th Light, and *Trieste* Motorised Infantry Divisions to advance towards El Adem, and the 21st Panzer Division to demonstrate against the British in the area of the Rigel Ridge and Knightsbridge. On the evening of 11th June the 4th Armoured Brigade was sent to intercept this move and bumped into the 15th Panzer Division south-east of Knightsbridge. From another British wireless indiscretion Rommel gathered to his delight that his opponent's planned an armoured attack to the south-east. He accordingly directed the 15th Panzer Division to halt and stand on the defensive, and issued orders to the 21st Panzer Division to advance south of Knightsbridge box on the morning of 12th June and attack the British armour in the rear. The 90th Light Division, in the meantime, was to push on to El Adem.

The 12th June dawned without any sign of a British attack, so Nehring ordered the 15th Panzer Division to take the offensive. At midday the 21st Panzer Division was thrusting into the flank of the 2nd and 4th Armoured Brigades, which were now caught between the converging attacks of two panzer divisions. Further east the 90th Light Division was containing the 29th Indian Infantry Brigade in the El Adem box.

The German armour was now further assisted by a sand haze, under cover of which their anti-tank guns moved forward and poured a heavy fire into the cornered British tanks.

The 22nd Armoured Brigade drove rapidly southwards from the Rigel Ridge to break the belt which was tightening round the 2nd and the 4th. This attempt, however, failed, and the 22nd suffered heavy tank losses from the 21st Panzer and the *Trieste*. By the evening the Germans broke through the flanks of the beleaguered armour. Remnants of the 4th Armoured Brigade made their way northwards to the region of Acroma, and what was left of the 2nd Armoured Brigade fell back with the 22nd Armoured Brigade to the neighbourhood of the Knightsbridge box.

At the start of this disastrous battle reinforcements had brought the British tank strength to 330, which was more than double the number which Rommel could muster. By the evening of 12th June the British had lost 260 tanks.

The next day Rommel tried to crown his success by cutting off the Knightsbridge box. He was foiled by a gallant defensive action by the British tanks, and when night came the Guards evacuated the box.

A rapid British withdrawal now became inevitable. The 1st South African and the 50th Divisions were ordered to withdraw from the Gazala line on the night of 14th June. The 1st South African Division got back along the coast road before it was cut. The 50th Division carried out a remarkable withdrawal by striking westwards through the Italians, and then wheeling south to pass round the old Bir Hacheim position.

In Tobruk were the 2nd South African Division and the 11th Indian Infantry Brigade. These were reinforced by the Guards Brigade and the 32nd Army Tank Brigade. To cover the troops retreating to the frontier a mobile force was formed of the 4th Armoured and 7th Motor Brigade, the former taking over the tanks remaining to the 2nd and 22nd Armoured Brigades.

The 21st Panzer Division, pushing on rapidly, attacked the 20th Indian Infantry Brigade which was holding El Duda and Sidi Rezegh. The 4th Armoured Brigade drove to their assistance and engaged in a terrific fight with the 21st Panzer. The British had the cruel disadvantage of the evening sun in their eyes, making accurate shooting impossible. The 4th lost nine tanks in this action, but fifty-eight still remained to them.

Relieved from outside interference, Rommel was now able to turn his attention to Tobruk. He attacked on 20th June at a point where an Indian infantry battalion, unprotected by any minefield, was holding a front of 3 miles. The Germans pierced these thin defences before the British tanks were able to concentrate against them.

When it did arrive the 32nd Army Tank Brigade attacked furiously. By 5 p.m. it had only seven tanks left; and at 6 p.m. the Germans entered Tobruk. General Klopper, commanding the garrison surrendered the next morning. Rommel captured 33,000 prisoners, some thirty tanks in running order, 2,000 serviceable and, to him, invaluable vehicles, 1,400 tons of fuel, and about 5,000 tons of provisions. Nevertheless Rommel had expected considerably greater quantities of fuel and he was bitterly disappointed that the defenders had had time to destroy so much. However, it was his captures at Tobruk which enabled Rommel to renew the pursuit so rapidly, and indeed of the vehicles which now carried his troops forward after the 8th Army, more than 80 per cent were British running on British petrol.

When Rommel reached the Egyptian frontier he had only fifty-eight German and Italian tanks left, but Ritchie considered he was too weak to stand there and fell back another 100 miles to Mersa Matruh.

On 25th June Auchinleck himself took over command of the 8th Army from Ritchie. Whilst the new commander was grasping the reins in his own extremely capable hands, disaster was still following in the wake of Gazala and Tobruk. Headquarters 13th Corps lost its head and ordered a retreat when none was necessary, and the newly arrived Headquarters 10th Corps was cut off in Mersa Matruh as a result. The Matruh force was ordered to break out, and most got away but the Germans captured 6,000 prisoners and an enormous quantity of equipment.

Back at El Alamein Headquarters 30th Corps was organising a position, and here the British forces, after some further mishaps but also after inflicting some checks on their enemy, arrived almost at the same time as the leading troops of the Africa Corps.

It looked like one more milestone to final disaster. It was in fact the springboard to victory.

CHAPTER XVI

Alamein

THE position to which the 8th Army had now retired stretched for 38 miles from the Mediterranean Sea, south to the precipitous plunge into the great Qattara Depression. It was this depression which made the Alamein defences so different from any others occupied in the Western Desert, for it could be traversed neither by troops nor vehicles and flanked the south of the British position with an area more impassable than the sea.

Parallel to the sea and some 2 miles from it ran the railway, and between the railway and the sea was the coast road, and north of the road a marsh. South of the railway the desert lay for miles almost without feature. But the monotony was broken by three low ridges, so low that they would have been hardly noticeable in any other landscape; but from the command they gave over this flat expanse they were to dominate the battlefield. These three features were the Miteiriya, Ruweisat and Alam Halfa Ridges, stretching in a rough crescent from west to east, overlapping each other, and varying in distance from 5 to 12 miles south of the railway. South of these ridges the ground gradually got more broken, with flat topped hills rising higher, till at the border of the depression they were some 700 feet above sea level.

A year previously, in July 1941, Auchinleck had spotted the potentialities of this position and had directed the preparation of defences which should constitute the final barrier to any enemy threat to the Nile Delta. These defences were based on four large "boxes" which, starting from the north, were located as follows: El Alamein railway station, close to the coast; Deir el Shein, a shallow depression at the west end of the Ruweisat Ridge 11 miles south of El Alamein; the head of the Bab el Qattara defile, 8 miles south-west of Deir el Shein; and Naqb Abu Dweis, 15 miles south-west of Bab el Qattara, and overlooking a track suitable for motor vehicles, which crossed the Depression and eventually led to the Wadi Natrun near the road from Cairo to Alexandria.

See map page 228

Plate 43. CROMWELL TANK MARK III WITH THE 6-POUNDER GUN.

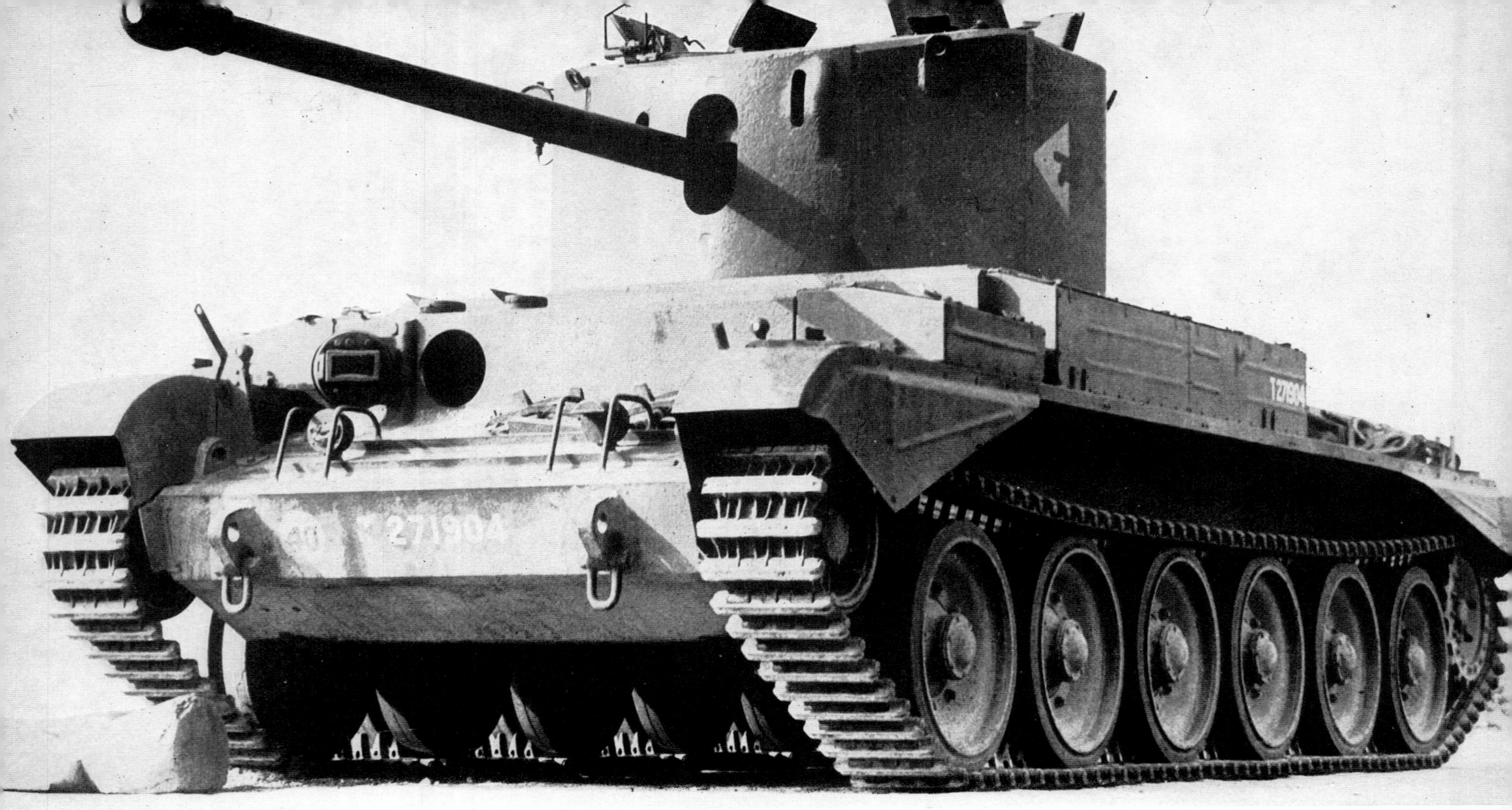

Imperial War Museum

Plate 44. CHALLENGER TANK WITH THE 17-POUNDER GUN.

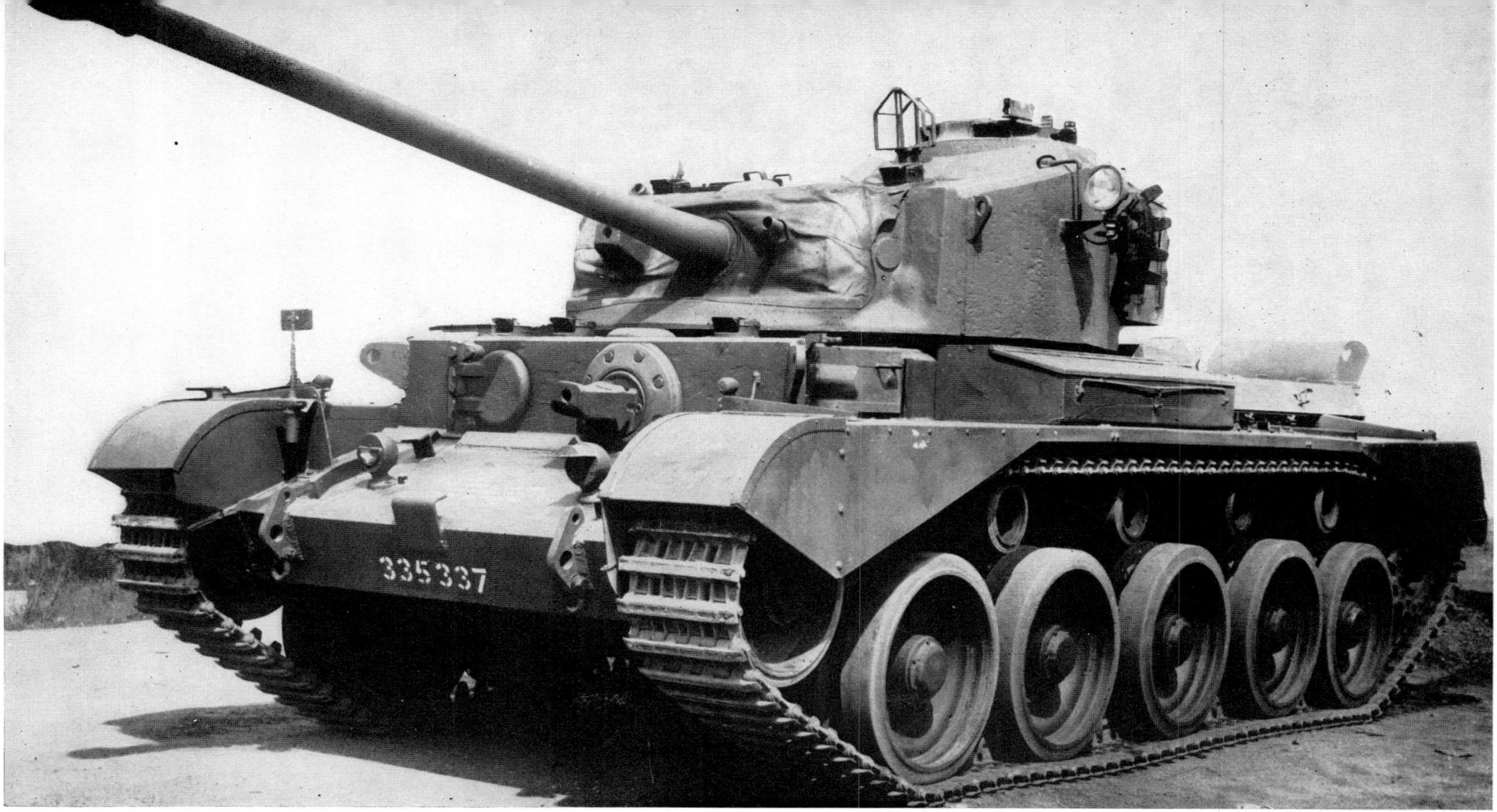

Imperial War Museum

Plate 45. COMET TANK WITH ITS 77-MM GUN.

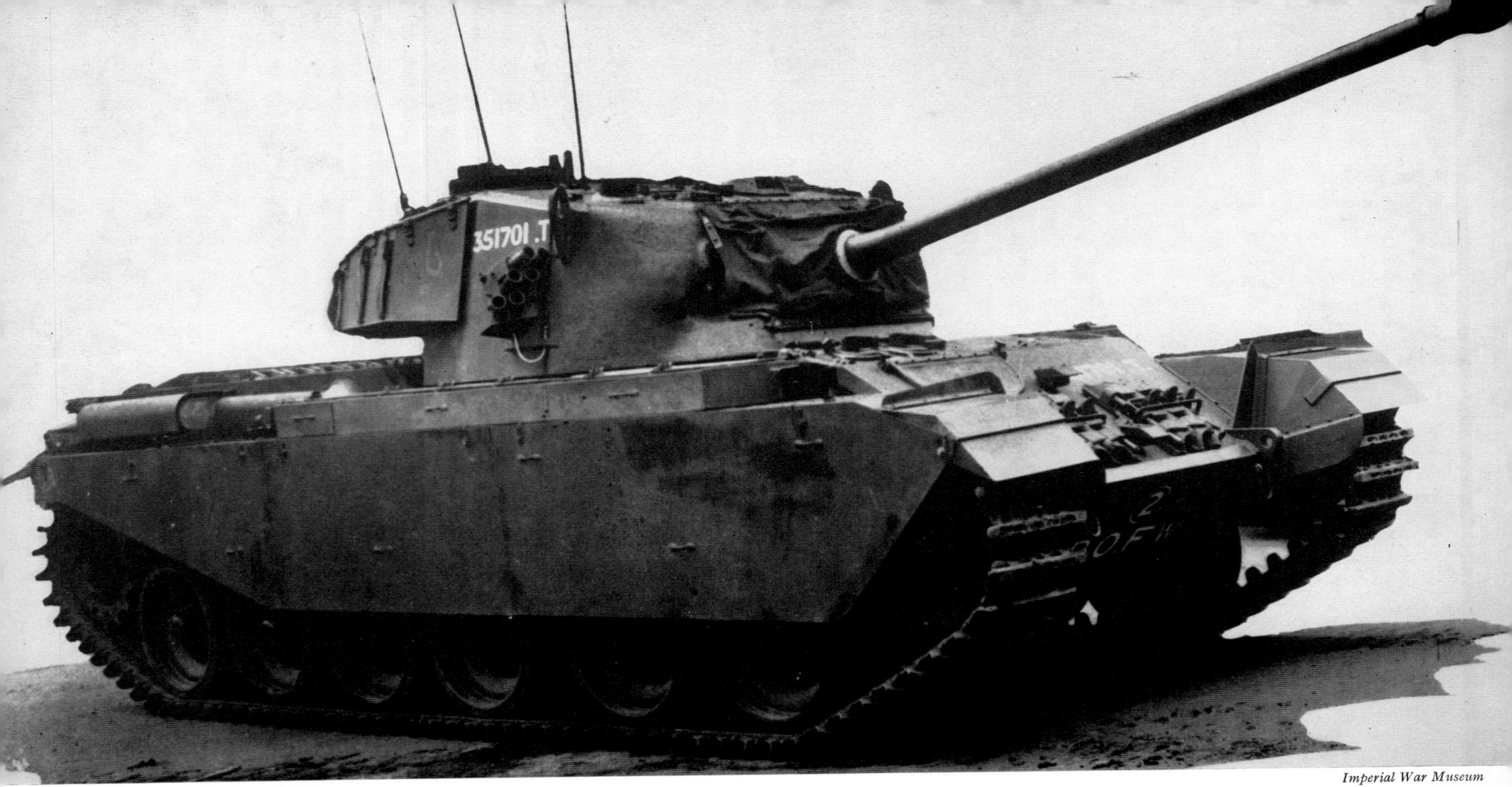

Imperial War Museum

Plate 46. CENTURION TANK MARK II, ARMED WITH A 17-POUNDER GUN.

The El Alamein box was held by the 1st South African Division. One brigade occupied the west and south faces with its right flank on the sea, and two mobile brigades were stationed to the south-east and east respectively. At Deir el Shein was the 18th Indian Infantry Brigade with nine Matilda tanks in support; Bab el Qattara was occupied by the 6th New Zealand Brigade; and the 9th Indian Infantry Brigade was at Naqb Abu Dweis.

The 7th Motor Brigade (the only formation remaining in the 7th Armoured Division) was mobile between Bab el Qattara and Naqb Abu Dweis. The remainder of the New Zealand Division was at Deir el Munassib, 9 miles south-east of Bab el Qattara. The 1st Armoured Division was held in reserve, with its 4th Armoured Brigade near to and south-east of El Alamein and its 22nd Armoured Brigade at the east end of the Ruweisat Ridge.

The northern sector of the defences from the sea to the Ruweisat Ridge was the responsibility of the 30th Corps, whilst the southern sector came under the 13th Corps.

By 30th June Rommel's strength in tanks had risen to fifty-five, but some of these were the light Pz. II's. With this somewhat meagre armoured force at his disposal he attacked before dawn on 1st July. The Africa Corps (the 15th and 21st Panzer Divisions) had been sent south on 30th June on a feint towards the Qattara Depression, but with orders to report back again that night. (The object of this feint was to pin the British armour which Rommel mistakenly believed was in the southern sector). The Africa Corps was then to drive to a point 10 miles south-east of El Alamein station, followed by a southward turn which Rommel hoped would bring it rear of the British defences. The 90th Light Division, followed by an Italian division was to go south of the El Alamein box and then swing north, cutting the coastal road and the British communications. Another Italian division was to go straight for El Alamein. The Italian 20th Corps (*Ariete* Armoured and *Trieste* Lorried Divisions) was to follow the Africa Corps. The right flank of this operation was to be covered by the *Littorio* Armoured Division and German reconnaissance units.

In the event the Africa Corps was first delayed by the bad going and sandstorms and was then bombed by the R.A.F. in the early morning. As a result its attack went in 8 hours later than Rommel had planned. The 90th Light Division also had troubles; it was hampered by the unexpectedly deep sand, lost its bearings and turned north much too soon. It thus ran straight into the El Alamein defences and was pinned to the ground by artillery fire from the 1st and 2nd South African Brigades and from the 4th Armoured Brigade. (At this time the 1st Armoured Division was concentrating in the neighbourhood of El Alamein; the 4th Armoured Brigade had already arrived with some forty tanks, and the 22nd Armoured Brigade was limping along to join it with about eighteen tanks operational and a number of others on tow.)

In the meantime the Africa Corps, in its southward movement, had run headlong into the 18th Indian Infantry Brigade in the Deir el Shein box. This brigade and its nine Matildas put up a most gallant fight before it was overwhelmed. Fighting behind half-finished defences and short of ammunition, it held off the 15th and 21st Panzer Divisions from 9 a.m. until 7.30 p.m. and destroyed eighteen tanks out of the fifty-five attacking it before succumbing to the enemy's great superiority.

At about 2 p.m. H.Q. 30th Corps had ordered the 1st Armoured Division to support the 18th Indian Brigade. However, owing to bad going, misunderstanding of orders and inaccurate information, no move took place until 4.30 p.m., and the few tanks which reached Deir el Shein arrived after the 18th Indian Brigade had been destroyed. But this Brigade's great fight had deprived Rommel of his chance of immediate and decisive victory.

Rommel gave orders for the attack to continue by moonlight, but heavy R.A.F. attacks made this impracticable, and he deferred further action until the following day. After being bombed throughout the night a very weary Africa Corps did not get going until 3 p.m. on 2nd July.

Auchinleck now went over to the offensive, with the intention of striking wherever the Africa Corps was not present. He hoped that the German armour would move to the assistance of a threatened spot, and that by varying the location of his attacks he might gradually destroy the Italian infantry whilst at the same time wearing out the Africa Corps.

In the belief that Rommel was preparing to attack El Alamein, with his German divisions, Auchinleck directed the 13th Corps to wheel north, pivoting on Bab el Qattara, to attack the enemy's right flank and rear. Communications with the 13th Corps were very poor, and it was 2 p.m. on 2nd July before the Corps began pushing northward with the New Zealand

Division and the remains of the 5th Indian Division. The 4th Armoured Brigade now started moving round the enemy's southern flank whilst the 22nd Armoured Brigade pressed him in front. The situation began to look dangerous for Rommel, who was now engaged in a fruitless attack on El Alamein, when through an appalling failure to appreciate the situation, the 4th Armoured Brigade was recalled.

On 3rd July the balance of armour was heavily in favour of the British. Rommel had only twenty-six serviceable tanks, whilst the 1st Armoured Division had over a hundred, of which thirty-eight were Grants. Early that morning the New Zealand Division struck north from the Bab el Qattara at the Ariete Armoured Division, capturing all its guns and seizing the west end of the El Mreir depression west of the Ruweisat Ridge. With this success Rommel's hopes of victory were again disappointed. With the 90th Light Division, the Africa Corps and the *Littorio* Armoured Division, he had been battling all morning against the 1st Armoured Division and the El Alamein defences. The fighting was fierce, and the 1st Armoured Division lost thirty-nine tanks. But the day was memorable, for the 8th Army had gone over to the attack and Rommel had been stopped in his tracks.

It was Auchinleck's intention to continue the same general plan on 4th July. The 30th Corps was to engage the German armour whilst the 13th Corps was to move round the enemy's southern flank and strike north at his line of communications. This plan might, and should, have succeeded but for two inexcusable failures. Firstly, the 13th Corps direction was so lacking in drive and enthusiasm that the advance was slow and ineffective (nor, for that matter, was there much energy in the 30th Corps behind the move forward of the 1st Armoured Division). Secondly, Rommel again learned of the British plan through indiscretions over the British wireless communications. Auchinleck ordered the attack to be pressed the following day, but there was no further progress.

All the available Grant tanks at this time were in the 1st Armoured Division. The 7th Armoured Division consisted of the 7th Motor Brigade and the 4th Light Armoured Brigade, equipped with Stuart and Crusader tanks and armoured cars. The division was given such light cavalry roles as protective reconnaissance and harassing.

On 6th July the 9th Australian Division began to arrive and

was allotted to the 30th Corps (now under command of Lieutenant-General W. H. Ramsden, who had replaced Norrie). With reinforcements the 8th Army now had about 200 tanks at its disposal.

Auchinleck now planned an interesting "left-right-left" sequence. On 7th July the 13th Corps, in accordance with Auchinleck's instructions, withdrew the New Zealand Division from the Bab el Qattara box. On the morning of 9th July Rommel learned of its evacuation and jumped to the conclusion that the 8th Army was retreating. He immediately occupied the box with the *Littorio* Division, and issued orders for the panzer divisions to advance on 10th July.

In the meantime Auchinleck, on the 8th July, had ordered the 30th Corps to attack, their first objectives being the sandy mounds of Tel el Eisa and Tel el Makh Khad, 3 and 6 miles west of El Alamein respectively. The infantry were then to exploit southwards to Deir el Shein and the armour westwards to the El Daba airfield. The 2nd Armoured Brigade was allotted temporarily to the 13th Corps to help keep the enemy armour in the south.

At 3.30 a.m. on 10th July the attack opened with a heavy artillery bombardment. By 10 a.m. the Australians had captured Tel el Eisa and the South Africans were in Tel el Makh Khad. In face of the Australian attack the Italian *Sabratha* Division panicked and fled. A scratch force of Germans was rapidly assembled from Rommel's main headquarters (he was in the south with his tactical headquarters) and just succeeded in preventing the Australians from exploiting their success.

This action had the desired effect on Rommel, for he gave up all ideas of advancing in the south and hurried the 15th Panzer Division north.

Having attracted half the German armour to the northern sector, Auchinleck now prepared to strike in the south. In order to keep the enemy's attention fixed towards the coast, the Australians attacked again on 11th July. This attack hit the *Trieste* Division with such vigour that the 15th Panzer Division only just succeeded in stopping a complete break through.

On 13th July Rommel put in an unsuccessful counter-attack against the El Alamein box. The next day he turned, equally unsuccessfully, on the Australians at Tel el Eisa.

At midnight on 14th/15th July the 8th Army attacked along the Ruweisat Ridge, with the 5th Indian Brigade of the 30th

Corps on the right and the New Zealand Division of the 13th Corps on the left. The New Zealand Division were to take Point 63 on the west end of the Ruweisat Ridge whilst the 5th Indian Brigade protected its right flank. If this attack was successful the 13th Corps was to exploit north-westwards, and for this purpose the 1st Armoured Division, less its support group, had been placed under its command.

By dawn the New Zealand Division had seized its objective, after driving back the Italian *Brescia* Division. It was then that inept co-operation ruined the success of Auchinleck's plan. The 1st Armoured Division had been given the preliminary task of protecting the New Zealanders' left flank, and to do this it was essential that tanks should have been close up to the infantry by daybreak. The armour, however, had been unhappily slow in its movements, and at dawn it was still very far behind the forward infantry. The 22nd Armoured Brigade was 8 miles away and the 2nd Armoured Brigade was very little closer. In the rapid night advance the infantry had left many enemy posts behind them, with the result that their artillery was unable to get forward. The German dawn reaction was a fierce armoured counter-attack, and the unfortunate New Zealand infantry battalion on which it fell, with no effective guns at its disposal, was practically destroyed.

On the right flank the 2nd Armoured Brigade arrived in the early afternoon to support the 5th New Zealand and 5th Indian Brigades. But the 4th New Zealand Brigade about Point 63 had still to rely on its own resources. At 5 p.m. it was again attacked by German tanks, with the result that the brigade headquarters was captured and Point 63 perforce abandoned to the enemy.

By 16th July the troops in the Ruweisat area were in a better defensive posture, and a renewed German attack was defeated with the loss of twenty-four tanks. The support group of the 1st Armoured Division had arrived by this time and its 6-pr guns played a significant part in the German repulse.

Auchinleck's next plan was another attempt to mislead the enemy and throw him "off balance". There was to be a double punch—the first to attract and hit the enemy armour, and the second to follow the first and break through the Axis defences.

At this time the 1st Armoured Division had 170 tanks, of which sixty were Grants. The 23rd Armoured Brigade, which had arrived in Egypt on 6th July with 150 Valentines, was also made available for the battle. But after 2 months at sea and without any desert training it was in no position to pull its full weight against the Africa Corps. It had a further and very serious handicap in that many of its wireless sets had not been "tropicalised".

The 13th Corps were to attack with infantry on the night 21st/22nd July; the objectives being Point 63 on the Ruweisat Ridge and Deir el Shein. Due in part to inadequate planning by the Corps staff, the attack was something of a disaster. The infantry went forward well and the 6th New Zealand Brigade reached the El Meir depression, just south of Point 63, but the armour which was to have supported the attack and protected the left wing was again not there. The commander of the 22nd Armoured Brigade had refused to move before dawn on the grounds that tanks could not move by night, and Corps Headquarters had not overruled this extraordinary assertion. The German tanks, unfortunately, did move by night, and the Africa Corps was in position to put in a dawn assault which cost the New Zealand Brigade 700 men and all its anti-tank guns. The 2nd Armoured Brigade, rushing up to assist, lost twenty-four tanks on mines. On the right of the New Zealand Division the 161st Indian Motor Brigade of the 5th Indian Division had reached Deir el Shein, but it too was counter-attacked at dawn and the battalion at Deir el Shein was destroyed by tanks.

The 23rd Armoured Brigade (less the 5th Royal Tank Regiment, which had been detached in support of the Australians) was supposed to pass through the infantry in the morning, as soon as a gap had been cleared in the enemy minefield, and exploit west for 3 miles towards El Mireir, whence the 2nd Armoured Brigade was to continue. The 23rd Armoured Brigade crossed its start line, according to schedule, at 8 a.m. and ran into some of the 161st Brigade withdrawing. There was no information as to whether the minefield had or had not been cleared. Nevertheless the Brigade Commander decided to advance and the 23rd swept past the New Zealanders' northern flank in the armoured equivalent of a "flat-out" gallop and, running straight on to the minefield, lost twenty tanks. German tanks and anti-tank guns now opened fire from in front and from either flank on the unfortunate brigade. After a very gallant fight the remains of the 23rd Armoured Brigade withdrew, but there were only eleven tanks left out of the 104 which it had taken into action.

After one unfortunate cavalry affair in the Peninsular campaign Wellington commented: "Our officers of cavalry have acquired a trick of galloping at everything". The charge by the 23rd Armoured Brigade was only the latest of many incidents which showed that the "trick" had not been entirely eliminated.

The second attack was to have been launched on the night 24th/25th July. However, the Commander of the 9th Australian Division insisted on a postponement of 48 hours. Auchinleck was forced to agree, but the delay probably ruined his plan for the Axis forces had time to recover and regroup after the 13th Corps attack. The infantry attack went well at first, but the German armour was there to greet it and, since there was delay in getting the British tanks forward, the attack failed.

A series of brilliantly conceived operations thus ended in disappointment and frustration. Auchinleck was denied the chance to turn his defeat of Rommel into decisive victory, for he was relieved as Commander-in-Chief by General Sir Harold Alexander, whilst Lieutenant-General B. L. Montgomery was appointed to the command of the 8th Army. There was also a change in Corps Commanders: Major-General Sir Oliver Leese went to the 30th Corps and Lieutenant-General B. G. Horrocks to the 13th Corps.

During August Rommel received some badly needed reinforcements. Two airborne formations arrived for employment in a ground infantry role—the German *Ramcke* Parachute Brigade and the Italian *Fulgore* Parachute Division. His tank strength was increased to 440; but only 200 of these were German gun-armed tanks, and of these 200 only 100 had the new long guns (27 Pz. IV's with 75-mm.'s and 73 Pz. III's with 50-mm.'s).

On the British side there took place one of those peculiar moves which were never considered necessary by the Germans. The 1st Armoured Division went back to refit and was replaced by the "green" 10th Armoured Division. Twice in the desert campaigns this practice had led to disaster. New arrivals in Egypt included the 8th Armoured Division, the 44th Infantry Division and the 51st Infantry Division. The 8th Armoured Division's 23rd Armoured Brigade had already had premature and expensive experience of desert warfare, but the 24th Armoured Brigade had not yet been used.

167

The unfortunate Gazala operations had resulted in a considerable reorganisation of armoured divisions. The 10th Armoured Division had originally two armoured brigades, the 8th and 9th. Both these, however, lost all their tanks to make good battle losses, and the 9th was still not re-equipped. The 10th Armoured Division was therefore allotted the 22nd Armoured Brigade of four regiments to make up its deficiency. It addition the 23rd Armoured Brigade was placed temporarily under command of the 10th Armoured Division, which thus had three armoured brigades at its disposal.

British tank strength rose in August to a total of 935, of which 194 were Grants. Of these, 713 (including 164 Grants) were immediately available to the 8th Army. More than half of the Grants were in the 22nd Armoured Brigade. (The Grant tank had acquired the nickname of "ELH", or "Egypt's Last Hope").

The 8th Army's next battle was fought on the position and in accordance with the plan which Auchinleck had bequeathed to his successor. From the coast south to Bab el Qattara deep and strong fixed positions had been constructed behind a thick belt of mines. From Bab el Qattara south to the Qattara Depression the mine belt continued but it was covered only by light mobile troops. Eastwards from Bab el Qattara defences had been laid out which terminated some 20 miles away on the eastern end of the Alam Halfa Ridge, so that the 8th Army presented a refused defensive flank to the south.

The object of this layout was to entice the enemy armour into an attack south of Bab el Qattara, and then to defeat it when it was between Alam el Halfa and the Qattara Depression. This, in the event, is what happened. Auchinleck had intended to finish the business by sealing the German armour inside the "bag" with an attack southwards close to the minebelt. But there was, unfortunately, no such triumphant finale.

The sector from the coast to Bab el Qattara was the responsibility of the 30th Corps, and it was held by the 9th Australian, 1st South African and 5th Indian Divisions. On the left of the 5th Indian Division was the New Zealand Division of the 13th Corps, and to the south of the New Zealanders the 7th Armoured Division (now consisting of the 7th Motor Brigade and the 4th Light Armoured Brigade) provided a mobile screen as far as the Qattara Depression.

Rommel planned to do exactly what the British hoped he

would; that is, to break through the southern sector of the 8th Army's front and push rapidly eastwards to sever the British communications. This operation was to be mounted with a night attack by the Africa Corps and part of the Italian 20th Corps, which was to pierce the minefield and to penetrate some 30 miles east before dawn. This force was then to wheel north to the coast. The 90th Light Division and the remainder of the 20th Corps were to follow the attack and were then to form a defensive flank to the north to protect the communications of the armoured force.

To defeat this move, the British plan envisaged, at last, the Napoleonic co-ordination of the mounted, infantry and artillery arms. In their defensive positions tanks lay hidden from enemy observation in the dips of the sand ridges, and in their close support were artillery and anti-tank guns and the sturdy masses of the infantry.

The defending armour consisted of the 10th Armoured Division with two armoured brigades, the 8th and the 22nd. The former had three regiments comprising eighty-four tanks, of which seventy-two were Grants; and the latter consisted of four regiments and 166 tanks, including ninety-two Grants. The Alam Halfa Ridge itself was held by the 44th Infantry Division of only two brigades. The 22nd Armoured Brigade occupied broken ground south of the western end of the ridge. The 8th Armoured Brigade was deployed some 10 miles south-east of the 22nd, with the task of barring Rommel's route if he should try to drive past the Alam Halfa Ridge. The 23rd Armoured Brigade was in Army reserve, located east of the Ruweisat Ridge.

At 2 a.m. on 31st August the leading columns of the Africa Corps reached the minebelt. Penetration, however, proved unexpectedly difficult, and the Axis armour was harried both by the British covering troops and the Royal Air Force. In addition the sand was much looser than expected, slowing down the speed of the tanks and making the going very difficult for the wheeled vehicles. It was 9.30 a.m., therefore, before the Africa Corps was ready for its eastwards advance—6 hours behind schedule. As a result its northern flank was too exposed to British observation for the long thrust which had been intended. The Africa Corps was accordingly ordered to make an early wheel to the left, which brought it face to face with the 22nd Armoured Brigade.

It was 1 p.m. before the Africa Corps moved forward to attack, and 5 p.m. when the German tanks were first spotted by the 22nd Armoured Brigade. In accordance with instructions, however, fire was not opened until the enemy was within a 1,000 yards.

During the terrific fight which followed the 22nd Armoured Brigade was badly battered by the new German guns. At one point the Germans succeeded in driving a gap through the defence, but tanks from the reserve charged over the crest behind the forward positions and restored the situation. At dusk the Africa Corps withdrew its mauled and sorely depleted armoured units; and, though this was not immediately apparent, Rommel's last chance of conquering Egypt had been defeated.

The following morning Rommel made one further effort to break the British defence, but he had too little petrol left for more than a local attack on the Alam Halfa Ridge which was easily repulsed.

On 2nd September Rommel started to withdraw. On the night of 3rd/4th September a British counter-attack was launched southwards from the Alam Nayil position, just east of Bab el Qattara, to cut the Axis armour off inside the British minefields. The Germans, as usual, reacted vigorously and there was insufficient strength in the counter-attack to breach their defence.

By 7th September Rommel had extricated his forces and they were all west of the British minefields. His tanks casualties had been heavy and, since he had had to evacuate the battlefield his damaged tanks could not be recovered and fell into the hands of the British.

During the weeks which elapsed between the battles of Alam Halfa and second Alamein there was a re-organisation and vast build-up of the 8th Army. The total number of British tanks rose to 1,080, and of these 210 were Grants and 270 were the newly arrived Shermans with 75-mm. guns mounted in the turrets. The Axis forces, on the other hand, could only muster 519 tanks, and of these 278, or more than half, were the indifferent Italian medium tanks and another thirty-one were Pz. II's with no gun armament. The only real battle tanks, the Pz. III's and IV's, amounted to 218, of which 118 had the new long guns. The thirty Pz. IV's with the long 75-mm. were probably the best tanks on either side. The British superiority in numbers was further emphasised by the large tank reserves in the depots. Rommel, on the other hand, had hardly any tanks in reserve to replace casualties. The effect of this lack of reserves was shown strikingly in the forthcoming battle; for although the British tank casualties were three times those of the Axis, the 8th Army had eventually a superiority of twenty to one.

Of anti-tank guns the British had 850 6-pr, or equivalent, against the Axis 454. Here, however, the superiority lay more in numbers than in quality; for none of the modified 3·7-inch anti-aircraft guns seem to have been deployed with the 8th Army, whilst 154 of the Axis anti-tank guns were either the formidable 88-mm.'s or the almost equally good captured Russian 76·2-mm.'s.

Tactically the Axis armour was to be extremely handicapped by shortage of petrol, owing to the sinking of so many oil tankers by the Royal Air Force. As a result the armoured formations had to be so split up and deployed that support could be provided when required without the necessity of any long mileage. The petrol required by an armoured division was very considerable. A British armoured division of the 1941 organisation needed perhaps a 1,000 gallons of petrol to move 1 mile across country.

The American Sherman tank was a great improvement on the Grant. The prototype, as the T6, had been completed in September 1941; and production of the new tank, now entitled the Medium M4, began in July 1942. It was introduced into the British Army as the Sherman, and went into action for the first time at the battle of El Alamein in October 1942. It weighed 30 tons, had a crew of five, was powered by a nine-cylinder 400-h.p. radial engine giving it a speed of 24 m.p.h., and had a range of 85 miles. The armament consisted of a 75-mm. gun in the turret with a co-axially mounted Browning machine-gun and another Browning in the hull. The armour thickness varied between 76 and 12 mm. There were two marks, Mark I with an all-welded hull and Mark II with a cast hull. The 75-mm. of the Sherman had a muzzle velocity of 2,050 which was greater than that mounted in the Grant, but which was less than the 2,461 of the Pz. IV's long 75-mm. By mid-1942 the first Crusaders armed with 6-pr guns were beginning to appear; but by the end of the year the 6-pr as a tank gun was already outdated, for it was an inferior weapon to the German long 75 mm. Recognising the superiority of the German gun, the War Office, at the beginning of 1942, had begun the planning of a 17-pr gun as a replacement for the 6-pr.

A new organisation was now introduced for the British armoured division which was very similar to that of the German panzer division. The latter, as we have seen, came about through a shortage of tanks, but German experience had shown it to be an admirably balanced fighting force. The new British division had only one armoured brigade of three armoured regiments, and one infantry battalion, the place of the second armoured brigade being taken by a three-battalion motorised infantry brigade. The support group was removed and the artillery was increased by the addition of another 25-pr regiment, so that there were now two field, one anti-tank and one anti-aircraft regiments. The armoured car regiment was retained.

Owing to the high proportion of armour now available, it was not possible to adopt this new organisation in its entirety, and two of the armoured divisions had a second armoured brigade. The armoured order of battle was: 1st Armoured Division (2nd Armoured Brigade), 7th Armoured Division (4th and 22nd Armoured Brigades), 10th Armoured Division (8th and 24th Armoured Brigades), 9th Armoured Brigade (under command of the New Zealand Division), and 23rd Armoured Brigade (employed in an infantry support role).

There were two broad alternatives on which a plan to defeat the Axis Army could be based: either to make the main attack against the enemy's weaker defences in the south, followed by envelopment; or to attack in the north where the defences were far stronger. It was considered by the British command that it would be easier to get decisive results from a successful attack in the north, because the enemy's line of communications, the coast road, ran north-westwards from his extreme left flank. A penetration in that area, therefore, would drive the opposing forces away from their lines of communication and threaten to isolate formations south of the breach. Envelopment from the south, on the other hand, might push the Axis troops towards their communications. It may be that Rommel's failure at envelopment from the south at Alam Halfa was another factor which influenced the decision which was taken to attack in the north. Nevertheless it was only the considerable British superiority in numbers and material which made such a decision practicable.

The Axis position was strong. The northern part was covered by minefields and defended localities which extended to a depth of 4 miles. One flank rested on the sea and some 15 miles inland switch lines ran westwards as a bastion against any penetration in the south. In the southern sector the defences were more slender. They were covered by about half the enemy armour, but this was the dispersion forced on Rommel by his petrol shortage.

Montgomery announced his plan for the battle as the destruction first of the enemy unarmoured formations and second of the hostile armour. He claimed this to be a reversal of the previous order of events and as his own idea. But, as we have seen, Auchinleck had already adopted this policy at the first battle of Alamein by striking first at the Italian infantry.

The second battle of Alamein was to open with a main attack in the northern sector by the 30th Corps and feint attacks in the south by the 13th Corps. The object of the main attack was to open two corridors through the minefields so that the armour of the 10th Corps could advance through them. The subsidiary attacks by the 13th Corps were intended to retain enemy forces, particularly the 21st Panzer Division, in that sector.

The 30th Corps attack was to be carried out by the 9th Australian, 51st Highland, 2nd New Zealand (with the 9th Armoured Brigade), and 1st South African Divisions. The 10th Corps, the exploiting force, consisted of the 1st, 8th and 10th Armoured Divisions, with, in reserve, the 5th Indian Infantry Brigade. In a holding position south of this attack was the 4th Indian Division, less one brigade. In the 13th Corps were the 7th Armoured Division, the 44th Home Counties Division, the 50th Northumbrian Division, the Free French Brigade Group and the Greek Brigade.

At 9.40 p.m. the second battle of Alamein opened with a bombardment of nearly a thousand guns—all the field and medium artillery of the 8th Army. In a short deluge of fire directed against located enemy batteries, nearly all the Axis guns were silenced. The firing then stopped for 5 minutes, before opening up once more at 10 p.m. against the enemy's forward positions. At the same time, under a full moon, the infantry of the 8th Army moved steadily forward to the attack.

Enemy opposition was stubborn, and it was daybreak before the southernmost of the two corridors was cleared. The 10th Armoured Division and the 9th Armoured Brigade therefore passed through in broad daylight and were held before the Miteiriya Ridge. The 10th Armoured Division had been partly delayed by petrol shortage. This was primarily due to tank crews keeping their engines running during the long stationary periods. In the congested traffic routes the replenishment of petrol proved difficult.

The 51st Division had been fighting slowly forward against stubborn resistance, and it was the afternoon of the 24th before the northern corridor was cleared and 1st Armoured Division, now a very efficient fighting formation, got through.

By the morning of 25th four armoured brigades, (the 2nd, 8th, 9th, and 24th) were deployed on the far side of the minefield. The enemy now counter-attacked strongly with the 15th Panzer Division and the *Littorio* Armoured Division, and lost some hundred tanks in the process. By the evening the 15th Panzer Division had only about thirty tanks left. In spite of this defensive success, however, the British armour was hemmed by the enemy anti-tank screen into a very restricted space and was unable to manoeuvre.

The next day the British armoured formations delivered a heavy attack against the ring contour named from the map "Kidney Ridge" (though the contour actually marked a depression). There was little progress and heavy tank casualties were caused by the enemy anti-tank guns. The 1st Armoured Division then attacked and captured the Kidney feature with its Motor Brigade.

On 27th October both the 15th and 21st Panzer Divisions were thrown into violent counter-attacks against Kidney. The bulk of these attacks fell on the 2nd Battalion The Rifle Brigade which knocked out thirty German tanks with its 6-pr guns. In all the Africa Corps lost fifty tanks in this unsuccessful attempt to recapture Kidney.

At this point in the battle there was a pause whilst Montgomery re-grouped his forces. The New Zealand and 1st Armoured Divisions were withdrawn into reserve. The 7th Armoured Division, (now no longer required by the 13th Corps owing to the failure to prevent the northward move of the 21st Panzer Division) was moved to the 10th Corps. Also from the 13th Corps came one brigade of the 44th Division and one brigade of the 50th Division. The former was placed under the command of the 7th Armoured Division and the latter went into the 30th Corps reserve.

The British armour had by now lost 200 tanks, but the 800 remaining were considerably more than the ninety which were all that were left to the Axis.

Rommel, who had been sick in Germany when the battle started, had by now returned, and was also re-grouping, with his armour disposed around the area of the main British attack.

On the night of 28th October the second phase of the battle started with the 9th Australian Division attacking northwards from the salient. This was only partially successful, and the tank regiment supporting the attack lost heavily. Further fighting in this area was indecisive and, moreover, the 90th Light Division had been moved near the coast to block any attempt at exploitation.

The 8th Army had now only sufficient reserve strength for one more big push. Montgomery, apparently, intended this final effort to be made as far to the north as possible. But Alexander's Chief of Staff, Major-General R. L. McCreery, insisted that the right point was just to the north of the northern-most corridor. This advice was accepted, and the British forces were once more re-grouped for a fresh attack on the original axis. The New Zealand Division was brought back into line, and all three armoured divisions were placed under the 10th Corps.

This, the third phase, started with an attack by the New Zealand Division with, under command, the 152nd Brigade (51st Division), the 151st Brigade (50th Division) and the 133rd Lorried Brigade (10th Armoured Division), and in support the 23rd Armoured Brigade and 360 guns. The attack made progress but was then held up by the anti-tank gun screen. The 9th Armoured Brigade was to go through when the first objective had been gained, but this was half an hour behind schedule, and it was dawn when the 9th Armoured charged through the 151st Brigade at the anti-tank gun screen on the Rahman track. It broke the screen, but was promptly counter-attacked by the enemy armour on both flanks and lost eighty-seven tanks. Nevertheless, it had knocked out a number of the anti-tank guns and held open a gap until the 1st Armoured Division (with the 8th Armoured Brigade under command) was able to pass through. After this gallant action the 9th Armoured Brigade had ceased to exist as a fighting force. But Montgomery had told the Brigade Commander that the forcing of this gap was of such importance that he must be prepared for a 100 per cent casualties.

After passing through the gap the 1st Armoured Division formed a defensive front and was then counter-attacked by the

Africa Corps from both north and south in an effort to pinch out the British penetration. This was the biggest armoured clash of the struggle and was known as the "Battle of Tel el Aqqaqir". The British tank loss was greater than that of the Germans, but the latter were left with only twenty-four tanks fit for action.

The next day, 3rd November, Rommel started to withdraw, but was ordered back by Hitler. At mid-day the 8th Armoured Brigade tried to get past Tel el Aqqaqir but was stopped by fire from hull-down tanks. The 51st Division, with the 23rd Armoured Brigade and the 5th Indian Brigade under command, then put in an attack to the south-west at 5.30 p.m.; but this failed with heavy loss.

That night the 5th Indian and the 154th Brigades, supported by one tank regiment and 360 guns, attacked in the same direction but more to the left. They hit the junction of the Africa Corps with the Italians, and at dawn they were through the enemy defences and 4,000 yards into open country. Through this gap and onwards rolled hundreds of British tanks.

Plate 47. THE BIGGEST TANK IN THE WORLD; THE 65-TON CONQUEROR ARMED WITH A 120-MM GUN.

Plate 18. THE CHIEFTAIN.

CHAPTER XVII

The Conquest of North Africa

THE opening of the pursuit after the second battle of El Alamein was curiously slow. There seemed to be little of O'Connor's sense of urgency without which successful exploitation is impossible. No properly organised pursuit started until 5th November and its subsequent conduct was indifferent. The armoured divisions tried to intercept Rommel by cut-off moves to the coast, but these moves were too slow and of too short a range to head off the fast running Axis columns. The Royal Air Force, instead of carrying out low-level attacks against the retreating enemy vehicles, made an ineffectual attempt to stop them by high-level bombing.

At Fuka, 60 miles west of Alamein, the 22nd Armoured Brigade caught up with the 21st Panzer Division, which had fifteen tanks left and no petrol. That night sufficient petrol reached the Germans for their wheeled vehicles and they slipped successfully away leaving the tanks behind.

On 6th and 7th November, when the head of the British advance was just east of Mersa Matruh, heavy rain bogged down all the vehicles which were pursuing across the desert, without hampering the Axis columns streaming along the coastal road.

A special pursuit force was now organised, consisting of the 7th Armoured Division and the New Zealand Division (the latter with the 9th Armoured Brigade still under command).

On 8th November the ground had dried out and the pursuit force got going. It might have been supposed that only supply difficulties would now stand in the way of a long and rapid desert move on the O'Connor model. But Montgomery forbade any "mad rush" forward. His reasons were, not only the possibility of outrunning supply, but also, surprisingly, that the pursuit force might give Rommel an opportunity for or : of his ripostes. Though it should have been clear to the 8th Army Intelligence staff that Rommel had nothing to riposte with. In fact the Africa Corps was now reduced to ten tanks and had insufficient petrol for any but the most limited action.

See map page 225.

On 11th November the 7th Armoured Division crossed into Cyrenaica, having covered 160 miles since 8th November, with the New Zealand Division one day behind. On 13th November the 22nd Armoured Brigade, of the 7th Armoured Division, entered Tobruk and then halted at El Adem for some days to carry out maintenance, the pursuit being continued by the 4th Light Armoured Brigade. Alexander, in his despatch, stated that Rommel's forces were withdrawing through the Djebel, and he commented that it was very tempting to drive across the desert to cut him off in the region of Agedabia; but Montgomery was determined to take no chances, and only armoured cars were allowed to take this route. This is a remarkable instance of the effect which the personality of a great commander, though in command of a vastly inferior force, can have on even a very able opponent.

The 22nd Armoured Brigade started off again on 18th November and one regiment reached Agedabia on 22nd November, having covered 260 miles over desert going. In the meantime the 4th Light Armoured Brigade had occupied Benghazi on 20th. On 23rd November the 7th Armoured Division was facing Rommel, who was back once more on his old positions about Agheila and Mersa Brega. Here he received reinforcements in the shape of the *Centauro* Armoured Division and elements of three Italian Infantry Divisions.

There was now a pause of a fortnight to bring up supplies and reinforcements for the pursuit force. The attack on the Agheila position was due to start on 15th December, but on 8th December it was apparent that the Italian troops were withdrawing. The attack was accordingly advanced to 13th December, and was launched after a heavy preliminary bombardment. However, there was nothing to hit as Rommel had evacuated the position on the night 12th/13th December. An attempt to intercept him failed.

On 16th December the pursuit force caught up with the Africa Corps near Merduma. The 7th Armoured Division attacked frontally whilst the New Zealand Division with its armoured brigade cut in behind the enemy and reached the coast. The Africa Corps had only sufficient fuel remaining for a direct attack, but on 17th December the German armour succeeded in forcing a way through the New Zealand curtain and getting away.

There was now a pause of a month at Notilia whilst the line

of communications was consolidated and the force replenished. The 8th Army was already 250 miles beyond its new advanced base at Benghazi.

In the meantime Rommel had deployed his forces on 29th December at Buerat. He had been reinforced from Tripoli but he was still much inferior in strength. He now had thirty-six German and fifty-seven Italian tanks to oppose the 8th Army's total of about 500 (magnified by the German Intelligence to 650). Nevertheless Rommel decided to stand and fight in a position where his defence would be assisted by some deep wadis. He intended, however, nothing more than a delaying action, and accordingly sent back the major portion of his infantry, the Italian, who were devoid of transport and thus incapable of conducting a rapid withdrawal.

On their side the British were suffering from supply difficulties and the forces which could be made available for an attack were limited to the 7th Armoured Division, the New Zealand Division and the 51st Highland Division.

On 15th January the British divisions advanced to the attack —the 51st astride of the coast road, whilst the 7th Armoured and the New Zealanders moved round the enemy's right flank. The 7th Armoured Division encountered the 15th Panzer Division in a sharp action. The 15th Panzer Division fell back in the direction of Tarhuna, and by the time the 51st Division attacked the remainder of Rommel's command were already withdrawing.

On 23rd January the 8th Army entered Tripoli. Further advance was now again held up by the administrative difficulties, and it was not till 17th February that British troops entered Medenine, beyond which the Axis forces were holding the formidable Mareth Line. By the following day the 7th Armoured and 51st Divisions were in the Medenine area.

During this approach march trouble had come to the Allies in the north where the 1st Army had been engaged with the massive German reinforcements which had been marshalled in Tunisia. On 15th February Rommel, who had taken back most of his armour from the Mareth Line, attacked the United States 2nd Corps with his own and Von Arnim's panzer divisions. The unpracticed American armour was routed with the loss of over a hundred tanks and chased through Kasserine Pass towards the Allied bases about Tebessa, endangering Allied positions further north. The German advance was finally checked by the

6th British Armoured Division. As a result of this disaster, Alexander (now in command of the 18th Army Group) requested assistance from the 8th Army to relieve the pressure. Montgomery accordingly ordered the 7th Armoured and 51st Divisions, together with the Free French contingent under the gallant General Leclerc, to probe the outer defences covering the Mareth Line. On 27th February these formations were reinforced by the New Zealand Division, the 8th Armoured Brigade, the 201st Guards Brigade, and part of the 50th Division.

By 5th March the 51st Division was deployed near the coast, the 7th Armoured Division was on its left, and inland on the extreme left was the New Zealand Division. Rommel had now returned and had three armoured divisions at his disposal. On 6th March he attacked with 160 tanks, but the British defence, which had over 400 tanks and 500 6-pr anti-tank guns, was too strong for him. The German attack was beaten off with the loss of over half their tanks, mainly from anti-tank gun fire.

The 8th Army was now faced with the formidable steel and concrete defences of the Mareth Line—built by the French to keep out the Italians and defended by the Germans and Italians against the British and Free French. In the coastal sector these defences had been constructed to make the maximum use of the Wadi Zigzaou, which had been formed by nature as an effective tank barrier. The inland flank.of the Mareth Line, 25 miles from the sea, rested at Toujane on the rugged Mahatma Hills. Twenty miles further west these hills dropped to a barren desert, and their north-western flank was protected against any hostile advance through this desert by a detached switch line covering the approach to El Hamma and the coast through the Tebaga Gap.

Montgomery's plan for the forcing of the Mareth Line comprised a frontal attack in the coastal sector combined with a wide out-flanking movement through the hills to cut the enemy's line of retreat about El Hamma.

The outflanking column was to consist of the New Zealand Corps (the New Zealand Division, the 8th Armoured Brigade, Leclerc's Free French contingent, an armoured car regiment and a regiment of medium artillery) followed in due course by the 1st Armoured Division.

On the night of 11th/12th March the New Zealand Corps started moving to its assembly area, about 30 miles south-west of Foum Tatahouine. This movement was completed on 18th

March, and the next day the advance started off westwards through a gap in the hills.

On 20th March the New Zealand Corps was approaching the Tebaga switch line. That night the 151st Brigade of the 50th Division attacked the enemy positions near the coast in order to draw the Axis reserves away from the route of advance of the New Zealanders. The brigade seized a bridgehead and the next day the 50th Royal Tank Regiment was pushed across the Wadi Zigzaou in support.

Most of the Africa Corps at this time was located south of Gabes in reserve. The Germans, however, reacted quickly to this threat and on the afternoon of 22nd they threw in thirty tanks and two infantry battalions against the bridgehead. The 50th Royal Tank Regiment, with most of its Valentines still fitted with 2-prs, fought at a disadvantage and by 5 p.m. they had lost about thirty tanks. By dawn on 23rd the 151st Brigade and the remainder of the 50th Royal Tank Regiment had withdrawn across the wadi. Nevertheless, for all its failure the attack had achieved part of its object, for it had kept the 15th Panzer Division away from the battle about the Tebaga Gap until 24th March.

On this same day of 23rd other forces were on the move to the west. The 1st Armoured Division started off to Foum Tatahouine on its way to join the New Zealand Corps and the 4th Indian Division began to move westwards to open a more direct route between the right and left flanks of the battle by seizing the Hallouf Pass.

Delayed 24 hours through having to await the passage of the 1st Armoured Division through the bottleneck of Medenine village, the 4th Indian Division eventually established themselves between Toujane and Mahatma by dawn on 28th. Moving quickly, they were on the outskirts of Gabes on the following day.

In the meantime, at 4 p.m. on 26th March the New Zealand Corps, with the 8th Armoured Brigade leading, had driven a hole through the Tebaga switch line, and through this went the 1st Armoured Division, heading for El Hamma 16 miles to the north.

The exploit of the 1st Armoured Division had been outstanding, for after a 200 mile approach march to join the New Zealand Corps, they had gone into battle within half an hour of their arrival. Their further advance to El Hamma took place in the dark and the town itself was reached at dawn. Large portions of the enemy had been left behind in this rapid advance and the divisional rear guard became engaged with some of these detachments which were trying to break through. In one of these little actions the 17-pr gun showed what it could do by knocking off the turret of a Pz. IV with one shot.

At El Hamma the enemy flank guards kept the 1st Armoured Division at bay until 29th, sufficiently long for the Axis troops to withdraw.

The enemy now retreated to the Wadi Akarit, a strong position south of the Tunisian plain. Here the Axis held a 12-mile front with one flank on the coast and the other on an impassable expanse of marsh and lakes. The position was dominated by a great rugged block of hills lying somewhat west of centre and rising to a maximum height of about 800 feet. From the eastern slopes of this feature an anti-tank ditch ran some 2 miles eastwards to another but much smaller height, the 500-foot high Roumana Ridge.

The central massif was seized by a brilliant night attack on 5th/6th April carried out by the 4th Indian Division under the command of Major-General F. I. S. Tuker. On the right of the 4th Indian Division the 50th and 51st Divisions attacked at 4.30 a.m. on 6th April, the former against the anti-tank ditch and the latter against the Roumana Ridge.

At 8.45 a.m. the Commander of the 10th Corps (1st and 7th Armoured Divisions) arrived · at Headquarters 4th Indian Division and Tuker pointed out that the way was clear for the armour to go through and finish the campaign in North Africa. The opportunity was not taken. It was not till 7 a.m. on 7th April that the 10th Corps started its advance and by that time the Germans had gone.

After this battle the 1st Armoured Division went off to join the 1st Army, and later on it was followed by the 7th Armoured Division, the 4th Indian Division and the 201st Guards Brigade.

The battle which was to herald the complete destruction of the Axis forces in North Africa took place east of Medjez el Bab in the valley of the Medjerda River. Two infantry divisions, the 4th on the right and the 4th Indian on the left, were to break the enemy's line. The 6th Armoured Division was then to drive through the 4th Division and the 7th Armoured Division through the 4th Indian Division. The 4th Indian Division had a regiment of 17-pr anti-tank guns at its disposal in case the new German Tiger tanks put in an appearance.

The attack had been planned to take place at dawn on 6th May, but at Tuker's insistence his division attacked on the night of the 5th/6th. The 4th Indian Division achieved complete surprise and by the morning the way was wide open for the armour to go through. The next day the 7th Armoured Division entered the city of Tunis and on 12th May all Axis resistance ceased in North Africa.

Apart from the lamentable episode of Dieppe in August 1942, the British Churchill infantry tank took part in active operations for the first time in North Africa. The origins of the Churchill lay in a specification, A20, for a successor to the Matilda. This design bore some outward resemblance to a First World War heavy tank, for there were sponsons on either side in which it was intended to mount 2-pr guns. Five prototypes were ready in mid-1940 but without any armament. That was as far as the A20 got, but it was used as the basis of a new design, the A22 or Mark IV Infantry Tank, which became the Churchill. The track suspension for this tank was derived from the old French B-1 Bis, and consisted of eleven small bogie wheels on each side, with each bogie independently sprung. Dr. H. E. Merritt, Director of Tank Design, worked at Vauxhall Motors Limited, together with Vauxhall engineers, on the design of the A22. After the evacuation from Dunkirk, and with the resulting acute shortage of military equipment, production of the new tank within 1 year was stated as an urgent requirement. And so, although design only started in July 1940, the first production models were delivered by June 1941. Such rapid production without proper field trials resulted inevitably in a crop of "teething" troubles, and it was a long time before the Churchill settled down into the reliable tank which it eventually became.

The first Churchill had frontal armour of 100-mm. thickness, but the 2-pr gun in the turret of this 38½-ton vehicle rather gave the impression of an elephant armed with a pea-shooter. In March 1942 the first Churchills fitted with 6-prs made their appearance, and units were getting these towards the end of the year. Three of them were tested at Alamein.

In the Tunisian campaign the Churchills, operating in close country, were very popular, and 120 of them were modified to take the 75-mm. guns as fitted to the Shermans. These modified Churchills were known as "NA 75's".

The Churchill carried a crew of five, had a range of 90 miles, and was powered by a 350-h.p. Bedford engine which gave it a speed of 15½ m.p.h. It was the last of the infantry tanks.

The Americans came into North Africa with their excellent M4 Medium, or Sherman, tank. This almost monopolised American tank production, for of 54,027 medium tanks built in the United States of America during the Second World War no less than 49,234 were M4's. The American armour made an unsuccessful debut in North Africa, but this was probably due to lack of training and the fact that the American army was going through an unfortunate period when the role of armour in battle was in dispute. There was a lot to be said for the American 1942-pattern armoured division. It consisted of a reconnaissance battalion, two armoured regiments (each of one light and two medium tank battalions), three battalions of self-propelled 105-mm. howitzers, and one armoured infantry regiment of three battalions carried in armoured half-track vehicles. For command in battle there were under divisional headquarters, two "combat commands", A and B, each of which was intended to assume command of any combination of divisional units. In 1943 American official thinking suddenly swung away from the idea of the armoured division as an assault formation, to a concept of a role somewhat similar to that of a cavalry division of the rifle era. Its employment in battle was considered to be limited to "pursuit and exploitation". As a result, a large portion of the tank strength was removed from the armoured divisions and allotted to the close support of the infantry. In addition the armoured divisions themselves were tied more closely to the infantry by their incorporation into corps, each consisting of one armoured and two infantry divisions.

The existence of a new German tank, the Tiger, has already been mentioned. This formidable 56-ton tank was produced as an answer to the Russian KV heavy tank and was first used on the Russian front in August 1942. The first mark had faults and a re-design was undertaken after experience with the first few. The Mark II was the most powerful tank in any of the contending armies, and it arrived in Tunisia early in 1943. It was armed with an 88-mm. gun and two 7·92-mm. machine-guns, had armour of 26–102 mm., and a speed, from a V-12 600-h.p. Maybach engine, of 25 m.p.h. Its great width of 12 feet 3 inches made it an out of gauge load on all railways and special arrangements had to be made for rail transport. It had one great disadvantage, for, unlike most German tanks, it was not mechanically reliable. Fortunately for the Allies, perhaps, there were not many Tigers in Tunisia and their influence on the course of the battle was slight.

The campaign in North Africa was one of the most interesting in the history of war, and from O'Connor's lightning victories till the capitulation of the German armies in Tunisia it was coloured by such clash of cavalry on the battlefield as had not been seen since the Napoleonic wars. It was a period when many leaders were feeling their way with this new type of cavalry, and when all too few had a clear appreciation of its nature. As we have seen there was a school of thought on the British side which held that an armoured brigade was akin to a fleet at sea and that it should manoeuvre and be employed as such. The disasters in the Western Desert were largely due to this misconception. O'Connor, on the other hand, saw that he had the mounted arm of a soldier's dream, and with his highly trained regular troops he made brilliant use of it.

It was Rommel who retaught later British commanders the lessons of Crecy and Agincourt, showing them the proper association of tanks and anti-tank guns—these latter day descendants of the mounted chivalry and longbowmen of the mediaeval English armies.

Only one British soldier demonstrated his ability to defeat Rommel on level terms, and that was Auchinleck. O'Connor, unfortunately, never had the chance, and Wavell never commanded in the field. Montgomery never fought him except with overwhelming superiority in strength.

One of the major difficulties which British commanders had to contend with was Winston Churchill's consistent failure to appreciate that against a first class army with first class equipment only full trained formations will do. If Rommel's Italian troops were of mixed quality, his Germans were excellent: trained to perfection and led by commanders with a sound knowledge of armoured warfare. Auchinleck had the best soldier material in the world, but his troops were all too often forced into battle for political reasons without being properly trained, and they were all too often led by commanders without the requisite ability for this fast moving mechanical conflict.

CHAPTER XVIII

The Invasion of Russia

O N 22nd June 1941, whilst Auchinleck was striving to roll
back Rommel's first tide of victory, the Germans launched
their attack on Russia.

In theory the vast mass of Russian tanks should have been
well able to deal with the onslaught of the formidable panzer
divisions. By 1941 the Russians had over 22,000 tanks, which
was a greater number than there were in all the other armies in
the world put together, and about four times as many as the
Germans had. The T-26's and BT's were still standard equipment and formed the bulk of the Russian armour. In addition
there were the multi-turret T-28 medium and T-35 heavy tanks.
All these were described in Chapter IX, and in 1941 they were
obsolescent. However, at the time of the German attack new
and vastly improved tanks, about which the Germans knew
nothing, were already in service in some quantity. There were
two types, the T-34 medium and the KV heavy. Both were
noteworthy on account of a well-shaped exterior, thick armour
and a heavy gun. They were, indeed, very fine fighting
machines, but there were certain disadvantages. The accommodation was cramped and tiring for the crew, there were no aids for
control, shooting and driving, mechanical failures were too
frequent, and vision was poor.

With all the above disadvantages, the T-34 was probably a
better tank than any in the possession of either the Germans or
the Western Allies. It was at first armed with a 1939 model
76·2-mm. gun 30·5 calibres long, which was a normal length
for a 75-mm. field gun. This was later replaced by the 1940
model of the 76·2-mm., which was 41·5 calibres in length and
had a muzzle velocity of 2,172, making it roughly comparable to
the 75-mm. of the Sherman. Like the BT from which it was
evolved, the T-34 had a Christie-type suspension. It was
powered by a V-12 diesel engine of 500 h.p. giving it a road
speed of 30 m.p.h. The armour varied between 20 mm. on
the belly and 75 mm. on the turret.

See map page 229.

The 46-ton KV heavy tank was also armed at first with the 1939 model of the 76·2 mm., and later with the 1940 version. The first KV's were used in the Russo-Finnish war of 1939–40. The KV had the same engine as the T-34, and therefore the slower speed of between 20 and 25 m.p.h. It's armour varied from 20 mm. to 100 mm. (There was a more heavily armed, but clumsier, version, the KV II, which was a failure and had a short life.)

The T-34 became eventually the most numerous of Russian tanks, and was used both in armoured formations and for close infantry support.

In 1940 the Russians introduced new organisations for their armoured and mechanised formations. A tank division consisted of two tank regiments (totalling 400 tanks), a motorised infantry regiment, and an artillery regiment. A motorised infantry division was organised similarly but had two infantry regiments and one tank regiment. Two tank divisions and one infantry division formed a tank corps. It had been intended that twenty tank corps should be formed by the autumn of 1941; but the German attack came before the re-organisation was anywhere near complete.

Compared with the enormous number of Russian tanks, the Germans at the time of their invasion of Russia had (excluding those captured from the French) about 5,300 tanks of all types. Of these some 3,200 were available for deployment against Russia, but there was an annual output of only about 1,000 behind them to replace wastage. Apart from their potential tank weakness, the Germans were suffering from such fuel shortage that not only were the number of motorised formations limited but much of the infantry divisional transport was horsed. The organisation of the panzer division was similar to that used against the British in North Africa.

The country with which the German panzer divisions were faced was very different to the Western Desert. The terrain was, indeed, wide and flat and much of it very open. But there were great areas of forest and swamp, and wide rivers which were bridged infrequently, and then by structures generally too frail for the passage of a tank. Most of the few roads were mere unmetalled tracks, which in dry weather were covered with a fine dust which clogged engines, and in wet weather became impassable ditches of mud. But it was the climate which was to ruin the fighting ability of the German army, as it had that of

Napoleon's *Grande Armée* 130 years before. For Hitler had calculated on a short summer campaign, and no provision had been made for winter clothing for the soldier nor for the protection of vehicles and weapons. As it happened the Russians could have been knocked out before the onset of winter, and it was only through the stupidity of Hitler and the brutality of Himmler's Gestapo that the German Army was denied decisive victory.

The German plan envisaged the adoption of the same major tactics which had served them so well in the West; that is, deep penetration and envelopment by the armoured formations combined with a frontal advance by the infantry mass.

The ultimate objective of the campaign was given as the line of the River Volga and thence north to Archangel, thus putting German territory beyond the range of the Russian bomber aircraft.

The offensive would be divided naturally into two halves by the immense barrier of the Pripet Marshes. Of the two army groups operating north of the Pripet Marshes, that on the right had the principal role. It was to break out of the area around Warsaw and destroy all the Russian armies in White Russia. The left army group was to advance from East Prussia in the direction of Leningrad, and it was to be joined by mobile troops from the army group on its right after success in White Russia. The objectives then were to be Leningrad followed by Moscow. The southern army group, advancing from Lublin, was given the general direction of Kiev, with the task of destroying the Russians on the line of the River Dnieper and then occupying the economically important Donetz Basin.

For this campaign the German forces were organised into three army groups, designated respectively North, Centre and South. Army Group North was commanded by Field Marshal von Leeb and consisted of the 18th Army (General von Küchler), the 16th Army (General Busch), and the 4th Armoured Group (General Hoeppner)—a total of twenty infantry divisions, three armoured divisions, and three motorised divisions. Army Group Centre, with the largest armoured component, was under the command of Field Marshal von Bock. In it were the 9th Army (General Strauss) and the 4th Army (General Kluge). With the 9th Army was associated the 3rd Armoured Group (General Hoth), and with the 4th Army the 2nd Armoured Group (General Guderian). In Army Group Centre there were a total of thirty-one infantry divisions, nine armoured divisions, seven motorised divisions, and, curiously, a horsed cavalry division. Field Marshal von Rundstedt commanded Army Group South, in which were the 6th Army (Field Marshal von Reichenau), the 17th Army (General von Stuelpnagel) and the 1st Armoured Group (General von Kleist. Of German troops, von Rundstedt had, all told, thirty infantry divisions, five armoured divisions, and four motorised divisions. In addition, however, he had the 3rd Italian Corps, a Hungarian Corps and a Slovak Division. Also, attached to him, were the 11th German/ Rumanian Army, the 3rd Rumanian Army, and the 4th Rumanian Army with the task of protecting the right flank of the attack. In general reserve to the whole German force were twenty-four infantry divisions, two armoured divisions, and two motorised divisions. The three army groups were supported, respectively, by the 1st, 2nd, and 4th Air Fleets.

To meet this formidable onslaught the Russians had no defensive plans at all. Their forces were strung out along the 1941 frontier without any reserve formations behind. The Russian Army at this stage, too, was neither very good nor very confident. Only 3 years had elapsed since Stalin's brutal purge had liquidated about 400, or half, of the Army's senior officers from brigade commander upwards, including many of the most able of Russian professional soldiers.

The Russian forces in the West were distributed into four groups. In the north was the Finnish Group (General Meretzkov) in the neighbourhood of Lake Ladoga, and so deployed as to renew the contest with Finland if necessary. It consisted of twenty infantry divisions, two cavalry divisions and five armoured brigades. Covering Leningrad and stationed in Lithuania and Latvia was the Baltic Group (Marshal Voroshilov) of nineteen infantry divisions, seven cavalry divisions and five armoured brigades. In the centre, about East Poland and Bielorussia, was the Bielorussian Group (Marshal Timoshenko) of fifty infantry divisions and two armoured brigades. Its primary task was to cover Moscow. Covering the Ukraine, in South-East Poland and Bessarabia, was the largest of the four Groups, the Ukrainian (Marshal Budienny), with sixty-nine infantry divisions, eleven cavalry divisions and twenty-eight armoured brigades.

The German attack opened at 3.15 a.m. on 22nd June with a heavy artillery barrage on the front of Army Group Centre.

At 3.50 a.m. the dive bombers of the 2nd Air Fleet went screaming into the attack. At 4.15 a.m. the 3rd Armoured Group, starting from Suvalki, and the 2nd Armoured Group, from Brest Litovsk, drove forward. They were to curve in and west of Minsk, some 200 miles away, with the object of encircling the whole of Marshal Timoshenko's Bielorussian Group. The attack took the Russians completely by surprise, and on 26th June, 4 days after it had started, Hoth's 3rd Armoured Group was around Minsk. The next day Guderian joined him with the 2nd Armoured Group and Timoshenko was surrounded. The climax came on 3rd July when in the battle of Bialystock-Minsk the Bielorussian Group was crushed with a loss to the Russians of 290,000 men taken prisoner, 2,585 tanks and 1,449 guns. This amazing victory gained by an armoured penetration and encirclement some 200 miles in depth, had been won within 11 days of the start of the campaign.

In the meantime the Germans had also been advancing on either wing. Army Group North had captured Dvinsk, and was across the Dvina, and Army Group South was over the River Bug and advancing on Latsk and Rovno.

On 7th July, after 3 days pause, Army Group Centre's panzer divisions were off again. Hoth moved on the left via Vitebsk, and Guderian on the right advanced via Mogilev and Orsha. Smolensk was occupied by Guderian on 16th July and Elnya, fifty miles south-east of it, on 22nd. At Elnya the Russians counter-attacked unsuccessfully, and Hoth, coming in towards Smolensk from the north completed another encirclement. In less than a month the two armoured groups had now advanced over 400 miles and had twice encircled the opposing Russian armies. Having regard to the country which had been traversed, it was an astounding achievement. The battle of Smolensk which now ensued cost the Russians another 185,487 prisoners, 2,030 tanks and 1,918 guns, by the time it ended on 8th August.

Whilst Army Group Centre was engaged in this great battle, Army Group North had broken through the Russian defences and was advancing on Novgorod, to cut Leningrad's communications with the interior, and Army Group South was driving rapidly towards Kiev.

At this juncture, when the complete defeat of Russia was as certain as anything can be in war, Hitler made the first of two blunders which assured the eventual salvation of his enemy and his own ruin. The first, his Directive 33, was a strategical blunder. The second, his unleashing of Himmler's brutal Gestapo into the Ukraine, was a political blunder; for it turned a people, who had been greeting the Germans as their liberators from Communism, into their bitter opponents and into enthusiastic supporters of Russia's fight.

Directive 33 halted Army Group Centre and removed its armour to assist in the operations of the two German wings. It thus saved Moscow, the great rail centre and hub of the country, which must otherwise have fallen to the Germans before the end of September.

This disastrous order dispatched Hoth north to cut the Russian communications between Leningrad and Moscow (thereby preventing interference with the attack on Leningrad) and Guderian south to join in Army Group South's planned encirclement of the Russian forces in the Kiev area.

In the meantime the twice-beaten Timoshenko, struggling back from Smolensk, had managed to save some half-million men from the wreckage of his armies, and with these he was hastily organising a defence of Moscow. In this task he was assisted by Hitler's refusal to agree to a continuation of the offensive against Moscow. He insisted that the objectives were Leningrad and the Ukraine, and that, in addition, the Crimea must be seized to prevent the Russians bombing the Rumanian oilfields.

Army Group South's intention was to destroy Marshal Budienny, whose Ukrainian Group lay in a great salient stretching nearly 300 miles from Trubechevsk in the north to Kremenchug in the south. The Army Group plan envisaged an outer encirclement of the enemy by armoured formations and an inner one by infantry formations.

To carry out this plan the 6th Army was to pin the enemy in front whilst the 2nd Army on its left attacked south from about Gomel and the 17th Army struck north from Cherkasy. Beyond this, in a wider swing, the 2nd and 1st Armoured Groups, respectively, were to advance southwards from Trubechevsk on Lokhvitsa, and northwards from Kremenchug on Lubny, the two groups meeting about 125 miles east of Kiev.

Tactically, if measured in terms of prisoners and booty, the battle (which lasted from 25th August to 26th September), was the greatest German victory in Russia. Strategically, according to Hitler's chief-of-staff, General Halder, it was "the greatest blunder of the eastern campaign". The enormous Russian losses included 665,000 prisoners, 3,719 guns, and nearly 900 tanks.

In the north things had not been going so well, for the Germans had twice failed to take Leningrad by assault. Hitler decided, therefore, to invest the city and go for Moscow after all. He was too late. The month spent fighting the battle of Kiev was too expensive in terms of the remaining campaigning weather. Nevertheless, it was a near thing; for the new battle, with Moscow as the objective, was planned with the customary German skill and was another brilliant tactical victory.

Army Group Centre was again to attack the battered Timoshenko, and Army Groups North and South were directed to reinforce it with armour. In this battle the enemy's centre was to be broken and the two halves encirlced. The immediate objectives were Viasma and Briansk. The 4th Army, with the 4th Armoured Group on its right, was to break through the Russian centre and then wheel north on Viazma. On the left wing the 9th Army, with the 3rd Armoured Group on its left, was to swing south towards Viazma. On the right wing the 2nd Army, with the 2nd Armoured Group on its right, had the task of enveloping Briansk. Army Groups North and South were to help; the former by covering the left flank and the latter by advancing on Kharkov.

The battle opened on 30th September on a front of over 300 miles. Guderian's 2nd Armoured Group, achieving complete surprise, broke right through the Russian defences, and by the next day had advanced 85 miles. On 2nd October the main attack was launched by the 9th and 4th Armies and by the following evening the Germans had advanced some 30 miles. On 4th October the 3rd and 4th Armoured Groups were converging on Viazma, whilst the 2nd Armoured Group, capturing Mitsensk with a detachment, was pushing towards Briansk. By 8th October the German pincers had closed on both Viazma and Briansk, and Timoshenko had suffered his third disaster. By the time mopping up had been completed on 20th October the Russians had lost 663,000 men taken prisoner, 5,412 guns and 1,242 tanks. Forward German troops were now at Mozhaisk, only 65 miles from Moscow.

But, as the battle drew to a close, the rain came down in sheets. The roads dissolved into liquid mud and the rapid German exploitation of their victory was brought to a halt. Moscow was saved.

In the south, where the weather had not yet affected operations, Army Group South gained a major success about the Azov Sea and captured 100,000 prisoners.

Von Kleist's and Guderian's commands now became the 1st and 2nd Armoured Armies respectively.

On the night of 3rd/4th November there was the first frost and a great drop in temperature. The roads now became usable again, but the unfortunate German soldiers without any winter clothing began to suffer from the cold. Nevertheless, tanks and transport could move again and preparations were made for the final assault on Moscow. The 4th Army, with thirty-six divisions, was to attack directly towards Moscow, whilst the armoured groups of Holt and Hoeppner were to envelop Moscow from the north and west respectively and Guderian's armoured army was to do the same thing from the south. Flank protection was the responsibility of the 9th Army on the left and of the 2nd Army on the right.

On 16th November in the bitter cold the half-frozen German troops advanced to a nearly impossible task. The 4th Army became engaged almost immediately in severe fighting and struggled slowly forward with difficulty. On the left flank Holt reached the Moscow-Volga Canal only 14 miles from Moscow on 28th November, with a tantalising view of the Kremlin towers; Hoeppner was just short of Zvietkova, about 25 miles west of Moscow; and Guderian, on the left, was nearing Columna, some 70 miles south-east of Moscow. The armoured wings, however, were getting dangerously isolated from the 4th Army. On 2nd December the advance of the 4th Army finally came to a halt in the forests round Moscow, with a few parties of troops actually in the suburbs of the city. The next day the 4th Army started to withdraw, and on 5th, the temperature being minus 32 degrees, Guderian decided that he would have to retreat.

The cold beat the Germans; not the Russians. The attack had been an astounding feat of endurance, but the 4th Army was now incapable of any further effort. Thousands of soldiers were incapacitated by frostbite, hundreds were frozen to death, and the intense cold put out of action weapons, aircraft, tanks and transport.

Marshal Zhukov, now commanding in the Moscow sector, followed up the German withdrawal with a vigorous counter-stroke. He now had many divisions from Siberia under his command, and these fresh and acclimatised troops broke through the German defence in several places. Everywhere along the long front the Russians were advancing and the Germans gradually withdrew into fortified areas based on supply depots where some shelter could be provided for the freezing troops.

When the year 1941 came to an end the Russian casualties probably amounted to the incredible figure of about 3,000,000. On their part the Germans had lost some 830,000 men, a very large proportion of their original strength, and, far worse, Hitler had ruined the fighting spirit of his army. It was still to fight well and stubbornly in Russia but it never regained the dash and drive of the formidable force which had so nearly shattered the Communist regime.

The original Russian armoured forces were practically wiped out in the battles of 1941. The German high command identified thirty-five Russian tank divisions as having been destroyed and another thirty as so depleted that they had been disbanded.

The halt and recession of the German offensive gave the Russians a breathing space to build up their armoured formations. They needed no incentive, for the seemingly irresistible power of the panzer divisions had been, as in the West, the dominant feature of the campaign. The excellent T-34 tank was now coming out in quantities from the Ural factories, and from the Western allies the Russians received over 12,000 tanks, including Matildas, Churchills, Tetrarchs, Valentines, Stuarts, Grants and Shermans. Fresh armoured units were rushed up from the interior and new ones were formed with picked troops. The basic formation of the new armoured force was the brigade. This, it was intended, should consist of a tank regiment of three small mixed battalions, a motorised machine-gun battalion, an anti-tank gun company and a mortar company. Lack of resources precluded the complete implementation of this establishment. Many of the brigades had only two tank battalions with the modest strength of twenty-three tanks each, and the infantry element was generally a rifle and not a machine-gun battalion.

The next higher echelon above the tank brigade was the tank corps. This was a variable organisation, but it normally comprised three tank brigades, a motorised rifle brigade, corps artillery and other troops. In striking power it was roughly the equivalent of a panzer division. There was also a mechanised corps of three motorised rifle brigades and one tank brigade.

Tank armies were formed which included corps of both these types. The number of tank brigades grew rapidly, and by the end of the war the Germans had identified 258, of which forty-nine were manned by troops of the Guard.

The new Russian tanks had impressed the Germans and specifications were produced for new heavy and medium tanks which should be a match for them. In the meantime, in 1942, Pz. III's and IV's with the long 50-mm. and 75-mm. guns respectively were drafted to the Eastern Front.

The German reply to the KV was the 56-ton Tiger Mark I, a total of 1,350 of which were built. By the autumn of 1942, as a result of battle experience, a new 68-ton version was produced, the Tiger Mark II, armed with an improved and formidable 88-mm. gun. Its calibre length was 71, and it had a muzzle velocity of 3,340 (3,708 with APCR ammunition).

The new German medium tank, the Panther, was inspired by the T-34 and had its distinctive sloping armour. It weighed 45 tons and was armed with a new 75-mm. gun with a calibre length of 70 and a muzzle velocity of 3,068. It appeared first in action in November 1942.

In 1943 Tigers and Panthers were produced in quantity and they were better than any tanks possessed either by the Russians or by the Western Allies.

By the winter of 1943–44 the Russians had evolved an improved model of the T-34 which they hoped would be more than a match for the Panther. It had a three-man turret and a long 85-mm. gun, adapted from their 1939 model anti-aircraft gun and comparable with the original German 88-mm. This new tank was known as the T-34/85. It was not, in fact, as good as the Panther, but with its powerful gun it was better than contemporary British and American tanks.

The new turret and gun was also fitted to the KV, which became the KV-85, but this was soon superseded by a new heavy tank built up on the KV chassis. This was the JS (Joseph Stalin) I with a 122-mm. gun and the remarkably low weight of 46 tons. It suffered, however, from the usual Russian tank troubles of insufficient space, with consequent discomfort for the crew and inadequate supply of ammunition. Its armour thickness varied from 30 to 110 mm. and it had a speed of 20 m.p.h. It was followed by a slightly modified version, the JS II. At the end of the war there was an improved mark, the JS III, in which the turret had been redesigned, and the maximum armour thickness and the speed had been increased to 200 mm. and 23 m.p.h. respectively.

In the later stages of the war the Germans and Russians were making very similar tactical use of their heavy and medium tanks. An attack against strong defences was usually led by the medium tanks, whilst the heavy tanks supported them from behind with their big guns.

CHAPTER XIX

Normandy and After

IN the invasion of Normandy in June 1944, a new tank entered the field for the first time; this was the British equivalent of the German Panther, the 27½-ton and 38-m.p.h. Cromwell.

The Cromwell was a descendant of the Crusader, and its descent had been long and laborious. Already before the end of 1940 the first steps had been taken towards the provision of a successor to the Crusader, and it was intended that it should mount a 6-pr gun and be protected by armour of a maximum thickness of 76 mm. Great cross-country speed was also considered to be essential, and it was hoped that the necessary power could be supplied by a suitable modification to the very successful Rolls-Royce Merlin aircraft engine. Unfortunately it was apparent that by the time the proposed tanks could be produced there was no prospect of any of these engines being available. The A24, or Cromwell Mark I, was therefore fitted with a Nuffield Liberty engine, giving it the modest speed of 24 m.p.h., which was slower than the Crusader. Presumably as its performance would not come up to the specification required for a Cromwell, its name was changed to Cavalier—a perhaps unnecessary slight on Price Rupert's Royalist cavalry. Only two or three hundred were built, and none went into action as gun-armed tanks.

The Cavalier was followed by the Cromwell Mark II, with the same hull and turret but with a better suspension. Its interior layout and the position of the radiator were designed to take the modified Merlin engine. None of these engines could yet be provided, but when they were fitted to the anticipated Cromwell Mark III little change in production would be needed. The Cromwell Mark II also had a Nuffield Liberty engine, and thus its name too was changed to Centaur, but with no possible offence to anybody. The Centaurs went into action as tanks rather accidently. Eighty were armed with 95-mm. howitzers and issued to the Royal Marines Armoured Support

See map page 230.

Group with a purely naval bombardment task. They were to support the landings on the Normandy coast whilst shackled to landing craft offshore. This did not apparently suit the Royal Marines, for the Centaurs shook off their shackles and followed the infantry inland.

The first real Cromwell appeared as a pilot model, the A27M, in January 1942. After trials it was apparently considered worthy of the name and genuine Cromwells were being turned out from the factory 12 months later.

There was a Cromwellian vogue at one stage of the war, and the name of this singularly unpleasant regicide soldier was applied in various directions. Cromwell's "plain russet-coated soldier who knew what he fought for and loved what he knew" was quoted ad nauseam to and received with ribald comment by the British soldiery.

The Merlin engine, as modified for the Cromwell tank, was re-named Meteor. Its performance was outstanding and the Cromwell was one of the fastest tanks of the war—too fast in fact for even its Christie suspension, and in later models the maximum speed was geared down to 32 m.p.h.

The Cromwell had a crew of five and an operational range of 165 miles. Its armour varied in thickness from 76 mm. to 8 mm., though in some later welded tanks this was increased respectively to 101 mm. and 11 mm. The earliest Marks, I to III, were armed with a 6-pr gun, as originally intended, together with two Besa machine-guns. It was soon apparent, however, that this gun was now too light and in Marks IV, V and VII a medium velocity 75-mm. was substituted for the 6-pr. The new gun was, however, still much inferior to the latest German 75-mm. tank gun. Two marks of Cromwell, VI and VIII, were armed with 95-mm. howitzers for close support.

The design of the Cromwell had been worked out by the Birmingham Railway Carriage and Wagon Company, in conjunction, as regards the engine, with Rolls-Royce. The former company were entrusted in 1942 with modifying the Cromwell to provide a tank which would increase the fire power of the armoured regiment. This new tank, entitled the Challenger, had the Meteor engine and the same speed (32 m.p.h.) of the later Cromwells. It was armed, however, with the much better 17-pr (76·2 mm.); of which the muzzle velocity of 2,950 approximated to the 3,068 of the Panther's 75-mm. The armour varied between 102 and 20 mm., there was a co-axially mounted ·30 machine-gun, and the suspension was improved. A few Challengers were used in the campaign in North-west Europe but their performance, in spite of the good gun, was disappointing.

Experience in North Africa had shown that the 75-mm. tank gun was fast becoming outmoded. In July 1943 Leyland Motors (by then undertaking the production of Centaurs and Cromwells) were given the task of designing a tank to carry a 17-pr gun. Previous 17-pr tanks, the Sherman Fireflies and the Challengers, had been modifications of existing designs. In the new tank, which was entitled the Comet, the layout and engine of the successful Cromwell were retained. Since welding of Cromwells had proved successful, the hull was all welded and the armour thickness could be increased to 101 mm./14 mm. without impairing performance. The gun was actually a modified 17-pr (called a 77-mm.) with a shorter barrel and the rather lower muzzle velocity of 2,575. In action it proved to be a good and accurate gun. The Comet weighed 32½ tons, had a speed of 29 m.p.h. and a range of 123 miles, and it was manned by a crew of five.

The first prototype was ready for test in February 1944 and Comets were reaching units in the following September. It was not until after the crossing of the Rhine in the final stages of the war in Europe that the Comet went into action, when it soon proved itself to be the finest British tank of the war.

In 1942, whilst the Cromwell was still undergoing its field trials, it was suddenly decided that the solution to the tank problem was to have only one basic tank but to make it in two types—one a cruiser tank for exploitation and the other a heavily armoured tank for infantry support. In pursuance of this idea a design was prepared for a Cromwell with 114-mm. armour weighing some 40 tons. Only one, the A33, was actually built, and then the new idea, like so many, died as quickly as it had been conceived.

Most of the tanks with which the British armoured divisions were equipped for the invasion were the Sherman "Fireflies" with their 17-pr guns. At the time they were the most formidable tanks in the Allied armies. All the armoured reconnaissance regiments of the armoured divisions had the fast Cromwells, as also, except for a few Fireflies, did the 22nd Armoured Brigade of the 7th Armoured Division.

Two major alterations had been made to the British armoured

division; one was the substitution of an armoured reconnaissance regiment with tanks in place of the armoured car regiment, and the other was the equipment of one of the two field artillery regiments and half the anti-tank regiment with self-propelled guns.

The number of armoured divisions in the British Army, however, had dropped considerably. As compared with a peak of eleven there were now only five. A principal reason for this was the return of a recurrent heresy that armoured divisions were only suitable for exploitation. Many of the armoured regiments made available by the disbandment of armoured divisions had been allotted to infantry support.

One very important addition to the British tank armoury was the swimming, or "Duplex-Drive" (DD), tank. This device had first been tried out successfully in 1941, and subsequently a number of Valentines had been fitted with it for training. For the invasion force some hundreds of Shermans were converted into DD tanks. The term "duplex-drive" meant that the tank was fitted with a propeller at the rear powered by the tank's bevel drive. Round the hull there was a deck to which was attached the bottom of a canvas screen. When raised by compressed air this formed a hull from which the tank was suspended in the water. Viewed from the shore the swimming tank looked like a small boat, and hence was inconspicuous amongst the mass of craft of an invasion fleet. Once the tank reached the shore the screen would be collapsed immediately and it could drive straight into action.

The American armoured units which landed in Normandy were still equipped with the M4 medium, or Sherman, tanks armed with the 75-mm. gun. A few months before the operation, however, steps were taken to produce a more powerful version. An experimental tank had been under development and a turret and 76-mm. gun which had been designed for it were fitted to some of the Shermans. It was not until after the invasion of Germany, however, that a few of them were ready to go into action. In the meantime work on the experimental tank proceeded, but it was developed as a heavy tank with a 90-mm. gun and entitled the M26, or Pershing. Some of these 41-ton tanks arrived in Europe in time to take part in the final battles of the war in Europe. The Pershing was powered by a Ford GAA eight-cylinder 500-h.p. petrol engine which gave it a speed of 20 m.p.h. The secondary armament consisted of a ·5 machine-gun and two ·30 machine-guns. A valuable feature was the low silhouette which it presented for its size.

The French armoured division had American equipment, but the organisation was French. Under divisional headquarters were three armoured groups, each composed of an armoured regiment, an infantry battalion, and a group of self-propelled 105-mm. howitzers. The divisional troops included an armoured regiment equipped with American M10 tank destroyers, and a reconnaissance regiment equipped with armoured cars and light tanks.

By 1944 the armoured establishment of most of the German panzer divisions was pretty low. The standard panzer division had only two tank battalions (of which one generally had Panthers and the other Pz. IV's), only one out of its three artillery battalions was equipped with self-propelled guns, and only one out of four infantry battalions had armoured carriers. Tank battalions now had only one type of tank, instead of, as in the earlier practice, being mixed units. The establishment of a tank battalion was four companies of twenty-two tanks each. In practice strengths were generally much lower and a normal complement was three tank companies of seventeen tanks each. By the end of the war the company strength had dropped to fourteen tanks. Some of the 1944 panzer divisions, however, still had three tank battalions, and some of the more favoured formations were on a special, or higher, establishment. In the *Grossdeutschland* Division, for instance, there were four tank battalions, of which one was equipped with Tigers, and six infantry battalions. The *Panzer Lehr* Division, which was to take a prominent part in the Normandy fighting, had only two tank battalions (though with four companies each) but there was a divisional headquarters company of Tigers, its infantry battalions had half-track armoured carriers, and all its artillery units had self-propelled guns.

SS divisions were better off than those belonging to the Army, because for political reasons they were given priority in equipment and personnel reinforcements. The first SS panzer divisions were formed in 1943 from existing SS panzer grenadier divisions. (A panzer grenadier division was a motorised infantry division with a tank battalion.) In 1944 there were twenty-five army panzer divisions and eight SS.

At the time of the Allied invasion of Normandy the German forces in France and the Low Countries consisted of two army groups and an armoured group known as Panzer Group West. In overall command was Field-Marshal von Rundstedt. Of the two army groups, the more important was Army Group B under the command of the British Army's old desert opponent, Field Marshal Rommel. It was composed of the 15th Army (General von Salmuth) of four corps totalling seventeen divisions, deployed between Antwerp and the River Orne in Normandy; the 7th Army (General Dollman) holding the coast between the mouths of the Orne and the Loire, consisting of three corps (of which one was stationed in the Channel Islands) made up of fifteen divisions; and the 88th Corps (General Christiansen) of three divisions, which was garrisoning the Netherlands. Of these thirty-five infantry divisions, twenty-five were stretched along the coast and ten were held back in reserve. Three of the reserve divisions were south of the Seine.

The other army group, G, was commanded by General Blaskowitz. There were two small sized armies, the 1st with five divisions which was responsible for the Biscay coast from the Loire to the Pyrenees, and the 19th with eight divisions watching the Mediterranean coast between Perpignon and Mentone.

Panzer Group West was under the command of General Baron Geyr von Scheppenburg, but his responsibilities were confined to administration and training, and he had no operational function. In the group were ten panzer divisions located as follows: the 1st SS Panzer Division (*Leibstandarte Adolf Hitler*) at Beverloo in Belgium, the 2nd Panzer Division at Amiens, the 116th Panzer Division east of Bonn, the 12th SS Panzer Division (*Hitler Jugend*) at Lisieux, the 21st Panzer Division at Caen, the *Panzer Lehr* Division at Orleans, the 17th SS Panzer Division at Poitiers, the 11th Panzer Division at Bordeaux, the 2nd SS Panzer Division (*Das Reich*) at Toulouse, and the 9th Panzer Division at Avignon. Of these, four were under Rommel's command: the 116th, 12th SS, 21st, and 2nd SS; but the only one he could touch without Hitler's permission was the 21st. The remaining six panzer divisions were in Supreme Headquarters reserve.

Most of von Rundstedt's infantry divisions were below normal German standards and they were handicapped by having mainly horse-drawn transport. In addition, the available air support was weak, for Field-Marshal Sperrle's 3rd Air Fleet, stationed in France, had only ninety bombers and seventy fighters.

In June 1944 there were in the United Kingdom fourteen British divisions, three Canadian, twenty American, one French, and one Polish—a total of thirty-nine armoured and infantry divisions. This was the same number as Rommel had at his disposal, including the four panzer divisions. But comparing the number of divisions in opposing armies is, if popular, a most inaccurate method of arriving at a true assessment of their relative strength. The Allied divisions were far stronger than the German in manpower, and an Allied armoured division had a greater number of tanks than the average German panzer division.

The Allied assaulting force under the command of Field Marshal Sir Bernard Montgomery consisted of the Airborne Corps (6th British, 82nd U.S., and 101st U.S. Airborne Divisions), the 1st U.S. Army (Lieutenant-General O. N. Bradley) and the 2nd British Army (Lieutenant-General M. C. Dempsey). The coast of Normandy selected for the assault stretched from Les Dunes de Varreville, on the east side of the Cotentin peninsula, to Cabourg, a few miles east of the mouth of the Orne. Five beaches had been selected, two allocated to the 1st U.S. Army ("Utah" and "Omaha") and three to the 2nd British Army ("Gold", "Juno" and "Sword"). The 7th U.S. Corps (Major-General J. L. Collins) was to land at "Utah", its 4th Division assaulting, followed in turn by the 90th and 9th. The 5th U.S. Corps (Major-General L. T. Gerow) had the "Omaha" beach and, appropriately, the 1st U.S. Division was to lead with the 29th on its right and the 2nd following. "Gold" beach was allotted to the 30th British Corps (Lieutenant-General G. C. Bucknall), the assaulting troops being the 50th Division and the 8th Armoured Brigade, which were to be followed in succession by the 7th Armoured and 49th Divisions. The 1st British Corps (Lieutenant-General J. T. Crocker) was to attack at both "Juno" and "Sword" beaches: the 3rd Canadian Division and 2nd Canadian Armoured Brigade landing at the former, and the 3rd British Division with the 27th British Armoured Brigade at the latter. Behind these formations were the 51st Highland Division and the 4th Armoured Brigade. The 1st and 4th Special Service Brigades were allotted to the 1st British Corps attack. The airborne forces were to guard the flanks of the attack.

The Allies aimed first at establishing a firm bridgehead on the Normandy coast, and then at seizing Cherbourg and the

Brittany ports. The 2nd British Army was then to attack strongly in the Caen area, threatening to break out through the German defences, in order to draw the enemy reserves. Once these were committed, the 1st U.S. Army (with the 3rd which was to be formed later) was to break through on the western flank and push southwards to the Loire. When this had been achieved the whole Allied army, pivoting on Caen, was to wheel left to front the Seine.

The prelude to the Allied landings had been a 3-months bombing onslaught with the aim of destroying bridges and railway locomotives, so paralysing the transport system and isolating the enemy forces in Normandy.

Early on 6th June British and American forces were landing on all five beaches. In spite of high seas the DD tanks were very successful, and they led in the majority of the assault landings. On the British beaches use was made of other specialised armour. It included "Crabs", or Shermans fitted with flails, and AVRE's (Assault Vehicles Royal Engineers), which were Churchills armed with a "Petard" and modified to deal with obstacles. (The Petard was a 12-inch spigot mortar which could throw a 25-lb. charge, universally known as a "Flying Dustbin", up to a distance of 80 yards.) The specialised armour preceeded the infantry, and where DD tanks failed to arrive the "Crabs" took over their assault role. On the American beaches the DD tanks were successful at Utah, but at Omaha the sea proved too rough and many were sunk.

The first landings, the airborne, took place at 2 a.m., and as soon as von Rundstedt heard of them he asked that the panzer divisions in reserve should be made available to him. However, it was more than 12 hours later that Hitler's permission was eventually obtained, by which time the Allies were ashore in strength. At first the German High Command held to their original appreciation that the main invasion would take place in the Pas de Calais, and they therefore regarded the Normandy attack as a feint. As a result von Salmuth's 15th Army was retained in its positions covering the Straits of Dover.

Rommel's intention was to hold the American attack with an infantry defence whilst he counter-attacked the British about Caen with the 1st Panzer Corps. Speed was obviously essential, and he gave orders that the attack should start early on the morning of 7th June, without waiting for the arrival of the *Panzer Lehr* Division, which was joining the Corps. However, any chance of success had been lost by Hitler's dilatoriness, and successive attacks by the 1st Panzer Corps on 7th and 8th were unsuccessful.

On their side the Allies were faced with some of the most difficult tank country in Western Europe. This was the *Bocage*, a patchwork of tiny fields bordered with tall thick hedgerows, and pierced by narrow winding and high-banked lanes. Under these conditions well-sited defensive posts could engage tanks at very short range.

By mid-June the Allied tank strength in Normandy, a week after the landings, already outnumbered the tanks available to the Germans by about three to one. Rommel could now dispose of some 600 medium tanks of which about 150 were Panthers and the remainder Pz. IV's. In addition to these there was a heavy tank battalion equipped with Tigers at Corps Head-quarters. The Allies had about 1,700 tanks, most of which were Shermans.

Between 13th and 15th June Rommel made an attempt to stop the American advance on Cherbourg by throwing the 17th SS Panzer Division against the junction of the 7th and 5th U.S. Corps; but the attack was unsuccessful, and 3 days later the Americans were across the Cotentin peninsula and had taken Barneville. On 27th Cherbourg surrendered. Two days before this the 2nd British Army had attacked Caen, but after making slow progress the British advance was brought to a halt by a heavy counter-attack delivered by the 1st and 2nd Panzer Divisions. The German armour in this sector was now rein-forced by the 9th Panzer Division, and also by the 10th, which had recently been transferred from the Eastern Front.

On 3rd July von Rundstedt, fed up with Hitler's inept inter-ference, resigned and was replaced by Field Marshal von Kluge.

In pursuance of his initial plan, Montgomery now directed the 1st U.S. Army towards the line Coutances-St. Lo, preparatory to a break out on the western flank. This attack was to be followed by the 2nd British Army striking at Caen.

The Americans attacked on 3rd July, but progress through the *Bocage* was disappointingly slow. Four days later the British, preceded by a heavy bombing attack, assaulted Caen. The bombing, however, proved a handicap, rather than a help, as the streets were filled with so much rubble that the tanks could not move and the Germans were able to withdraw at their leisure to the south bank of the Orne.

By 10th July the Americans had come to a halt and the British had been stopped at Caen. At this stage Rommel was reinforced by four infantry divisions from the 19th Army. He used them to replace the panzer divisions in the Caen sector, and began moving the latter towards the Americans.

This movement of the panzer divisions threatened the whole Allied plan, and it was necessary to attack again to stop it. The 2nd British Army was accordingly directed to feint with its right and then to attack with its armour about Caen. It was hoped that this would draw the German tanks away from the American sector, and enable the 1st U.S. Army to break out to the south.

The feint attack by the 12th and 30th British Corps on the night of 15th July had some initial success in drawing German attention, but then unfortunately enemy air reconnaissance spotted the steady flow of vehicles over the bridges crossing the Orne as the 8th British Corps moved to its forming up areas.

For this Operation, "Goodwood", Lieutenant-General Sir Richard O'Connor's 8th Corps had been made entirely armoured and consisted of the Guards Armoured, 7th Armoured and 11th Armoured Divisions. These three divisions were to follow each other into the small bridgehead over the Orne, north-east of Caen, and strike south towards Falaise. This entailed moving on a one-divisional front for a distance of 4 miles before there would be sufficient elbow-room for them to fan out on to a three-divisional frontage. The attack was to be preceded by a very heavy air bombardment. The tanks would then advance over an area which had been neutralised by the bombers and behind a creeping artillery barrage.

However, Rommel had been anticipating an attack in this area for some time, and he had prepared a defence organised in five successive belts. In front were two infantry divisions, and behind them was the 21st Panzer Division, strengthened by an additional Pz. IV battalion and a Tiger battalion. In the rear of the 21st Panzer Division the villages about the main railway line from Caen to Paris were each manned by an infantry company with anti-tank guns. Next came the crest of the Bourguébus Ridge along which was the enemy's gun line of 88-mm.'s, field guns and six-barrelled mortars. The final belt lay in the villages on the plateau south of the ridge which were to be occupied by the infantry of the 1st SS Panzer Division if the other belts were penetrated. In reserve were the Panther battalion of the 1st SS Panzer Division and a battle group of the 12th SS Panzer Division.

The air attack did indeed have a stunning impact where it hit, but unfortunately it stopped short of the Bourguebus Ridge. But this was Rommel's last battle of wits with his old enemies, for on the evening of 7th July British aircraft attacked his car and he was dangerously wounded, and recovered only to be murdered by Hitler.

At 2 a.m. the next day, 18th July, the 11th Armoured Division, leading the British attack, began to move over the Orne bridges, and at 7.45 it crossed the start line behind the artillery barrage. Behind the 11th came the Guards Armoured Division, which deployed well to its left, and then the 7th Armoured Division, which came up between the two.

With the enemy still reeling under the effects of the tremendous bombing, the initial progress was easy; but in the zone of defended villages and hamlets the Germans had remained under cover whilst the air attack was in progress, and had then come out and manned their anti-tank guns. Here the advance slowed up, and it was 9.20 before the leading tanks reached the railway, only 40 miles from the start line. And then in front of the dominating and undisturbed Borguebus Ridge the attack slowed to a halt.

Little progress was made the next day, and then heavy rain and a resultant morass of mud brought the battle to an end, with a loss to the British of over 150 tanks.

But if the attack had been a tactical failure it had been a strategic success, for most of the panzer divisions were now facing the 2nd British Army.

On the Allied right flank the 1st U.S. Army's offensive had been planned for 21st July, but the weather which had stopped the 8th Corps enforced a postponement till 25th. This operation, "Cobra", was also preceded by a heavy air attack. Three infantry divisions led the attack, followed by another infantry and two armoured divisions. The German resistance was stubborn, and after two days fighting only 5 miles had been gained. But the Germans had reached their limit. Owing to the withdrawal of German armour to meet the "Goodwood" threat, the Americans had been faced only by the *Panzer Lehr* Division, and this, with only fourteen tanks left, was now forced to withdraw.

There was now a gap which the 2nd U.S. Armoured Division

penetrated on the night of 26th July, and by the following morning it had driven through it to a depth of 4 miles. On 27th the gap was exploited by a rapid advance south-westwards towards Coutances and the western coast. To seal this gap the Germans, on 27th, rushed up the 2nd and 116th Panzer Divisions from the Caen sector, but they were attacked heavily from the air and arrived too late to stop the break through. On 31st July the 4th U.S. Armoured Division was through the Avranches bottleneck and out into the open country. It was followed by a flood of armour, part of which swung westwards into Brittany, whilst the remainder drove east towards the Seine.

About the end of July and the beginning of August there were certain changes in the higher organisation of the Allied Armies. On 23rd July the 1st Canadian Army (Lieutenant-General H. D. G. Creaver) became operational and, together with the 2nd British Army, formed the 21st Army Group. On 2nd August the 3rd U.S. Army was formed under the command of Lieutenant-General George S. Patton. It included the 8th, 12th, 15th and 20th U.S. Corps. Lieutenant-General C. H. Hodges was appointed to the command of the 1st U.S. Army, consisting of the 5th, 7th and 19th U.S. Corps. These two armies made up the 12th Army Group under Bradley.

On 30th July another, mainly armoured, attack was launched in the British sector. The 8th and 30th Corps attacked from the Caumont area to try and break out to the south-east and exploit towards the River Orne. Little progress was made on 30th against a stubborn enemy defence. On 31st, however, an armoured car troop of the Household Cavalry discovered a track in the Foret l'Eveque which, through some extraordinary oversight, was neither mined nor guarded and which led southward through the enemy's positions. That night the whole of the 11th Armoured Division was moving down the track, and the following night forward elements of the Division were in Vire, some 40 miles south of the coast. Towards this same town were advancing the 5th and 19th U.S. Divisions, and Dempsey therefore directed O'Connor to vacate Vire and to wheel the 8th Corps towards Flers, 20 miles east of Vire. However, German reinforcements were being rushed up and this move brought the 11th Armoured Division into contact with the 9th SS Panzer and 21st Panzer Divisions.

The German mobile defence of this wide gap in their front was masterly. It consisted of a large number of detachments, each consisting of two or three tanks, about a company of infantry, and some six-barrelled mortars. The offensive handling of these detachments created such an impression of strength that the 8th Corps advance came to a halt to await the arrival of more infantry. The 30th Corps, on the left of the 8th Corps, had made little progress, and by 6th August this near breakthrough had come to a stop.

Meanwhile the advance of the American 3rd Army was going well. On 2nd August it had captured Rennes, and the next day Bradley ordered Patton to leave the minimum force for the reduction of the German troops in Brittany and to drive on Paris.

Von Kluge appreciated rightly that only an immediate withdrawal to the Seine could save him from decisive defeat. Hitler would not hear of it and ordered him to attack from Mortain against Avranches with eight of his nine Panzer divisions in order to cut Patton's communications. Given some sort of equality in the air, this would have been a stroke in the Rommel tradition, but with the immense air forces at the disposal of the Allies such an attack was to invite disaster. In fact, the largest force which von Kluge could disengage for this operation included only four panzer divisions, with a total of less than 250 tanks.

The concentration of the counter-attack force was soon spotted by air reconnaissance and the Americans reacted quickly to the threat against this very sensitive spot. Bradley deployed five infantry divisions to meet the German thrust and ordered Patton to have three divisions on the enemy's south flank. He then attacked about Vire on 6th August, so compelling the Germans to weaken the counter-attack force in order to protect their right flank.

At 1 a.m. on 7th August General Hausser, now commanding the 7th German Army, launched his attack. Any German armoured attack was formidable, and this one had penetrated for 7 miles by dawn. But as soon as an early morning mist had cleared to show the roads round Mortain crowded with German columns, the Allied air forces swept on them; and soon all movement had stopped on roads hopelessly blocked with masses of destroyed and burning transport.

Montgomery now moved to surround the 7th Army. He directed the 1st Canadian Army to attack south on the axis of the Caen-Falaise road against Hausser's right rear, and he requested

Bradley to order Patton's 15th Corps northwards from Le Mans towards Argentan to meet the British. On 10th August von Kluge spotted the development of this thrust and applied, without success, for permission to withdraw. On 11th August the 15th U.S. Corps (in which was the 2nd French Armoured Division) captured Alençon, Hausser's main supply base, and on 13th August it reached Argentan.

The 2nd Canadian Corps had, meanwhile, attacked south-wards on the night of 7th August with six armoured regiments and six infantry battalions, the latter carried in converted self-propelled gun carriages ("Kangaroos"). This force consisted of the 33rd British Armoured Brigade, the 2nd Canadian Armoured Brigade, a brigade of the 51st (Highland) Division and a brigade of the 2nd Canadian Infantry Division. The remainder of the above two infantry divisions were to clear up villages left behind by the armoured columns.

This night operation resulted in considerable confusion amongst the attacking columns, but in spite of this it was successful and all the objectives were seized.

In the next phase, on the afternoon of the 8th August, the 4th Canadian and 1st Polish Armoured Divisions were to pass through and thrust towards Falaise. But the afternoon was too late to exploit, and the attack was too slow when it got going; with the result that the Germans, reacting with their usual speed, closed the gap which the night attack had opened.

Hausser was now in an impossible position, with his army occupying a salient 40 miles in depth and 15 miles in breadth, and so he started to withdraw without consulting Hitler's wishes in the matter.

Bradley used the American halt at Argentan to replace the 15th U.S. Corps by the 5th Corps of the 1st U.S. Army, so that the 15th could continue its advance on Paris. Patton's army was making good progress. On 16th August the 12th U.S. Corps captured Orleans and the 20th U.S. Corps took Chartres. The 15th Corps, moving via Dreux, was over the Seine at Mantes, north-west of Paris, on 19th August. On this same day the Allies, attacking from north and south, at last sealed Hausser's escape route; and now within an area 10 miles by 5 the remnants of fifteen German divisions were being continu-ously attacked from the air. Hitler's reaction was to replace the unfortunate von Kluge by Field Marshal Model.

On 20th August the 2nd Panzer Division broke through **the**

Canadians and held open a gap sufficiently long to allow over a third of the 100,000 trapped Germans to escape. This unfortunate mishap was due to the Allies using insufficient forces to contain the Germans. However, most of the German tanks and guns within the Falaise pocket had to be abandoned, and nearly as much was lost subsequently in the withdrawal across the Seine. Altogether the Normandy battle cost the Germans 500,000 men, 1,500 tanks, and vast numbers of guns and vehicles.

By 31st August the Allies had a considerable superiority in numbers. At General Eisenhower's disposal were twenty-three infantry divisions and the equivalent of fifteen armoured divisions. The enormous logistical back-up for these formations is shown by the number of troops in France, which amounted to 2,000,000 men, or 50,000 for every division in the field. Vehicles in the force totalled some half million. In fighting soldiers the Allies had a two to one superiority, but in material the odds in in their favour were far greater. In tanks, for instance, after the end of the battle of Normandy they had a numerical superiority of about twenty to one.

In spite of the vast administrative resources, petrol supplies alone were insufficient to launch all four of the Allied armies in rapid pursuit of the beaten enemy. Montgomery proposed a thrust by one army by way of Belgium into the North German plain, where the great superiority of the Allied armour could be exploited to the best advantage. Eisenhower, however, rejected this. From its position such a thrust would necessarily fall to the lot of the 2nd British Army, and the 3rd U.S. Army would have to be halted. Eisenhower is said to have rejected Montgomery's proposal for two reasons; firstly because he thought that a "pencil-like thrust" was militarily unsound, and secondly (according to Chester Wilmot in *The Struggle for Europe*) that to halt the 3rd U.S. Army in order to place everything at the disposal of the 2nd British Army was not practicable "because the American public would never stand for it". That the people of any nation should wish to see its troops foremost in victory is understandable; but no such consideration influenced Montgomery's conduct of the battle of Normandy, and one hopes that Eisenhower's decision was based solely on the first of his reasons.

The plan which Eisenhower adopted was to advance on a broad front with priority on his left, but also to push the 3rd

U.S. Army eastwards to join up with the 6th Army Group, which had landed in the south of France and was advancing northwards along the valley of the Rhone. As a plan it was singularly uninspiring and it invited trouble—which it got.

In the British sector the pursuit had started on 17th August, before the end of the Falaise battle, when the 1st Corps with the 7th Armoured Division under command pushed forward towards the Seine. Its advance was delayed by a very thorough destruction of bridges and culverts and by the very enclosed country of which the Germans took every advantage to impose delays.

On 21st August this sector and the 7th Armoured Division came under the command of the 1st Canadian Army. On 22nd August the 51st (Highland) Division, also under Canadian command, came up in support, and on 23rd Lisieux was captured. The enemy forces now withdrew 25 miles eastwards to the River Risle.

Meanwhile part of the 15th U.S. Corps, which had seized Mantes, together with the 19th U.S. Corps were moving along the left bank of the Seine to try and get behind the Germans holding up the British and Canadian advance. Enemy resistance, however was strong, and the Germans eventually succeeded in withdrawing across the Seine, though leaving most of their major equipment behind.

The Americans now withdrew to their own sector, and the 2nd British Army, at last free from the Falaise battle started its long and successful armoured drive to the north. The 43rd Division crossed the Seine at Vernon, 15 miles downstream from Mantes, and through it on 28th August went the 11th Armoured Division. Two days later the Guards Armoured Division followed and took a route to the right of the 11th.

On the morning of 31st August, after a 30-mile night drive, the 11th Armoured Division entered Amiens. Eleven miles to its right the Guards Armoured Division crossed the Somme at Corbie. On the same day the 7th Armoured Division, having been halted for rest and maintenance, crossed the Seine at St. Pierre, and drove 30 miles on to Poix. The next day it was on the Somme, with the 11th Armoured Division 40 miles ahead. On 2nd September Dempsey ordered the 30th Corps, with the 11th and Guards Armoured Divisions under command, to capture Antwerp and Brussels. The following day these orders were complied with, the Guards Armoured Division entering Brussels and the 11th Armoured Division seizing Antwerp.

At Antwerp the advance on the docks was so rapid that they were captured undamaged. On 5th September the 7th Armoured Division, coming up on the left, entered Ghent.

In this remarkable armoured advance the British divisions had covered 230 miles in 7 days, an average of over 30 miles a day. The 2nd British was now the leading Allied Army. The 1st U.S. Army was approaching the River Meuse between Namur and Sedan, and the 3rd U.S. Army was out of fuel and stationary between Verdun and Commercy. On the left the 7th Armoured Division was leading the advance of the 1st Canadian Army, and engaged in bitter fighting with the retreating Germans, whilst much further to the south the Canadians were fighting for Le Havre.

During the following week the 1st U.S. Army drove through the Ardennes to reach the German frontier and the Siegfried Line. On its right the 3rd Army, against strong resistance, managed to secure a bridgehead across the Moselle between Nancy and Metz.

On 7th September the advance of the 2nd Army was continued. The Guards Armoured Division moved north-east from Louvain, and on 8th September crossed the Albert Canal 40 miles to the east of Antwerp. The 11th Armoured Division, which had been moved from Antwerp to the right flank, came up on the right of the Guards Armoured Division, and the 50th (Northumbrian) Division advanced on the left of the Guards. Progress was slow, for the country, intersected by numerous rivers and canals, restricted movement and the German troops fought stubbornly.

On 10th September the leading troops reached the Meuse-Escaut Canal at a point some 15 miles north of the Albert Canal. The Guards Armoured Division managed to seize the De Groote bridge intact, and on 13th September the 50th Division captured a second bridge. The 11th Armoured Division was less successful for every bridge on its route had been blown.

The 2nd Army was now to mount an operation designed to gain control of the Rhine crossing at one stroke. On 17th September the 30th Corps was to attack with the Guards Armoured Division, followed by the 43rd (Wessex) and 50th Divisions, whilst the Airborne Corps was to drop ahead from Eindhoven to Arnhem with, in succession from the south, the 101st U.S. Airborne, the 82nd U.S. Airborne and the 1st British Airborne Divisions. The 8th Corps, with the 11th Armoured

Division once more under command, was to protect the 30th Corps' right flank.

On 19th September, 2 days after the start of the attack, the Germans struck at the supply route with small armoured columns and hard fighting was necessary to drive them off. At Arnhem German counter-attacks were mounted in overwhelming strength and after a gallant struggle the bulk of the airborne garrison was captured, and this briefly held bridgehead over the Lower Rhine was lost. Hopes of a rapid end to the war vanished with the failure at Arnhem, but great results had nevertheless been achieved. On the right flank the 11th Armoured Division entered Geldrop, due east of Eindhoven, on 21st September, making contact with the 101st U.S. Airborne Division, and on 25th September it reached St. Anthonis near the River Maas (or Meuse).

In the meantime the Germans were still on the south shore of the Scheldt estuary and on the island of Walcheren, and these areas had to be cleared before Antwerp could be used for Allied shipping. Operations to achieve this started on 6th October and were completed successfully on 8th November. By the end of November all German resistance south of the Maas had ceased and the entire attention of the 21st Army Group could be directed towards the conquest of Germany.

Optimism, however, proved to be premature. The Germans were now to take advantage of Eisenhower's linear advance, and to make one final bid for a decision in their favour in the West. By stripping the Russian front of armoured reserves eight re-equipped panzer divisions had been massed in two panzer armies under the command of Field Marshal von Rundstedt. The German plan was to plunge once more across the Meuse, cut the Allied line, and make for Antwerp. On 16th December von Rundstedt's forces, advancing through the narrow winding roads of the Ardennes, struck suddenly and unexpectedly at unprepared positions weakly held by the 1st U.S. Army, and broke through. Brussels was immediately threatened and the 30th British Corps was rapidly redeployed to cover the city.

By early January the German advance had been stemmed, and with the failure of von Rundstedt's armour, as with Ney's cavalry at Waterloo, went the enemy's last, even if very remote, chance of victory.

CHAPTER XX

Nuclear Age

IT was apparent at the close of the Second World War that the explosion of a nuclear bomb had ushered in a new era of warfare. It was difficult at first to visualise the role of the traditional weapons and forces in this new military age. At the same time, whilst the problem was considered at countless staff exercises, it was clear that the United States of America had a monopoly of nuclear weapons, and that there was therefore no immediate need to determine how equipment, organisation and tactical doctrine should be modified.

The position changed all too quickly, but when the increase in the number and power of weapons available to the opposing sides was such as to ensure mutual destruction, it became more and more likely that the opening stages, at anyrate, of a major war would be fought with the so-called conventional forces. At the same time these forces would need to be so organised and equipped as to be able to fight under the conditions of nuclear war, and it was apparent that armoured forces were well suited for these conditions.

The development of military opinion in the nuclear age, then, was reflected to some extent both in the organisation of armoured forces and the design of armoured fighting vehicles. The United States, feeling secure perhaps in its sole possession of this beastly weapon, lost confidence in the continued value of armoured formations and thought that the tank itself might have little future in the face of the new and formidable anti-tank weapons which could be brought against it both from the ground and from the air. Only one armoured division was retained, and the surplus tank units were distributed in battalions and companies under the command of divisional and brigade headquarters respectively.

The Russian policy was entirely the opposite. Firstly, the Russians, having no nuclear weapons, depended absolutely on their conventional forces; secondly, their narrow escape from decisive defeat by the German panzers had made a deep impression on them—an impression which had been strengthened by the successes of their own new armoured formations against the weakened Germans in the later stages of the war. When, a few years after the war had ended, the Western Allies had demobilised, the Russians still maintained the formidable total of some fifty tank and mechanised corps.

British policy lay somewhat between the two. Faith in the value of the armoured division remained, though there was much difference of opinion as to its exact role, and this was reflected in frequent changes of organisation. At first the latest wartime organisation was retained except that divisional reconnaissance was once again entrusted to an armoured car regiment whilst the armoured brigade was increased in strength to four armoured regiments. Before long, however, there were further modifications, some of which only lasted a short time. The infantry brigade was raised to four battalions but later again reduced to three. Both artillery regiments and the anti-tank regiment (R.A.C.) were equipped with self-propelled guns, but the latter unit was later abolished.

But of greater importance than this military fickleness was that at last the British Army was once more leading the world in tank design. The new Centurion tank had appeared in 1945, just too late to take part in the War, and it was undoubtedly the finest tank in existence. It was armed with a 17-pr gun, of the same pattern as mounted in the Sherman Firefly, and had armour of a maximum thickness of 76 mm. It weighed 50 tons, had a crew of four, and its Rolls-Royce Meteor IVA engine drove it at a speed of 22 m.p.h. The suspension was partly covered by skirting plates, which gave it a distinctive appearance.

The Centurion was developed through many marks. The Mark II was noteworthy for its auto-stabilised gun platform which enabled the tank to move without deflecting the gun from its target. Mark II's proved their value in the Korean campaign of 1950, when Centurions were used in action for the first time.

The Mark III of 1948 was the first to be equipped with the high velocity 83·9 calibre 20-pr gun, and in 1959 this still first-class tank was armed with the very successful British 105-mm. gun, which has become a standard NATO tank weapon.

A regiment equipped with Centurions is normally composed of three squadrons, each of fifteen tanks, with another three tanks on regimental headquarters. Three of the squadron tanks are headquarters vehicles and the remainder are distributed in four troops each of three tanks.

The Centurion has been widely sold abroad and the Commonwealth and foreign armies which have used it include those of Canada, Australia, South Africa, the Netherlands, Denmark, Sweden, Switzerland, Iraq, and Egypt. There is a DD version which is driven through the water by twin propellers.

The American Army after the end of the war was armed in the main with the 76-mm. gun version of the M4, or Sherman, and the three medium battalions in the sole remaining armoured division were equipped with these tanks. The heavy battalion of the division had the 90-mm. gun M26 Pershing tanks and reconnaissance was carried out by M24 light tanks. American policy at the time was that these three classes of tank should be replaced by new designs for the same functions; and development of three new types was accordingly started in the late 1940's. However, the first major crisis over the access to Berlin, and other aspects of increasing Russian hostility, led to the Americans taking more rapid steps to modernise their armour. There were some 2,000 of the Pershings which had been put in store after the end of the war and many of these were now taken out and fitted with new engines and transmissions. Reclassified as medium tanks they were also redesignated "Pattons".

The Patton tanks came out in three series. The first one, the M46, displayed certain weaknesses during the Korean War and was markedly inferior to the Centurion. The next mark, the M47, was accordingly fitted with a turret which had been intended for the projected new medium tank and with a more powerful engine which increased its speed to 37 m.p.h. The first M47's were turned out in 1951, and they were subsequently used, not only in the Army of the United States, but also in those of Western Germany, France, Italy, Belgium, Spain, Greece, Turkey, Japan, and Yugoslavia.

A better version of the Patton came out in 1948. Entitled the M48, it weighed 44 tons and was very similar to its predecessor except for improvements to hull and turret. This new tank became the standard equipment of the three medium tank battalions of the armoured division. In the meantime development of the projected new medium tank had been stopped.

At about the same time as the introduction of the M48

Patton the four armoured infantry battalions in the armoured division were equipped with full-track armoured personnel carriers in place of the earlier half-track vehicles.

French armoured formations had finished the war equipped with American tanks, but in 1946 the French started to develop two tanks of their own; one of which should be a battle tank and the other a much lighter vehicle which could be transported by air. The battle tank was designated AMX50, and a few prototypes, armed with a 120-mm. gun, were ready in 1951. But it was a very expensive vehicle and no further production was undertaken.

The lighter tank, the AMX13, on the other hand, was a triumph in design, and was enthusiastically received when it appeared in 1949. It weighs only about 15 tons, but is armed with a high velocity 75-mm. gun of 61·5 calibre length and 3,280 approximate muzzle velocity. Its maximum armour thickness is 40 mm., it has a speed of 40 m.p.h. with a range of 208 miles, and it is manned by a crew of three. Production started in 1952 for the French Army, and it has been subsequently sold to Austria, Switzerland, Israel and Venezuela.

The Russians ended the war with large numbers of their T-34's, T-34/85's and JS-III's. The first post-war medium tank was the T-44, which was evolved from the T-34/85, with a better chassis and a lower silhouette, but with the same armament and armour. A still later development in this series was the T-54, the production of which started in the early 1950's. By 1955 it had become the standard equipment of the medium tank regiments and of the tank battalions in the mechanised infantry regiments. A descendant of the admirable T-34, it is a good and reliable tank. The armament has been improved and it has a 100-mm. gun of 54-calibre length and three machine-guns of which one is anti-aircraft. Its weight of 36 tons is little greater than that of its predecessors. The turret and track assemblies are better and the driver has night vision instruments.

The Korean war gave something of an impetus to the development of armour. British forces in Germany were reinforced, and no less than three out of the four divisions were armoured. In 1954 armoured regiments were given greater fire power with the arrival of the largest and heaviest tanks in existence—the 65-ton heavily armoured Conquerors, armed with a 120-mm. gun. Six were allotted to each armoured regiment and one troop in each of two of the three armoured squadrons was equipped with them. The purpose of these heavy tanks was to provide fire support for the Centurions by engaging the enemy heavy tanks and self-propelled guns. In addition to its 120-mm. gun the Conqueror has two machine-guns, one co-axially mounted and the other in the cupola for anti-aircraft fire. The tank is driven by a Rolls-Royce Meteor IVB engine which gives it a speed of 22 m.p.h. It has a crew of four.

The Conqueror was developed from the Caernarvon, an experimental design with the same chassis but with a Centurion turret mounting a 20-pr gun.

At about this time another British tank, the Charioteer, was issued to the Territorial Army for use as a tank destroyer in place of the self-propelled anti-tank gun. It was also sold to Jordan and Austria. The Charioteer made use of the Cromwell chassis on which was fitted a new turret carrying a Centurion pattern 20-pr gun. Its weight was 28½ tons and its speed was 31 m.p.h. Its characteristics were high fire power combined with comparatively thin armour.

In the early 1950's the French Army started experiments with a new type of armoured formation based on the AMX13 tank and their ingenious EBR reconnaissance vehicle, which runs on four wheels on the road and has four more in the centre of the chassis which are lowered for cross-country work. In 1954 an experimental armoured brigade took part in manoeuvres in Germany. The core of the brigade was an armoured battalion group called a "Regiment Inter-Armes', or RIA. It consisted of a headquarters squadron, a light car reconnaissance squadron, two armoured squadrons equipped with AMX13 tanks, an infantry company, and a 120-mm. mortar battery. There were two of these RIA's in the brigade as well as a brigade reconnaissance squadron equipped with EBR's.

The RIA's were a success and the following year they formed part of a new type of mechanised division incorporating an infantry regiment and divisional troops. However, this, with its small tank component of two squadrons, was hardly an armoured formation.

In 1954 the American Army heavy tank battalions and the U.S. Marine Corps were equipped with a new heavy tank, the M103, with a role similar to that of the British Conqueror. It weighs 54 tons and is armed with a 120-mm. gun and coaxial and anti-aircraft machine-guns. It has a crew of five and a speed of 21 m.p.h.

Four years later there was a new American medium tank, the M60, developed from the M48. It has the same chassis as its predecessor, but it has a diesel engine and an improved turret in which is mounted the British designed 105-mm. gun, together with co-axial and anti-aircraft machine-guns. It weighs 46 tons, has armour of 110 mm., and is manned by a crew of four. Its issue to tank battalions started in 1960.

In 1957 the Russians produced a new heavy tank, a development of the JS-III and known (the former initials having declined in popularity) as the T-10. It is armed with a 122-mm. gun of 43-calibre length and with the usual complement of machine-guns. It replaced the JS-III's in the heavy tank regiments. Not much information about it has yet been released, but it has been estimated that it weighs 50 tons, has armour of 200 mm. thickness, and can move at 25 m.p.h.

In 1955 the British armoured divisions were once more re-organised, and this time in a most extraordinary fashion; the infantry component being so reduced as to result in a formation which war experiemce should have shown to be extremely ill-balanced. There were no brigade headquarters; instead, the four armoured regiments were directly under divisional headquarters. There was only one infantry battalion, one medium artillery regiment and a regiment of armoured cars for reconnaissance. The next year one of these armoured divisions was broken up and its four armoured regiments were incorporated in the infantry divisions. At about the same time it was officially proclaimed that the role of the armoured division was limited to exploitation.

By 1957 the weakness of the new armoured division had presumably been appreciated, for in that year there was another and even more radical re-organisation. The division in the British Army was replaced by the brigade group as the basic organisation, and there were two kinds of brigade group—armoured and infantry. The armoured brigade group consists of three armoured regiments, one infantry battalion in armoured carriers and one artillery regiment equipped with 155-mm. self-propelled howitzers, together with Royal Engineer, Royal Signals, and service units. The infantry brigade group is somewhat similar in composition, but there are three battalions of infantry and one armoured regiment. These two formations are, indeed, copied from the organisations adopted for the Russian tank and mechanised infantry regiments. A divisional headquarters may command any number of brigade groups. It is apparent, however, that a division consisting of one armoured and one infantry brigade group would approximate to the balance of armour and infantry which was found to be most successful in the armoured divisions of the Second World War.

The most important British armoured development in recent times, however, has been the appearance of the new Chieftain tank. This remarkable vehicle shows promise of being by far the finest tank design in existence. It was officially approved for production on 19th July 1963 for issue to armoured regiments in 1965. Production was entrusted to the Royal Ordnance Factory at Leeds and Vickers-Armstrong at Newcastle-upon-Tyne.

The Chieftain is just over 50 tons in weight, but has a very low profile. It has a Leyland 700-h.p. multi-fuel engine which gives it a speed of 25 m.p.h. and considerably greater range than could be afforded by any conventional petrol engine. There is also a three-cylinder subsidiary engine. Its gun is the most outstanding yet mounted in a tank. It is a 120 mm. very high velocity weapon with a flat trajectory which makes it effective against armour at far greater ranges than have previously been achieved with a tank gun. Its armour piercing ammunition is the APDS, or "sabot", type, which was first used in 1944 in the 6-pr guns of Churchill tanks. This ammunition discards its outer jacket after leaving the muzzle of the gun, will penetrate armour at a very acute angle and will then shower metal splinters round the inside of a tank. The high-explosive ammunition is a "squash-head" shell which, apart from its normal HE use, is effective against heavy armour and concrete emplacements. The breech block is of new design with which a bagged charge can be used instead of the heavy and bulky brass cartridge case. The gun is ranged by a machine-gun firing rounds of tracer ammunition. Other machine-guns are mounted co-axially and for anti-aircraft use in the cupola. There are infra-red headlamps for night driving and infra-red viewers for the commander and gunner. It has a crew of four. Of this tank a recent Secretary-of-State for War has said, "In the Chieftain we have a winner. It meets all NATO requirements for the 1970's, and there is not another tank in the alliance that does this".

Both the French and the Germans have produced a new tank. In the first design stages the French were developing a tank for both countries, but differences of opinion as to the type of engine resulted in further design being undertaken separately.

Three prototypes of the French 30-ton tank led the 1963 Bastille day parade down the Champs Elysees. It has a crew of three, a speed of over 40 m.p.h., weighs 32½ tons and is armed with the British 105-mm. gun.

The German "standard" tank is remarkable. It weighs 39 tons, has a crew of four, is fitted with a Daimler-Benz 830-h.p. multi-fuel engine, is as fast as the French tank, and has the same British gun. It can pass through water up to a depth of 13 feet and has a *schnorkel* device fitted to the turret which enables it to stay submerged indefinitely and to fire its gun whilst under water. Some 1,500 of these tanks are being made for the West German Army.

There have been suggestions that, in view of the number and accuracy of modern anti-tank weapons, the day of the tank is over. But apart from the particular suitability of the tank for the nuclear battlefield, there will always be a need in war for cavalry. It may be that, like the horse, the tank will eventually become unsuitable for the shock of battle. But, if so, it will be essential to find a replacement. Aircraft cannot undertake the task, because in a ground attack role they are a form of artillery. Cavalry must be able to occupy and hold ground.

In 1962 there was demonstrated an ambulance called a "Hoversled". This was a platform supported on an air cushion which was maintained by a motor-driven electric fan. It could carry two wounded men and could be pushed by medical orderlies or towed behind a vehicle. Perhaps here lies the future replacement of the tank—a new type of armoured vehicle which can skim across country at very high speeds and with sufficient lift to surmount all the obstacles of the hunting field.

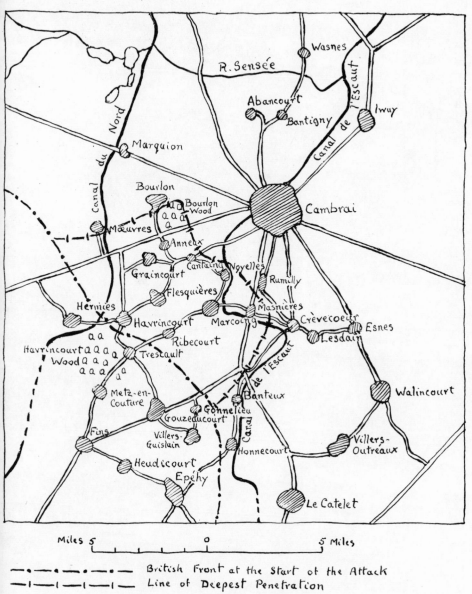

Miles 5   0   5 Miles

—·—·—·—·— British Front at the Start of the Attack
—|—|—|—|— Line of Deepest Penetration

THE BATTLEFIELD OF CAMBRAI 1917

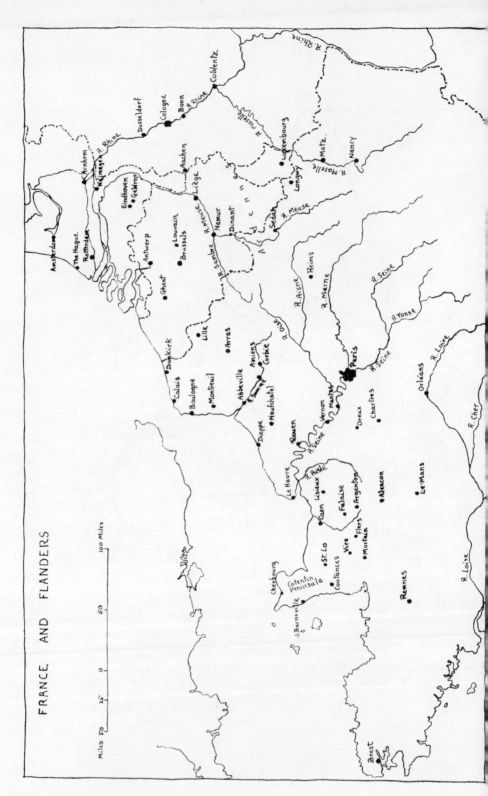

FRANCE AND FLANDERS

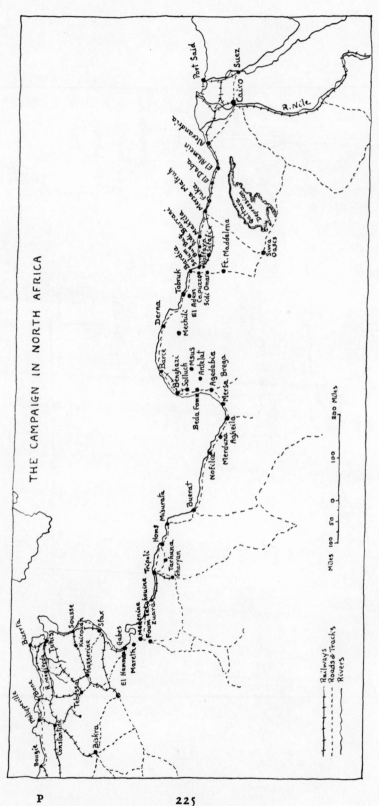

THE CAMPAIGN IN NORTH AFRICA

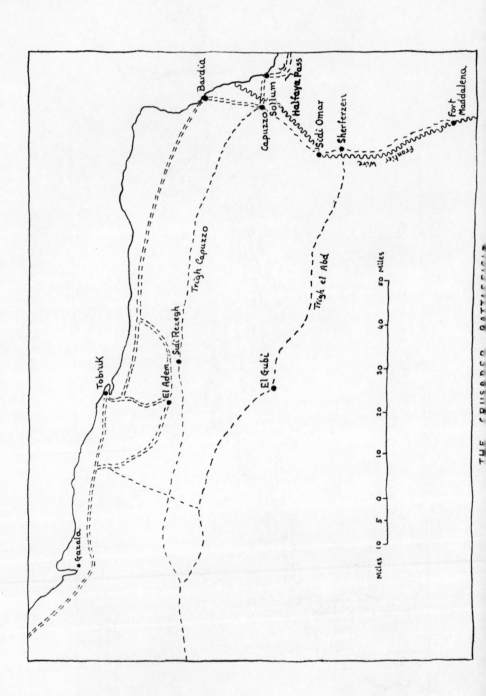

THE CRUSADER BATTLEFIELD

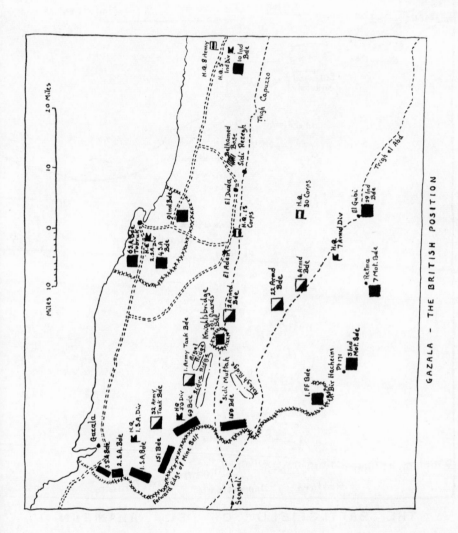

GAZALA – THE BRITISH POSITION

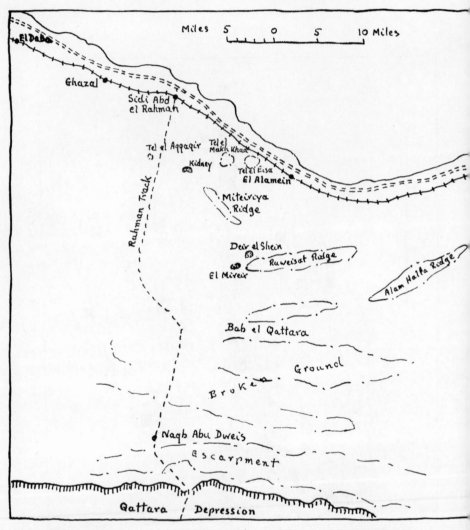

Miles 5 0 5 10 Miles

El Daba

Ghazal

Sidi Abd
el Rahman

Tel el Aqqaqir

Tel el
Makh Khad

Kidney

Tel el Eisa

El Alamein

Miteiriya
Ridge

Deir el Shein

Ruweisat Ridge

Alam Halfa Ridge

El Mireir

Bab el Qattara

Broken Ground

Rahman Track

Naqb Abu Dweis

Escarpment

Qattara Depression

THE BATTLEFIELD OF EL ALAMEIN

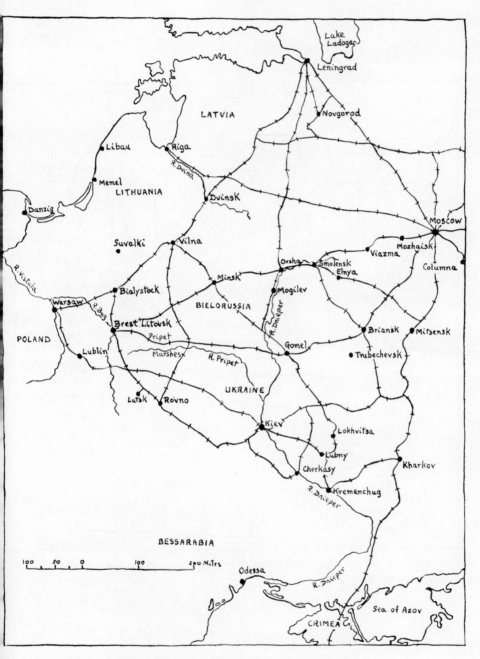

THE GERMAN INVASION OF RUSSIA

229

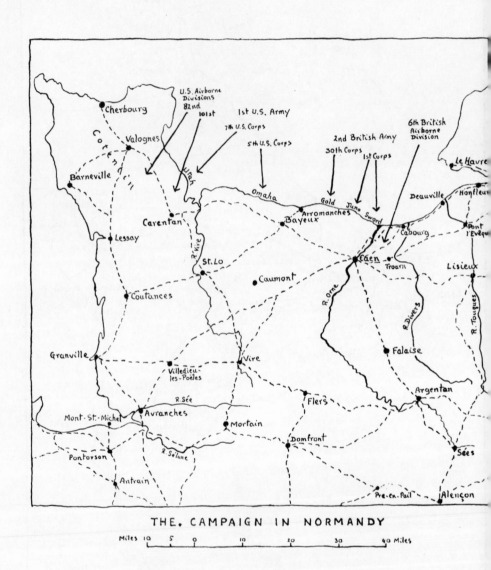

U.S. Airborne
Divisions
82nd
101st

1st U.S. Army

7th U.S. Corps

5th U.S. Corps

2nd British Army
30th Corps
1st Corps

6th British
Airborne
Division

Cherbourg

Le Havre

Valognes

Cotentin

Deauville

Honfleur

Barneville

Omaha

Gold
Juno Sword

Pont
l'Evêque

Arromanches

Bayeux

Cabourg

Carentan

R. Vire

Utah

Caen

Troarn

Lisieux

Lessay

St. Lo

Caumont

R. Orne

R. Divers

R. Touques

Coutances

Granville

Falaise

Villedieu-
les-Poêles

Vire

Mont-St.-Michel

R. Sée

Avranches

Flers

Argentan

Mortain

Pontorson

R. Sélune

Domfront

Sées

Antrain

Pre-en-Pail

Alençon

THE CAMPAIGN IN NORMANDY

Miles 10 5 0   10   20   30   40 Miles

Appendix

CHARACTERISTICS OF THE PRINCIPAL TANKS DESCRIBED IN THIS BOOK

I. GREAT BRITAIN

Name by which generally known	Armament	Armour (Maximum)	Speed (m.p.h.)	Weight (tons)
1. Marks I to IV (Male)	2 × 6-prs 4 m.g.	12 mm.	3·7	28
2. Marks I to IV (Female)	6 m.g.	12 mm.	3·7	27
3. Whippet	4 m.g.	14 mm.	8·3	14
4. Medium C	4 m.g.	12 mm.	7·9	19½
5. Mark V (Male)	2 × 6-prs 4 m.g.	14 mm.	4·6	29
6. Mark V (Female)	6 m.g.	14 mm.	4·6	28
7. Vickers Medium Mark II	3-pr 3 m.g.	8 mm.	18	16
8. Vickers Armstrong Light. Marks I to IV	1 m.g.	14 mm.	32	4¼
9. Vickers Armstrong Light. Mark VI	2 m.g.	14 mm.	35	5¼
10. A.9. Cruiser	2-pr 3 m.g.	14 mm.	23	12
11. A.10 Cruiser	2-pr 1 m.g.	30 mm.	16	14
12. Infantry Tank Mark I	1 m.g.	65 mm.	8	11
13. Infantry Tank Mark II or Matilda	2-pr 1 m.g.	75 mm.	15	26½
14. A.13 Cruiser	2-pr 1 m.g.	30 mm.	30	14
15. Crusader Mark I	2-pr 3 m.g.	40 mm.	27	18¾
16. Crusader Mark III	6-pr 2 m.g.	52 mm.	27½	19¾
17. Valentine (Mark VIII (Mark XI	2-pr 6-pr) 75 mm.)	65 mm.	15	17
18. Tetrarch	2-pr 1 m.g.	16 mm.	37	7½
19. Churchill (later Marks	2-pr 6-pr)	100 mm.	15½	38½
19. Cromwell	75 mm. 2 m.g.	76 mm.	38	27½
20. Challenger	17-pr 1 m.g.	102 mm.	32	31½
21. Comet	77 mm. 2 m.g.	101 mm.	29	32½
22. Centurion	17-pr 2 m.g.	76 mm.	22	50
(Mark III (Mark X	20-pr) 105 mm.)			
23. Conqueror	120 mm. 2 m.g.		22	65
24. Chieftain	120 mm. 2 m.g.	—	25	50

Appendix

Name by which generally known	Armament	Armour (maximum)	Speed (m.p.h.)	Weight (tons)

II. GERMANY

Name by which generally known	Armament	Armour (maximum)	Speed (m.p.h.)	Weight (tons)
1. A7V	57 mm. 6 m.g.	30 mm.	8	33
2. Pz I	2 m.g	15 mm.	24	5½
3. Pz II	20 mm. 2 m.g.	35 mm.	30	10¼
4. Pz III	50 mm. 2 m.g.	57 mm.	25	22
5. Pz IV	75 mm. 2 m.g.	85 mm.	25	23
6. Panther	75 mm. 2 m.g.	120 mm.	29	45
7. Tiger	88 mm. 2 m.g.	150 mm.	25	56
8. Standard	105 mm.	—	40	39

III. FRANCE

Name by which generally known	Armament	Armour (maximum)	Speed (m.p.h.)	Weight (tons)
1. Schneider	75 mm. 1 m.g.	25 mm.	5	14½
2. St. Chamond	75 mm. 4 m.g.	25 mm.	5	25¼
3. Renault FT	37 mm.	22 mm.	6	7
4. Renault R 35	37 mm. 1 m.g.	40 mm.	12½	11
5. Hotchkiss H 35	37 mm. 1 m.g.	40 mm.	17½	11½
6. Somua S 35	47 mm. 1 m.g.	40 mm.	29	19½
7. B-1 Bis	75 mm. 47 mm. 1 m.g.	60 mm.	18	31
8. AMX 13	75 mm.	40 mm.	40	15
9. AMX 30	105 mm.	—	40	30

IV. UNITED STATES OF AMERICA

Name by which generally known	Armament	Armour (maximum)	Speed (m.p.h.)	Weight (tons)
1. M2 Medium	37 mm. 8 m.g.	52 mm.	30	17
2. Stuart	37 mm. 2 m.g.	40 mm.	36	12½
3. Grant (M3)	75 mm. 37 mm. 1 m.g.	57 mm.	26	28
4. Sherman (M4)	75 mm. 2 m.g.	76 mm.	24	30
5. Pershing (M26)	90 mm. 3 m.g.	110 mm.	20	41
6. Patton (M48)	90 mm. 3 m.g.	110 mm.	37	44
7. M103	120 mm. 2 m.g.	110 mm. (?)	21	54
8. M60	105 mm. 2 m.g.	110 mm.	—	46

Appendix

Name by which generally known	Armament	Armour (Maximum)	Speed (m.p.h.)	Weight (tons)
V. RUSSIA				
1. BT	45 mm 2 m.g.	15 mm.	37	13½
2. T-28	76·2 mm. 3 m.g.	36 mm.	27	29
3. T-35	76·2 mm. 2×45 mm. 3 m.g.	45 mm.	20	45
4. T-34	76·2 mm. 2 m'g.	75 mm.	30	28
5. KV	76·2 mm. 3 m.g.	100 mm.	25	46
6 T-34/85	85 mm. 2 m.g.	75 mm.	30	30
7. JS-1	122 mm. 2 m.g.	110 mm.	20	46
8. JS-III	122 mm. 2 m.g.	200 mm.	23	46
9. T-54	100 mm. 3 m.g.	85 mm. (?)	34	36
10. T-10	122 mm. 3 m.g.	200 mm. (?)	—	50 (?)

Index

Index